CHILD ART

CHILD ART

By
WILHELM VIOLA

Author of
" Child Art and Franz Cizek "

WITH ILLUSTRATIONS

SECOND EDITION

UNIVERSITY OF LONDON PRESS LTD
WARWICK SQUARE, LONDON, E.C.4

CG106937-X

First Printed	.	.	.	.	.	1942
Second Edition	.	.	.	.	.	1944
Reprinted	.	.	.	1945, 1948, 1951, 1952, 1960

UNIVERSITY OF LONDON PRESS LTD

Warwick Square, LONDON E.C.4

SHOWROOMS OVERSEAS

41 Shortland Street, AUCKLAND C1, New Zealand
425 Little Collins Street, MELBOURNE, Victoria, Australia
558 George Street, SYDNEY, New South Wales, Australia

AGENTS OVERSEAS

Brazil Dr J. E. Bloch, Caixa Postal 8675, SÃO PAULO

Canada Clarke, Irwin & Co. Ltd, Clarwin House, 791 St Clair Avenue West, TORONTO 10

Egypt and the Sudan Dino Judah Nahum, 44 Sharia Sherif Pasha, CAIRO (P.O. Box 940)

The Far East Donald Moore Ltd, Macdonald House, Orchard Road, SINGAPORE 9 (P.O. Box 1742)
with branches in
Hong Kong 707 Gt China House, Queen's Road Central
Japan Shimura Building, 4–1 Kojimachi, Chiyoda-ku, TOKYO
Malaya Great Eastern Life Building, Ampang Road, KUALA LUMPUR
represented in
Indonesia by Gunung Agung, Kwitang 13, DJAKARTA

India Orient Longmans Private Ltd, 17 Chittaranjan Avenue, CALCUTTA 13 (P.O. Box 2146)
with branches at
Nicol Road, Ballard Estate, BOMBAY 1 (P.O. Box 704)
36A Mount Road, MADRAS 2 (P.O. Box 310)
24/1 Kanson House, Asaf Ali Road, NEW DELHI 1

East Pakistan Mr N. Mahmood, Orient Longmans Private Ltd, 17 Nazimuddin Road, DACCA

West Pakistan Longmans Green & Co. Ltd, Hayat House, 14 Hall Road, LAHORE

South Africa Mr H. B. Timmins, 109 Long Street, CAPE TOWN (P.O. Box 94)

Printed & Bound in England for the University of London Press Ltd
by Hazell Watson & Viney Ltd, Aylesbury and Slough

PREFACE TO SECOND EDITION

A SECOND edition has become necessary less than thirteen months after this book was first published. Letters which I received and the experience gained after a number of further lectures made me add a few new paragraphs. I have tried to clarify some misunderstandings of Cizek's ideas and to answer several questions. I should like to thank all the writers of letters, and the publisher for providing additional space (which means more paper).

W. V.

SHIRLEY, BIRMINGHAM,
January 1944.

PREFACE

THIS book is a result of the many hundred questions which I have been asked after my lectures on Child Art and of many visits to schools in Great Britain. It could not have been written without the inspiration which I received from very kind audiences all over the British Isles. It could never have been written without Franz Cizek, the man who knows more about Child Art than anybody else, and whose voice I always seem to hear. I could not have accomplished my task without the Selly Oak Colleges Library and the generous guidance of Mrs. Edith Adams, Dr. H. G. Wood, and Mr. Anthony Noble, as far as the English is concerned. I started my first talk in English by saying : " Please, do not corrupt my English ! " If Mrs. Adams did not entirely change my " Austrian accent "—do not blame her.

W. V.

SELLY OAK COLLEGES.

CONTENTS

CHAPTER I

THE DISCOVERY OF CHILD ART

IT is strange that scarcely anything done by children has been preserved which is older than a hundred years. True, we possess some works by young painters. Dürer's self-portrait when he was thirteen is one of them, but this was certainly " corrected " or finished when he was older. We have hardly anything from anonymous young children, whereas we, fortunately, possess a great number of documents of primitive art, some tens of thousands of years old. We have in our museums examples of peasant art, executed centuries ago. Why no Child Art ? If we recall the attitude of the average adult towards the child as recently as one or two generations ago we come to the conclusion that the child was regarded as something inferior, as a being to become grown-up as soon as possible. It is clear, then, that his drawing or modelling was considered of no importance. How many of us have heard it said in our childhood : " Do make something ! Don't waste your time and paper. Don't scribble ! " The widow of the Tyrolean painter Bachlechner, who came from one of the Dolomite valleys where for centuries the peasants did exquisite wood carvings, told me how her husband was beaten by his father when a boy of five, until his fingers bled, because he was doing some wood work.

What we possess of Child Art is only a few decades old. The term " Child Art " itself is very young. Two generations ago nobody dreamt that every child is a born artist, which does not mean that every child should or could become an artist. The discovery of Child Art is parallel with, or perhaps a consequence of, the discovery of the child as a human being with his own personality and his own particular laws.

We find passages in *Rousseau* which show that the great man (great in spite of all his shortcomings) had a vision of the child being a personality of his own. He says : " The child is not a small grown-up, he has needs of his own, and a mentality adapted to these needs." I found in *Herbert Spencer's* book on education a recognition of the child as an artist. In this book, written between 1854 and 1859, are words which sound almost revolutionary. " The spreading recognition of drawing as an element of education is one among many signs of the more rational views on mental culture now beginning to prevail. . . . What is it that the child first tries to represent ? Things that are large, things that are attractive in colour, things round which its pleasurable associations most cluster—human beings

7

from whom it has received so many emotions ; cows and dogs which interest by the many phenomena they present ; houses that are hourly visible and strike by their size and contrast of parts.   And which of the processes of representation gives it most delight ?   Colouring. . . . The question is not whether the child is producing good drawings.   The question is, whether it is developing its faculties. . . . *During early childhood no formal drawing-lessons are possible*.[1]   Shall we therefore repress, or neglect to aid, these efforts at self-culture ? or shall we encourage and guide them as normal exercises of the perceptions and the powers of manipulations ? . . . it must happen that when the age for lessons in drawing is reached, there will exist a facility that would else have been absent. . . . From what has been said, it may readily be inferred that *we condemn the practice of drawing from copies*[1] ; and still more so, that formal discipline in making straight lines and curved lines and compound lines, with which it is the fashion of some teachers to begin."   This was written more than eighty years ago.   I am afraid Herbert Spencer would find to this day schools where little children are made to copy.

In 1887 the Italian *Corrado Ricci* wrote a booklet, " L'arte dei bambini " (The Art of the Children).   There, as far as I could find out, a term relating to Child Art was used for the first time.   In the same year *Alfred Lichtwark*, a German, published a book, " Die Kunst in der Schule " (Art in School), in which it was stated " that the child in his representation of things simplifies according to laws which are valid for all times and all peoples, and we have recognised the relation between the first attempts of the child and those of primitive men."   Eternal laws in Child Art and the relation between Child Art and primitive art ! In 1895 *James Sully*, in his " Studies of Childhood " (new edition with corrections and additions published in 1903, from which I quote), speaks for the first time, as far as I know, of " child-art."   Although he warns us of the " adult's fallacy, the tendency to judge children by grown-up standards," he speaks of the " misrepresentations " of small children (" wrong " proportions, " wrong " division of space, " wrong " number of legs in their animal pictures, two eyes in profiles, three-sided houses, " errors " of perspective, exposure of objects which are covered by others, etc.) ; yet he states : " The art of children is a thing by itself," and, which is more important, *"The little artist is still much more of a symbolist than a naturalist."*   Further, " Crude, defective, self-contradictory even, as these early designs undoubtedly are, they are not wholly destitute of artistic qualities.   The abstract treatment itself, in spite of its inadequacy, is after all in the direction of a true art, which in its essential

[1] The italics are mine.

nature is selective and suggestive rather than literally reproductive."
There can be no doubt, Sully, with all his limitations, was far ahead
of his time, and so was *Ebenezer Cooke*. This is revealed by his paper,
" Our Art Teaching and Child Nature," read before the Education Society
and published in the " Journal of Education " (December 1885 and January
1886). Ebenezer Cooke deals with the discussion at the Art Section of the
International Conference on Education. Health Exhibition, 1884, and some
passages seem to be worth quoting :

" Mr. Ablett offered an easy practical suggestion. We admire Greek and
Japanese freedom, precision, and beauty. Yet the brush, their special
instrument, is not used generally: its point hardly at all for drawing with
colour. The ' thoroughly sound training in outline drawing,' rare in the
schools of this country, of Mr. Sparkes, was to Mr. Ablett ' a dreary discipline
of copying lines; originally the Greek decorator drew his design directly
with the brush, because it was a shape admirably adapted to that instrument to make. No lead pencil outline can give any conception of the apt-
ness of the original design, or any of the technical power the Greek enjoyed.
Freehand ! What freedom does a lead pencil give compared with its facile
colleague the brush ? ' This passage is connected all round with other
questions. Its strong blow at the usual freehand outline is supported by
history and nature. Muscular sense is the element underlying all, even the
questions of materials and instruments. . . . Mr. Sparkes thinks of copying
only, not of the child expressing its thought. . . .

9

"All intellectual growth results from exercise of faculty or function. Mr. Sully is not alone in saying,—'Training a faculty means regular calling it into activity by supplying the conditions of its existence. . . .' If the faculty is not cultured when possible, we may never gain the higher forms, and may weaken others. Rousseau and Froebel held that each age had its own completeness, and that the later stage was only perfected through the perfection of the earlier. . . .

"It is possible to use the apparatus and neglect the spirit. It is more difficult to evolve expression, to exercise imagination, to stimulate voluntary mental activity, than to teach mechanically. Its drawing can easily be used for the lower purpose. The teacher who is literal, or slave to a system, may regard it as a series of copies of lines, with little aim beyond exactness, cramming order in, not evolving it, attempting no exercise of imagination, but suppressing it by neglect. Imagination some teachers consider their enemy. Accuracy is ever opposed to it. . . . Froebel makes it the very centre of his system ; for his aim is education, not instruction, still less decoration. The unfolding of all the child's powers, the easiest and best,—the only way,—is to use its own natural activities. He finds the child a creative being, with active imagination. He accepts the fact, adapts his teaching to it, and supplies materials, for 'exercise strengthens faculty.' For him, imagination has the wide and full scope of Mr. Sully, perhaps even fuller. . . .

"To give to the child what may be suitable to the teacher,—the results, the science, the organised knowledge—instead of letting it follow its nature and acquire the knowledge first, is to reverse the order of mental development. To drag the child through all the interminable routine, copying lines only, and exercising only its fingers, exacting exactness, and cramming an order which should be evolved slowly, with no gleam of joyful invention, no stimulating discovery, is to forget the whole spirit of the founder. . . .

"If the nature of the child is a guide, we need revision ; in early stages, reversal. It wants colour, imagination, movement, life. We give dull, flat copies—motionless, dead. It asks bread, we give stones,—crystals in the Kindergarten, casts in Art Schools. . . . The appeal, of old, was to a sympathetic, interested parent ; not to a teacher, or system, desiring fruit before flower. . . .

"The choice is between accuracy and interest, technical skill and child-nature. . . . The child's attention is aroused and sustained by interest. It is a power not to be neglected. The teacher who includes child-nature in his subject—its progressive capacity, its extending interests, as they develope,—will try and get this and all natural forces on his side. . . . The nature of the child can no more be altered by us. We must study, sympathize, and conquer, by obeying it."

But both Sully and Cooke were only forerunners of another man. *Herbert Read's* introduction to the beautiful catalogue of the British Council's Exhibition of British Children's Drawings for North and South America, 1941–1942, contains the following passage : " Though the ultimate place of art in the educational system is far from being a settled question, it has won some degree of recognition as a subject, especially in the primary stages, and this recognition has been won largely as a result of the revolutionary reform which has taken place in the conception of art teaching in Europe and America. The history of this movement goes back some fifty years, to pioneers like Ebenezer Cooke and James Sully ; but it was Professor Cizek in Vienna who first demonstrated both the aesthetic and psychological advantages of releasing the creative impulse which is present in all children ; and it was he who had the difficult task of vindicating the aesthetic value of the drawings thus produced by children. During this same period of forty years, a growing appreciation of primitive art and revolutionary developments in modern painting have helped to bring children's art within the general range of aesthetic appreciation."

At the end of the nineteenth and the beginning of this century a few German teachers tried to reform the old methods of teaching art. One of them was the Hamburger *Götze*. He heard of an Austrian who had started practical work with children in Vienna. His name was *Franz Cizek*. Götze paid him a visit and was so impressed by what he saw that he reported to the Austrian Minister of Education what an important work was being carried on in Vienna.

Cizek was a painter, not a teacher, although I believe that every true artist is also a teacher. Franz Cizek was born in 1865 at Leitmeritz, a small town in Bohemia, then Austrian. His name is Czech, but I do not know how much (or little) Czech blood he has inherited, but this I think is not of great importance. In old Austria it was not easy to find one's racial background. Cizek came to Vienna when he was twenty, and entered the Academy of Fine Arts. He lodged with a poor family, where, fortunately, there were children. These children saw him painting and drawing, and they wanted, as Cizek has so often related, " to play painter too." Out of his genuine love for children, one of the reasons of his success, he gave them what they asked for—pencils, brushes, and paints. And beautiful works were created by them. It was a happy coincidence that Cizek was in close contact with the founders of the " Secession " movement, a kind of revolution of young painters and architects against the old academic art.

He showed his friends—among them important men like Klimt, Olbrich, Moser, Otto Wagner—the drawings of his children, and these artists were so thrilled that they encouraged Cizek to open what they scarcely liked only to call a school, but for which they had no other name.   There children should be allowed, for the first time, to do what they liked.   Now a long fight with the school authorities began.   They saw no necessity for an institution such as Cizek wanted to establish.   They turned the project down.   But this did not discourage him.   He made a new application.   And this time the School Board asked him to submit a programme for his new school.   Cizek wrote down the immortal words : " *To let the children grow, develop, and mature.*"   This programme they found entirely inadequate.

It was in 1897 that Cizek got the permit to open his very first Juvenile Art Class.   It was a private enterprise, but the experiment proved so successful that, in 1903, a comparatively early date, the State offered him rooms in the State " Kunstgewerbeschule."   This was, fortunately, the only material support he ever had from the State, and it proved a blessing, for it saved him from any interference in his work.   There was no inspector, and no curriculum, no time-table, and no superior.   In many countries State interference has proved to be a fatal influence on new enterprises.

This Juvenile Art Class Cizek carried on until 1938.[1]   Forty years were spent in humble and loving observation of thousands of children whose ages ranged from four to fourteen years, including some children of two years of age.   In these experiments and careful study of the children's works, which Cizek called " documents," he discovered the eternal laws which are followed unconsciously by the young creators.

It was perhaps no mere chance that it was in Austria that Child Art was discovered.   Those of us who were young in the years before the World War

---

[1] It may interest friends of Franz Cizek what I heard in Summer 1943 from Miss *Emma Cadbury*, America, who kept contact with Vienna until 1941.

" If only Prof. Cizek had gone to England," she wrote, " perhaps he might have finished his book. . . . [See footnote, page 171.] I think he was still having a children's class in the Spring of 1941, and was still negotiating with the Yale University Press. . . . He evidently was working on the book.   In January 1940 he sent a report about the book to the Yale University Press, with an Index. . . .   In July 1941 he told Miss N. that ' if the text were not used by the Yale University Press for finishing the book, the text would go to the Archiv der Stadt Wien.' . . . She gathered that he had made a record of this, perhaps in his will.   On August 14th, 1941, she wrote : ' . . . He did not look any worse than when I saw him before, but to see a blind painter is pathetic.   He is very grateful for all you do for him, though he would, of course, have liked to go on with his book, which is now impossible.'   That was my last news of him.   In April 1941 Miss N. wrote that ' the school has a subvention from the municipality as far as the premises are concerned.   A pupil pays 10 R.M. a year, and costs of course are at least tenfold.   He keeps the school for pure idealistic reasons and as a source of material for the completion of his work.' . . .   She had written of his being very poor—only on Sundays having full dinners. . . ."

had a feeling that it was a time of sunset in Austria after centuries of rich culture. Suddenly new life flamed up in literature (Rilke, Hofmansthal, Schnitzler, Schönherr), in music (Mahler, Schönberg), in art (the Secession-ists, Adolf Loos). It was a last contribution that the best of the old Austria had to give to the world.

Cizek was one of the contributors. Thousands came to Vienna every year to see his work, the greatest numbers coming from Great Britain and America. Long before he was appreciated in his own country (if he ever was) his name was familiar to many English-speaking people. One of the memor-able occasions which I shall never forget was the visit of the Maharaja who was carried in a chair to the Juvenile Art Class a few weeks before the "Anschluss." Years before, Rabindranath Tagore came to see Cizek and wrote a poem for him.

First came Cizek, and then followed the psychologists. This is important. Child Art is primarily Art. But it is good that psychology has proved what Cizek as an artist had intuitively said years before. A long list of psycho-logists have occupied themselves with Child Art.

In 1904 *S. Levinstein*, Leipzig, published " Untersuchungen über das Zeichnen der Kinder bis zum 14. Lebensjahre" (Inquiries about the drawing of children until the 14th year of age). Although some of the ideas of Levinstein are antiquated, most are valid to this day, and certainly were decades in advance of the time when he published them. " Children have no conception of proportion." To-day we would say, they have proportions different from the adult. But more important : " Signs and pictures are a language for the child. To draw means describe, not represent. He draws something because he wants to say something about it." Levinstein reminds us that the ancient Greeks had only *one* word for describe, draw, register, engrave, and write.

William Stern said at the third congress for Experimental Psychology in Frankfurt-on-Main in 1908 : " Everyman experiences himself as the centre of the space surrounding himself, but this space is only conquered by steps. In the second year—with some children even earlier—the capa-city is developed to recognise objects which are pictorially represented. Already in their fourth year children begin to come out of the stage of mere scribbling." And in his " Psychology of Early Childhood up to the Sixth Year of Age " William Stern made this extremely important statement, that " *Scribbling is to drawing much what babbling is to speech.*" Later another psychologist, *Karl Bühler*, in his book " The Mental Development of the Child " (1919 ; English version 1930), dealt further with the striking parallel between language and drawing. But his belief that the child draws synthetically is contradicted by the Swiss *Piaget*, who stated in his work " The Child's Conception of the World " that " in drawing, children give only the detail and neglect the synthesis." Piaget speaks of the juxtaposition in the child's drawing as well as in his thought. Karl Bühler's attitude towards Child Art is mainly based on Sully, Levinstein, and another man, Georg Kerschensteiner, who also was a pioneer.

Kerschensteiner, who was then superintendent of the Munich schools, published in 1905 a book, " Die Entwicklung der zeichnerischen Begabung " (" The Development of the Graphic Gift "), which was the result of the examination of 300,000 drawings and pictures of 58,000 Munich schoolchildren. It was the idea of a man of genius to collect and analyse so great a number of children's works, and to draw conclusions from certain features which again and again appeared. I do not think anything like it had been done before. Although Kerschensteiner certainly did all he could to exclude the influence of adults, a certain influence of the teacher remained. But the sheer overwhelming wealth of material is a certain guarantee that the observations made have weight, observations which confirmed Sully's and—to a certain extent—Levinstein's views. (Both authors were known to Kerschensteiner.) The Munich pedagogue found that the child cannot represent space, the third dimension, and further, that drawing from imagination is easier for the child than drawing from nature. How revolutionary Kerschensteiner was is shown by this sentence in his work : " Drawing from objects or models in the class is forbidden as a rule." He pointed out the fact, surprising to most people, that the best work did not come from the children of artists, sculptors, architects, or well-to-do families and parents of high intellectual culture in general, but mostly from children of simple, even poor artisans. On the other hand, Kerschensteiner, who was very progressive, believed that " the boys exceed the girls in all types of drawing, except certain kinds of decorative design, in which the girls do better than the boys." How far this view was due to predominant convictions of the time or simply went back to the fact that at that time boys had more opportunities in schools than girls is difficult to say. In any case, Kerschensteiner's view on boys' greater creative ability was contradicted in Germany itself. (Ernst Linde states in " Art and Education ": " So far, we have not succeeded in finding a difference in the drawings of boys and girls up to twelve.") And much later, the American *Florence Goodenough* stated in her work " Measurement of Intelligence by Drawing " that " school statistics have almost invariably shown that girls, on the average, make more rapid progress through the grades than boys ; that they are more often accelerated and less frequently retarded. . . . It is possible that the aesthetic sense develops earlier with girls than with boys, and that their higher ratings may be partly accounted for on this basis."

But apart from smaller details Kerschensteiner's work is of great importance in the history of Child Art. Yet the man who was for decades a leading personality in the democratic German education had not enough influence seriously to reform German art teaching. Twenty-three years after Kerschensteiner had published his work, the German Wulff could say in his book " The Art of the Child " (1928) : " The task of art teaching is to educate the average talent so far as it can be educated, that is to represent reality directly from perception as it is seen and not as merely imagined."

After the World War, 1922, *G. F. Hartlaub* published " Der Genius im Kinde " (The Genius in Child), which defended with great warmth the child's urgent necessity to create, and analysed many aspects of Child Art.

There was another German who had a clear view of Child Art : *Gustaf Britsch* in his work " Die Theorie der bildenden Kunst " (Theory of Pictorial Art), 1931. His practical influence also was not very great, and his disciple *Kornmann* met real opposition. Cizek said repeatedly that what Britsch and Kornmann had found mostly in theory was proved in his own fifty years of practical work with children.

America's contribution to Child Art is due to the tremendous opportunities given to a great many courageous women and men in her schools after the World War. In no country besides Great Britain was the new gospel more heartily welcomed. America added a new chapter : the use of children's works for all kinds of tests.

In England names like *Tomlinson, Richardson, Gibbs, Eccott,* are familiar to everybody interested in Child Art. The great exhibition of 1938 in the London County Hall, with its hundreds of beautiful pictures done by ordinary London schoolchildren, will remain unforgettable to the thousands of visitors. At private exhibitions like the one at the Zwemmer Gallery, London, in 1937, children's paintings were bought for five and ten guineas apiece. Could that have happened a generation ago ? We can now see that the general public have slowly begun to appreciate a child's graphic expression. The battle for Child Art from twelve to fourteen years of age is won, but how far does the ordinary person understand or appreciate real infantile art ? Are all children, for instance, allowed and encouraged to scribble ? Is there still no elementary school in any country, or shall I say in English-speaking countries, where children are no longer forced to copy ? There is still much to be done by those who fight for Child Art, and that means for the child against the so often very stupid adult.

CHAPTER II

CHILD ART AND PRIMITIVE ART

THE best way to understand Child Art is to study primitive art, both of races that lived tens of thousands of years ago and the art of living primitives. The most superficial observer must be struck by the similarity between the art of primitive man and Child Art. In both there is a lack of perspective, of the third dimension, except in Negro sculpture, of shadows; in both there is an inability to represent space. Proportions are different from ours. (The hopeless adult would say "wrong.") The right angle is predominant and obtuse and acute angles hardly occur. (The right angle is not in mathematical exactitude.) There is in both first a representation of men and animals, because they are alive and show movement. This, of course with exceptions, cannot yet be represented. When plants appear it is a sign of maturing. Therefore ancient Egyptian Art is not purely primitive. There is hardly any synthesis or composition. Neither the primitive nor the young child produces from nature. "Only those who are no more part of nature draw from nature." But the optical memory of primitive and child is enormous. Their eyes are better than ours. They see details which we never see, but details only, not the whole.

Both produce from *imagination*. "Imago" is a beautiful Latin word, and the translation "mental picture" is entirely inadequate. Neither of them wants to copy nature. They have no use for right perspective, right proportions, etc. Experiments have proved it. When small children were given pictures of known objects in strong perspective, the children misunderstood the pictures. (Passy, " Notes sur les dessins d'enfants," " Revue philosophique," 1891). Egyptian peasants were given pictures of animals executed in a modern way faithful to nature. They did not recognise animals which were familiar to them. Sir Gardner Wilkinson wrote in " The Manners and Customs of the Ancient Egyptians," vol. II (London, 1841) : " The mode of representing men and animals in profile is primitive, and characteristic of the commencement of art (see prehistoric remains in the British Museum) : the first attempts made by an uncivilised people are confined to it ; and until the genius of artists bursts forth, this style continues to hold its ground. From its simplicity it is readily understood ; the most inexperienced perceive the object intended to be represented ; and no effort is required to comprehend it. Hence it is that though few combinations can be made under such restrictions, those few are perfectly intelligible, the eye being aware of the resemblance to the simple exterior ; and *the modern* (written in 1841) *uninstructed peasant of Egypt, who is immediately struck with and understands the paintings of the Theban tombs, if shown an European drawing, is seldom able to distinguish men from animals ; and no argument will induce him to tolerate foreshortening, the omission of the parts of the body concealed from his view by the perspective of the picture, or the*

(From " The Supposed Errors in Drawing common to Beginners," by Habib Georgi, Cairo.)

FIG. 1.—FROM THE ROCK TOMBS OF AMARNA.   FIG. 2.—GLASS, DRAWN BY A CHILD.

Compare circles used for bread loaves and straight line for plate in ancient Egyptian drawing (Fig. 1) with circle for top and straight line for bottom of glass in Child's drawing (Fig. 2). Further compare these two with the drawing of the fountain in the village square, by a boy aged 8 (Picture 4, Plate III).

introduction of shadows, particularly on the human flesh." [1]   When Chinese peasants were given modern pictures of animals, they did not recognise them.

The Inspector of Drawing in the Ministry of Education, Cairo, Mr. *Habib Gorgi*, in a paper read to the VIIIth International Congress for Art Education, in Paris, 1937, entitled, " The Supposed Errors in Drawing common to Beginners, Their Relation to the Revival of Racial Art," points out that " if left alone to follow his own bent, the child when drawing a glass will

[1] The italics are mine.

draw a circle for the top and a straight line for the bottom. In the same way, the ancient Egyptian artist used to draw a straight line for a plate and complete circles for loaves of bread on the plate." (See pictures, page 17. The Egyptian Loaves of bread were made round.) One can compare with those drawings the fountain in the village square done by a boy of eight in Cizek's school (Picture 4, Plate III). In further examples the author shows how both the modern Egyptian child and the ancient Egyptian exaggerate the dimensions of one subject while they show the others small.

Some people would contend that our modern Egyptian children are simply the descendants of those ancient Egyptians and therefore reveal a certain heritage in their drawings. It would be foolish to deny that there is something like a national inheritance, that, for instance, Mexican children's drawings differ from Russian or Chinese, but, and this is an essential point, there is something approximating to an eternal child who follows—unconsciously—eternal laws in his production, and these laws are the same, to a large extent, as those which guided and still guide the primitive. Those laws are independent of time and nation. The idea that there is an eternal, or if the word is permissible, an international child, has some consolation in our time. But one has to add : The child is perhaps only 80 or 90 per cent. child, the rest is national heritage. In some children the proportion might be 95 to 5.

The young child produces like a primitive also for biological reasons. We all believe in the biogenetical law, that we repeat in our life from birth or pre-birth the history of mankind. (The Ontogenesis is the Phylogenesis.) Why, then, should the child who repeats the history of mankind biologically not also repeat it in his production ? Why should there not be a connection between Easter Island statues and plaster-of-Paris modellings of a youngster ? Why should there not be an Easter Island, an Egyptian, an early Greek, an early medieval stage ? Would it not be surprising if it were otherwise ?

G. A. Stevens (in " Educational Significance of Indigenous African Art," 1935) says : " Primitive art is the most pure, most sincere form of art there can be, partly because it is deeply inspired by religious ideas and spiritual experience, and partly because it is entirely unselfconscious as art ; there are no tricks which can be acquired by the unworthy, and no technical exercises which can masquerade as works of inspiration." I remember some words of *Sir William Rothenstein* at the opening of a Cizek exhibition in London in 1934 : " Simplicity as well as wisdom comes from the Gods." He was sitting under a huge picture of a girl, in brilliant colours, with a house and human figures in quite " wrong " proportions, but of a strength rarely attained by a grown-up civilised artist.

Can the comparison between Child Art and primitive art go too far? Is there an absolute identity in the reasons for the creation of both? Yes in both, as *Gregor Paulsson* put it (" The Creative Element in Art," 1923) : " The first impulse toward graphic expression has its origin in the desire for emotional outlet, the pleasure derived from the objectification of emotion." The pleasure motive certainly is there, but others stress the *animism* of primitives. Is there, too, that striking parallel which we have so often observed in both child's and primitive's work? And do we know enough of the religious conceptions of children other than what has been introduced by adults to be entitled to apply Freud's doctrine of the origin of primitive art to Child Art? *Freud* in " Totem and Taboo ": " Only in one field has the omnipotence of thought been retained in our own civilisation, namely in art. In art alone it still happens that man, consumed by his wishes, produces something similar to the gratification of these wishes, and this playing, thanks to artistic illusion, calls forth effects as if it were something real. We rightly speak of the magic of art and compare the artist with a magician. But this comparison is perhaps more important than it claims to be. Art, which certainly did not begin as art for art's sake, originally served tendencies which to-day have for the greater part ceased to exist. Among these we may suspect various magic intentions." In a footnote Freud mentions S. Reinach (" L'art et la Magie," in the collection " Cultes, Mythes et Religions "), who thinks " that the primitive artists who have left us the scratched or painted animal pictures in the caves of France did not want to ' arouse ' pleasure, but to 'conjure things '."

But we should perhaps refrain from rejecting a comparison which at first sight may look paradoxical. In the same chapter (when dealing with the taboo rules to which the women of savage tribes are subject, and dealing with the possibility that these taboos may also serve aesthetic purposes, an explanation which may expose him to the reproach of attributing a most improbable delicacy of psychic activities to contemporary savages) Freud says : " But I think that we may easily make the same mistake with the psychology of these races who have remained at the animistic stage that we made with *the psychic life of the child, which we adults understood no better and whose richness and fineness of feeling we have therefore so greatly undervalued.*" [1] Perhaps we have lost that direct contact with childhood which primitives never have lost.

----

[1] The italics are mine.

Primitive art existed long before language existed in our sense, and that is one of the reasons why it existed. The primitive wanted to express himself. It cannot be chance that we have documents 20,000 years old, in graphic but not in written language. Primitive art and Child Art are first expression, not representation. There is an urgent desire in both to express themselves. Language for them is too abstract. Therefore they express themselves in a picture language. This explains the tremendous power of expression in primitive and Child Art.

We find traces of creative expression already among animals. The building of nests, the spider's web, the " drawing " by chimpanzees if chalk is given to them, the collecting of boxes by monkeys similar to the " playing " with boxes by small children.[1] If we go even further—to plants and crystals —we come to the question as to whether life in all its forms is not shaping, forming, creating, " gestalten " ?

Against the comparison of primitive art with Child Art it has been argued that the oldest cave drawings or Bushman paintings are very faithful to nature. Hunted game, for instance, is so well " represented " that we clearly recognise the species. Sometimes movements are so perfectly rendered that the camera could scarcely do it better. There is one answer to this argument : Even the most faithful " representations " of animals were not done from nature. The fact of the drawings being done in caves would make it impossible. And another objection : Why are there so few scribblings of primitives ? Though we may not possess them, it does not mean that they have never existed. It may be that only those primitive works have survived which correspond to a later stage in Child Art.

As the child more and more mixes imagination with memory, so the primitive more and more drew from memory. Just as the Chinese landscape painter did and does. The nearness of some primitive art to nature certainly exceeds that of the young child in general, but this is the only difference, and it is perhaps less a difference than a differentiation.

The lack of perspective in primitive and Child Art goes back to a lack of depth-experience. *Oswald Spengler* in his " Decline of the West " pointed to the fact that the principle of perspective is only known to the West. He further stated that " the want of perspective in children's drawings is emphatically not perceptible to the children themselves." Neither did the primitive perceive it. About this lack of perspective or depth-experience Spengler makes the following important suggestion :

[1] *Wolfgang Köhler* (" The Mentality of Apes ") : " The anthropoid apes show a certain spontaneous interest in weaving grass, leafy branches, and other pliable material into a kind of rude circle in the midst of which they will then contentedly squat."

" For the involuntary and unqualified *realisation of depth,* which domin-ates the consciousness with the force of an elemental event (simultaneously with the awakening of the inner life), marks the frontier between child and . . . Man.   The symbolic experience of depth is what is lacking in the child, who grasps at the moon and knows as yet no meaning in the outer world, but, like the soul of primitive man, dawns in a dreamlike continuum of sensations.   Of course the child is not without experience of the extended, of a very simple kind, but there is no world-perception ; distance is felt, but it does not yet speak to the soul. . . . It is *perspective* that begins to awaken a premonition of something passing, fugitive and final.   The very words of distance possess, in the lyric poetry of all Western languages, a plaintive *autumnal* accent that one looks for in vain in the Greek and Latin. The late poetry of the withering garden avenues, the unending lines in the streets of a megalopolis, [1] the ranks of pillars in a cathedral, the peak in a distant mountain chain—all tell us that the *depth-experience* which con-stitutes our space-world for us is in the last analysis our inward certainty of a Destiny, of a prescribed direction, of *time,* of the *irrevocable.*   Here, in the experience of horizon as future, we become directly and surely con-scious of the identity of Time with the " third dimension " of that experi-enced space which is living self-extension."

If one thinks of early medieval painters with their figures behind and above each other, their lack of " right " perspective, and their precious independence of time and space, one will enjoy the following observation of Spengler : " In a picture it is possible to set the things inorganically above another or side by side or behind one another without any emphasis of perspective or interrelation, i.e., without insisting upon the dependence of their actuality upon the structure of space which does not necessarily mean that this dependence is denied.   Primitive men and children draw thus, before their depth-experience has brought the sense-impressions of their world more or less into fundamental order."

The first colours used by stone-age man in his outlines were red and yellow or brown.   The favourite colour of healthy young children is red, which is the colour of our life-blood, of movement, love, revolution.   Speng-ler's contribution in this sphere : " Yellow and red, the classical colours, are the colours of the material, the near, the full-blooded.   Red is the charac-teristic colour of sexuality—hence it is the only colour that works upon the beasts. . . . It is pure blue that etherealises the Madonna's mantle.   This relation of the colours has established itself in every great school as a deep-felt necessity.   Violet, a red succumbing to blue, is the colour of women no

[1] Spengler's huge modern city, the symbol of our culture.

longer fruitful and of priests living in celibacy.   Yellow and red are the popular colours, the colours of the crowd, of children, of women, and of savages.   Amongst the Venetians and the Spaniards high personages affected a splendid black or blue, with an unconscious sense of the aloofness inherent in these colours.   For red and yellow, the *Apollinian, Euclidean-polytheistic* colours, belong to the foreground even in respect of social life ; they are meet for the noisy, hearty market-days and holidays, the naïve immediateness of a life subject to the blind chances of the Classical Fatum, the point-existence.   But blue and green—the Faustian, monotheistic colours—are those of loneliness, of care, of a present that is related to a past and a future, of destiny as the dispensation governing the universe from within."

In the British Museum can be seen the facsimile of a Chinese mural painting executed 1575 B.C.   It is a monkey with rocks and flowers.   And the monkey is in blue.   This use of blue shows that China already 3,500 years ago had an old culture, for we have no reason to think there existed blue monkeys.   The anonymous Chinese artist used purposefully that " wrong " colour—just like a young child would use " wrong " colours.

The lack of right proportions in primitive and Child Art goes back to the fact that both want to create or represent what is most important to them. They are not illogical.   Neither are they allogical, to use Madariaga's description of the British.   Primitives and children have a different logic, and a logic which is as right as an adult's logic, perhaps even " righter."

One of the most striking features of ancient Egyptian and infantile art is their " writing " of pictures on lines.   The writer of this book had a wonderful experience at the Nursery School Association Summer School in August 1941 in Cambridge with three- to six-year-old children.   Some of them painted, others drew.   Suddenly a three-year-old girl detached herself from her painting group.   I asked her what she wanted.   " I want to write a picture," she replied.   Meaning, of course, she wanted to draw.

The ancient Egyptian, like the young child, puts eyes in front in profiles, and both do it for the same reason.   They do not want to draw things as they are seen, but what they know of them.   Therefore, if a very young child draws a profile, he sometimes puts even two eyes in it.   Or, if he draws a rider sitting on a horse in profile, he will show both legs.   In a picture of a house he will frequently depict what is inside.

Primitives and children produce out of a surplus of energy.   They are innately creative.   This opinion is questioned by *Margaret Mead,* a scholar who has lived among the relatively little influenced inhabitants of Samoa and New Guinea.   Among both she made her foremost study the growing up of children and adolescents. Her main discovery in Samoa was that adolescence there " is not necessarily a time of stress and strain," or, in other words, there was no puberty problem, very important in Child Art. Her experience among " a relatively untouched people, the brown sea-dwelling Manus of the Admiralty Islands, north of New Guinea," brought her to the conclusion that the " creative child " is not an established fact. I quote from Margaret Mead's " Growing up in New Guinea " (1931) : " Those who believe that all children are naturally creative, inherently imaginative, that they need only be given freedom to evolve rich and charming ways of life for themselves, will find in the behaviour of Manus children no confirmation of their faith." But the author herself weakens that view in her following statement : " Artists they have none, but they, *richer than their neighbours, buy their neighbours' handiwork*.[1] To the arts of leisure, conversation, story-telling, music and dancing, friendship and love-making, they give scant recognition. . . . The ideal Manus man has no leisure ; he is ever up and about his business, turning five strings of shell money into ten." Margaret Mead repeatedly stresses the importance of trade, not production, to the Manus adult. " Trade is the most important thing in life."

The children of the Manus were encouraged by Margaret Mead to draw in her presence. " The children were given perfect freedom. I provided them with pencil and paper and smooth surfaces upon which to do their work. They were neither praised nor blamed ; the very small children were sometimes encouraged, but only in the most general terms. For months these children avidly covered sheet after sheet of paper, throwing themselves whole-souled into this new and amusing occupation. In their work most of the tendencies which we find highly developed in the arts of different peoples were present in the efforts of individuals, conventualisation, realism, attempted perspective, symbolism, arbitrary use of design units, distortion of the subject to fit the field, etc. But, and this is the decisive point, there was no work produced which could be called art. On the canoe prows, on the betel spatulas, on the rims of bowls were carvings of real beauty made by neighbouring tribes. But the children had no precedent for drawing, and their work shows this lack. Working without a guiding tradition their efforts are interesting but they lend no support to the theories of those who hope for great things when the potentialities of children are pitted against the adult world. And yet there is no reason to argue from any racial theory of ability that these people simply lacked an artistic gift, because the wood-carving of their neighbours

[1] The italics are mine.

of the same race ranks with the finest work of its kind. Had every child been set to work with a penknife the results would in all probability have been far higher."

The last sentence gives us a ready answer. The Manus children could not express themselves by graphic means, but they might have done so in carving. Their neighbours of the same racial origin did so, and their wood-carving " ranks with the finest work of its kind." Our Manus only bought from them. A striking parallel with our mainly consuming Westerners ! Further, in the Manus children's drawings Margaret Mead found nothing that she would have called art, meaning Western art ; but does that necessarily mean that it was not there ? We needed a long time to discover the symbolism and beauty in primitive art, and we even now have only just begun to see it.

The wave of enthusiasm for primitive art and Child Art is a kind of renewal of Rousseau's " Retour à la nature," but it is less artificial. It is a consequence of our longing for the unbroken, unsophisticated, strong, and sincere. And therefore it can make us hopeful.[1]

[1] *Captain K. C. Murray* sent me the following letter from Africa : " In peace-time I am an Education Officer in Nigeria, specialising in art and handwork. I was responsible for getting up the exhibition of Nigerian work at the Zwemmer Gallery in 1937.

" I have just been reading your book and like your point that Child Art is different from Adult Art and has its own ' laws ' . . . I would not go so far, however, as you apparently do, in equating Primitive and Child Arts. The aesthetics of laws of Child Art change and develop according to the growth of the child, but those of a Primitive Art remain constant : there is no steady progression. Also, Primitive Art is in a sense mature in its technique. The child feels his way to the result ; but the primitive, the West African sculptor, for example, knows the qualities of his materials and of his tools and goes about his work according to a regular system. It could be argued, of course, that Negro Art is not a proper example as not being truly primitive. I would, however, differentiate Primitive Art from Mature Art by its technical limitations and by its limitations in expression. In Primitive Art there is mastery of tools and materials in some directions but not in all. Tools, while adapted to the purpose in view, are not the ' last word.' Other instruments are possible that would be more effective from the point of view of production, although not necessarily from the point of view of aesthetics. Secondly, Primitive Art expresses emotions of a comparatively simple kind, although it may do so with considerable mastery. . . . Child Art expresses feelings that have been hardly consciously formulated. . . .

" My experience as a teacher has been with Africans, and chiefly with adolescents. These have been more uncontaminated by civilisation and its accompaniments than have European children, and probably puberty is not such a time of stress. I have not had the difficulties, therefore, that teachers in Europe seem to have. It has only been necessary to arouse interest and create confidence. . . ."

I did not intend to equate Primitive and Child Art, I only wanted to show some striking parallels. In addition to those mentioned, both—primitives and children—draw first. Even if young children paint, it is as a rule a drawing of lines with the brush first. " The conceptions of children and of primitive peoples are not visual but are to a high degree bound up with the self. . . . The world is not so much perceived as an external object, but is built up from within and coloured by the artist's own emotional experiences." (*Victor Loewenfeld,* " The Nature of Creative Activity.") *Dr. Ruth Griffiths* points out the love for vivid contrasts and direct opposites. People are very big or very little. And *Herbert Read* says : " Art . . . in the Stone Age was a spontaneous exercise of innate faculties, as art still is with young children and savages."

CHAPTER III

THE PSYCHOGENESIS OF CHILD ART

Pure unity of " Gestalten " (forming and shaping).

|

Differentiation of colour, form, and space.

|

Introduction of characteristics ⎱ *Byway to conven-*
(enrichment by perception and ⎰ *tionalism, natural-*
experience) . . . . . . ⎰ *ism, illusionism.*

|

Introduction of types.

|

Real infantile Art. ⎰ Abstract-symbolic stage (Egypt).

|

Rhythm of spirit and hand . . . ⎰ *Byway to ornament,*
decorative art

|

Scribbling and smearing stage.

(Begin at the bottom and read upwards.)

These are the stages of Child Art which *Cizek* distinguishes after fifty years of experience with thousands of children. No age limits are given, because the stages are not severely separated from each other but are overlapping. The transition from one stage to another is a gradual and continuous process. There is nothing abrupt in growing. In addition to that, children are individualities, and in any of the different periods into which childhood is divided one child will remain longer than another.

The first three stages—scribbling, rhythmic, and abstract-symbolic stages—represent an overflow of vitality. The very first stage, the scribbling and smearing stage, is of extreme importance, and much evil has been unconsciously caused by parents who did not encourage or even allow their children to scribble. This scribbling is an absolute necessity for a child and it should begin between eighteen months and two years of age. The opinion that it generally and merely is an imitation of activities of adults has hardly any confirmation in facts. It is partly an activity of muscles, partly an expression.

25

Another opinion must be qualified. It may happen that a child scribbles without any aim and afterwards sees by chance some meaning in the lines. One has also rightly observed that a small child does not always begin by saying: " I shall draw a man or a house " and afterwards does it, but rather the other way : he first draws and says afterwards : " This is a man " or " This is a house." But from this observation we must not draw the conclusion that the child as a rule produces unintentionally. Lines are not shaped to a house by chance. The child creates intentionally. It is not essential whether it is done consciously or unconsciously or half-consciously. What counts is, that the very young child produces entirely from imagination. It is there, within himself. " It " (Freud's famous " it ") creates. How could we otherwise explain the production of blind children ? Or a small baby, sitting on sand, and immediately forming and shaping that material ? He wants to express something which he cannot express by words or, much more difficult, in spoken language. He may want to express things, he may want to express hopes, fears.

Rhythm is the origin of all art (music, dance), rhythm is life (breathing and pulsating, day and night). The child finds great satisfaction in rhythmic production, or we may call it more modestly, repetition. A figure, a line, is repeated in his drawings, colours are repeated. We find drawings of quadrupeds with eight or ten legs. It is not only the incapacity to count (again the parallel with primitives, who sometimes have no word for more than three), but the joy in repetition. And here again a parallel with language. " *And* he did this, *and* he did that, *and* . . ." It is rhythm. It is sometimes meaningless rhythm, at least for us adults, as in both drawing and nursery rhymes.

The scribbling stage, rhythmic stage, abstract-symbolic stage, is one way to describe the development of Child Art. Another way, and Cizek himself has indicated it, is the following : First the child produces out of a kinetic or dynamic desire, which does not mean that he represents movements, but that the movement, life being movement, is within himself, and wants an outlet. (There are other outlets, besides drawing, painting, modelling.) He will produce human figures, " a man." He will, at first, make no distinction, just a man, as later he will draw " an animal," and still later " a bird " for instance, or " a fish." No differentiation. But out of " a man " the father will come, and the mother. First he will draw the father, for instance, and name him afterwards ; gradually he will come to the period when he will draw and simultaneously say : " Now I am drawing father." Be on your guard and do not smile about the " clumsiness " of the drawing.   There is more work and effort in the little child's scribbling than in some pictures of adult artists.[1]

When drawing or modelling with clay, they will put parts together.   They cannot create a whole.   They do not see and they do not think as a whole, but only in detail.

The symbolic in Child Art is underlined by all psychologists.   Primitive art, too, is symbolic.   Not knowing the meaning of all the symbols is no reason to doubt their existence.   Sometimes children do not know themselves or cannot express by words what they mean.   We find symbolism in early medieval painters and even in some modern painters.   The young child is symbolic in form and colour, but his work is not entirely symbolic, or not always so.

The formation of types in the child's production is a sign that he is leaving the early infantile stage.   But we must be aware that the child's types have nothing in common with an adult's scheme.   Only adults and those children who imitate adults are schematic.   The unspoilt child is tremendously creative.

The child gradually comes closer to nature—because of more experience. He does not go with closed eyes through the world.   Out of this greater experience and knowledge of things more and more characteristic details appear in his works.   Now, for some children or even for most children in our civilisation the temptation of nature is too great.   They become naturalists or illusionists.   They create the illusion that the drawing is the real thing, mixing picture with reality.   This tendency towards naturalism is a decline and a byway from the straight way of Child Art as shown in the graph.   We already had a similar byway before, when some children at the stage of rhythmic production fell for ornament.   The sideway to naturalism occurs between ten and fourteen, and is much more frequent than the earlier one to ornament.   It is not always naturalism ; it may be a tendency to caricature, or it may be towards the strongest form of naturalism, illusionism.   All of which are declines.

The right way should go from introduction of characteristics to differentiation of direction, colour, form, and space.   The right angle becomes an obtuse and acute angle.   The word " differentiation " must be understood in the right sense.   The child does not proceed from wrong

---

[1] Dr. Ruth Griffiths distinguishes 11 *drawing stages* :
1. A stage of *undifferentiated scribble*. 2. *Rough geometrical shapes* appear. 3. *Combination of lines and squares.* 4. *Combination of circles and lines.* 5. *Juxtaposition of many objects.* 6. *Tendency to concentrate on one object at a time.* 7. *Further juxtaposition.* 8. *Partial synthesis.* 9. *The pure picture.* 10. *Multiplication of pictures.* 11. *Development of a theme.* (" A Study of Imagination in Early Childhood.")

to right or from making mistakes to what is correct, as so many people think, but from no or little differentiated to more differentiated. From the right to the acute angle is a good example.

And another view must be corrected. There is no progress in Child Art or in art in general, dear as this conception may be to many good people. Why, we may ask, should van Gogh be more than Rembrandt ? Who would dare to put a contemporary writer higher than Shakespeare only because he has wireless and aeroplane at his disposal ? Or is Shakespeare more than Dante and the Italian greater than Euripides ? There is no progress, only a natural and slow growth both in art and in Child Art. There are people nowadays who put the early Italian higher than Raphael, and there is something to be said for it. Cizek would prefer, as a rule, the work of an eight-year-old to that of a fourteen-year-old child. We must give up the superstition that something is better because it is more modern ; that merely means it is nearer to us. Yes, the fourteen-year-old's work is easier to understand, but that does not mean that it is stronger, more genuine, or better.

Few children, alas, go the ideal way to " Gestalten "—for various reasons most of them stop earlier ; but the tendency of the educationist (parent or teacher) should be to guide the child the right way towards pure " Gestalten."

One could describe that way thus : From creating out of pure imagination the child produces more and more from memory and—nature. There is no clear break which would separate the different stages. They are overlapping, for hardly any child produces out of sheer imagination. Whilst another fact is : Few even small children are 100 per cent. imaginative in our civilisation. Some may be 90 per cent., others 80, 70, down to 20 per cent. imaginative. Some children, because of heritage, or the influence of adults, will be born copiers. Again, the task of the educator is to encourage by every means the imaginative side, that is to say the creative impulse.

Besides the decline towards naturalism there is a decline towards mannerism (sheer skill). This is another kind of " repetition," but it has nothing to do with that early rhythmic stage. Just like the mere copying of nature, " repeating " of nature has nothing whatever to do with the rhythmic stage.

Every young child is creative, but in a different degree, and in different *media*. The old school (and old-fashioned parents) knew only drawing. But a child may have no sense for drawing, perhaps because of biological reasons, yet still be a wonderful painter, or he may reject both drawing and painting and produce excellent creative sculpture work. Or the little girl may have no use for any of the three media, but do very good embroidery work or paper cutting. Children are naturally different.

As for the simple-minded, the picture, first of all, tells a story, so the child produces his pictures. He wants to tell a story. He adds detail to detail. One thinks of medieval picture stories, or woodcuts. The love

PAINTING BY A LEEDS GIRL, AGED 7.
The house is in blue, the tree in red, and the sky in orange.

of many children for comicals goes back partly to that preference for stories in picture form.

The greatest mistake of the old-fashioned art teaching was not knowing that a young child produces what he knows, not what he sees. This is done unconsciously. And he selects from what he knows the most important or what he regards as important. There is a wise and artistic economy in this selection. "Selection also is art," says Herbert Read.

The child does not, and does not want to, represent nature. I had the following experience when I visited Blenheim School, Leeds, and saw the children painting. One girl of seven caught my attention. She had just finished the painting of a house in bright blue, and went on to make a tree in red. When finished, she painted the narrow sky—oh that wonderful narrow sky of small children !—in yellow. Three " wrong " colours. Now, this girl definitely preferred her colours to the natural ones. She had seen a house, a tree, and the sky, so there was no question as to whether she knew the natural colours. But later, when I was speaking in a teacher's course on that particular child's painting, a teacher suggested that the girl might be colour-blind or had a distorted sense of colours. As a matter of fact, colour-blindness is extremely rare among females, but I wrote to Leeds, and a few simple tests proved beyond any doubt that our little girl was absolutely normal in her colour sense. But she was an artist in choosing her own colours.

I once worked with two girls of five and six in a London suburb. When I started to tell them a little story which they should depict, they told me at once that they had been to " Punch and Judy " the day before, and they were so interested in that great event that I naturally asked them to make a picture of Punch and Judy. They had a twofold easel at their disposal, bright colours, and large brushes, and they began at once. The five-year-old girl did a big red Punch, and herself in a corner in profile (the eye of course " Egyptian," that means in front), both on the one side, but half of the paper remained blank. Now, " filling the space " is one of the things Cizek would suggest to a child who leaves blank spots. A picture is also something very real : the filling of a certain space. A child may just forget to fill a certain space, or he may be a little lazy. So I was going to ask her if it would not be nice to make something in addition to Punch and herself. But I had no need to ask. Suddenly the girl said to herself : " I shall make a door, a blue door." And she did. She painted a big blue door. She even said, while painting : " I must leave a space for the knocker." Which she did. I had my suspicion about the blue door, and I asked the mother afterwards if there was a blue door or any door at the Punch and Judy show. Her answer was in the negative. Our little girl had invented the door in order to fill the space, and it was blue because of that unbroken " right angle " of colours (red and blue). Needless to add, there was not the slightest influence by adults.

Another story which has become almost famous. The Cizek children, or most of them, had been to a circus, and so the subject he suggested the next Saturday afternoon when they met was " circus." A little girl painted an elephant, and she painted it in purple, but this child had seen an elephant. Cizek tactfully inquired why the elephant was painted in purple, and the reply was : " Don't you know, Herr Professor, grey is not sufficiently exotic for an exotic animal like an elephant." Cizek was very pleased.

But this story has a nice little continuation, which is told by *Hilda Wally Oldham* in her book " Child Expression in Colour and Form." " A little boy from an infant school which I visited had just been to a circus, and he drew me an elephant with a man sitting on its back. He went further than Cizek's girl in his desire to do justice to this miraculous animal. The boy was five years old and it was the first time that he had seen an elephant. He painted the head, trunk, and body bright blue, the tusks, legs, and tail bright brown, while the man, being of no significance compared with the elephant, was dressed in sombre black."

How certain children set about what they want to draw was proved to me in a Glasgow Nursery School. It was almost a slum school, and I thought the children would need a little story as a suggestion for a picture. I told them what I thought to be a vivid story about a boat and some sailor's children, a two-minutes story, at the end of which I asked them if they would like to draw or paint my story. They said nothing, but went to their papers and started to draw or to paint. After a few minutes I began walking around (this is the right place of a teacher in an art room) and looked at their work. None of my children were drawing or painting my story, but drew an animal, a house, or something else that had no connection with my well-intended story. Those children did not need my suggestion. They knew what they wanted.

To a psychologist Cizek once said : " First the child speaks, then he learns the grammar, not the other way round." He meant to say : First they are creative, and only much later comes the grammar of drawing and painting. This is the right way.

The young child is more perfect than the older child, he is richer, happier. The first years of life are the most important. We all know that. Therefore Child Art in a child's earliest years is of extreme importance.

Cizek once said : " *There is so much of the summer and the autumn, but the spring never comes again.*" And Francesca Wilson wrote about Cizek : " The age he loved most was from one to seven."

CHAPTER IV

FROM TALKS WITH CIZEK

THERE are many wrong impressions regarding Cizek's ideas. So I shall try to let Cizek speak for himself. I will begin with some sentences culled from a delightful little book, published by *Francesca Wilson* in 1921 and to-day hardly obtainable outside the British Museum. Francesca Wilson is a Birmingham teacher, who with *Bertram Hawker* saved Cizek after the last war when the Juvenile Art Class was in danger of being closed for lack of funds. Then, under the auspices of the " Save the Children Fund," Francesca Wilson and Bertram Hawker organised Cizek exhibitions in Great Britain, which had a great success, morally and financially. Francesca Wilson came in close contact with Cizek, and as a result of her talks with him she published three booklets, " The Child as Artist, Some Conversations with Professor Cizek," " A Lecture by Professor Cizek," and " A Class at Professor Cizek's." From this personal source she revealed the man and his work :

" How do you do it ? "

" But I don't do it. I take off the lid, and other art masters clap the lid on—that is the only difference."

" But you must show them some things ; you must at some time have pointed out to them their mistakes in proportion. Don't you point it out so that the child should learn and improve ? "

" But on the contrary. Children have their own laws which they must needs obey. What right have grown-ups to interfere ? People should draw as they feel."

" But what about Nature ? "

" We want Art, we don't want Nature."

From talks with Cizek between 1924 and March 1938, which I render as far as possible verbatim.

" There was always psychology in art. But to consider Child Art from a psychological piont of view—as it has been done in recent years— is against my conviction. Art is not realised psychology, but the forming and shaping of life. All true art contains psychology, but so wonderfully dosed as only nature can dose. If an olive tree grows, this tree contains in its sap all aromatic essences and so perfectly dosed as no druggist or chemist could dose. The same applies to art. Art is the most comprehensive subject.

" Nothing here is made, but it has grown like flowers. Vienna was the right soil, because where nations and cultures meet, art originates. Where little mixing occurs, usually little art is produced.

" Child Art was disregarded, ridiculed, and scoffed at. Even now people visit me who, when I show them real infantile work, only laugh. I estimate very highly those things done by small children. They are the first and purest source of artistic creation.

" The influence of school often is bad. There children must observe things which they never should conscientiously observe. That which is strongest in art is what one talks about least.

" The child creates subconsciously. What originates from the conscious is thought out, what comes from the subconscious is touching. Everything great has originated from the subconscious. Art more and more dries up because it is supplanted by the intellect, and from the subconscious only a few produce any more. The time for art is over perhaps. In its place probably technique will come. The latter can reach a very high level, of course, an immense accomplishment, but it will be something different from art or another kind of art.

" The most beautiful things in the creating of the child are his 'mistakes.' The more a child's work is full of these individual mistakes the more wonderful it is. And the more a teacher removes them from the child's work the duller, more desolate and impersonal it becomes.

" Even to-day people admire what is imitation of nature. The more faithfully nature is copied the more the work is admired. Real creativeness remains something to smile at for some people.

"If a child is used to drawing a tree, then he masters the task with ease. But if he is not used to doing it, he has to struggle. I like making children do what they are not accustomed to do. Creative art begins when the child starts struggling to find the right form. When he has the form at his finger-tips, the work becomes empty and manneristic. Mere mechanical skill is dangerous. I like to say to a child : 'Make something which you have never made before.' Then something truly childlike will result.

"Everything memorised is worthless. The least of the things experienced within is more valuable than the most skilful imitation.

"I have liberated the child. Previous to me children were punished and scolded for scribbling and drawing. I have saved them from this treatment. I said to them : What you do is good. And I gave mankind something which until I came had been spurned. I have shown parents the creative power of children. I have kept the parents away from the children. 'Entrance prohibited for grown-ups.' Formerly parents and teachers suppressed the best things in children. But I have done all that not from the point of view of the pedagogue, but as a human being and an artist. Such things are not achieved from pedagogy but from the artistic and human or from human artisticness.

"The child is born with creative power, but at a certain age this power begins to decline. Either mannerism or naturalism appears, as a substitute for creative power.

"Man begins to take nature as a criterion for his art. Nature is his crutch and he uses nature as an excuse for everything inartistic. 'It is like nature.' He begins to confuse art with nature. Instead of creating, the copying of nature begins—with or without a model.

"Young children usually are more sensible than teachers and parents suppose. Their brains are still fresh, they conceive many things in the shortest time which grown-ups do not understand, for they are too anxious.

"*Child Art is an art which only the child can produce.* There is something that the child can also perform, but that we do not call art. It is imitation, it is artificial."

CHAPTER V

THE TEACHER

LET us state a simple fact first. One cannot teach art. Nobody can. No Cizek, no society, no state can produce artists. Artists are born. And only those who cannot be prevented from becoming artists, who would sacrifice everything for art, can or should become artists. What the community can do for them is to make their life a little happier. (Usually artists are persecuted—in their lifetime.) Perhaps one out of a thousand is an artist. Very likely artists are those who remain eternally children.

School has nothing to do with the education or training of artists. It is beyond its possibilities. But what school can and should do is to encourage and not to suffocate the innate creative capacity of children. That is within the scope of school. Now the question arises : What is the right attitude of the teacher ?

What Cizek once said in the presence of Francesca M. Wilson about the ideal parents (" There are three types of parents—first, those who are always fussing after their children, controlling and correcting them and trying to make them walk in the same paths as themselves ; then the infinitely pre-ferable variety, who neglect their children altogether ; and lastly, the ideal kind, who watch their children from a distance and are ready with encourage-ment and friendship when that is needed ") goes for the teacher also.

The most important function of the teacher in an art room, and perhaps in every other school room also, is to create a *creative atmosphere*. If he succeeds in that, half the game is won. How this creative atmosphere is produced is an almost entirely personal matter. Some will do it with a few words, perhaps with a gesture or with the question asked : " What are you interested in to-day ? " Some will use the room itself and decorate it with highly coloured pictures (if possible by the children themselves). Much depends on the room, but not everything. The most modest " art " room with an excellent teacher is preferable to the best equipped room with a bad teacher. That applies to school buildings in general, but I would not say it to members of education committees who are responsible for the financial side of education. I have been to slum schools where beautiful work was done in overcrowded ugly rooms. But the ideal, of course, would be a real art room and a real teacher.

Next to the creating of a creative atmosphere, and closely connected with it, is what a great Englishman, *Dr. Rendel Harris*, put in these admir-

able words : " The secret of teaching is to get *en rapport* with your audience." Without this " rapport " the teacher is lost. But how to get it
is again a personal question.

Then you must *take the child seriously*. He knows at once if you take
him seriously or not. But it has no sense—quite apart from the moral
side—to simulate or to be a demagogue. The demagogue in school is a
very illuminating subject, and he is as great an enemy of good progressive
education as demagogy in political life is the mortal enemy of democracy.

Modern psychologists have discovered that every man, young and old,
and even entire nations, need three things to feel happy, and *Caroline
Graveson* has framed the need in the most precise words : *Love, security,
and significance.*

Love. But it must be genuine love, nothing artificial, copied, nothing
for the " head " or inspector or member of the education committee, nothing
tailored. And " dear child " is not enough. Only those should be allowed
to enter a classroom who are full of genuine love towards children.
The entrance of others should be forbidden. (And if we were wise we should
forbid them the entrance to a teachers' training college. We must not
forget that some people, at least in some countries, become teachers just as
they would become judges or attorneys, because of—let us hope unconscious
—sadism.) We cannot have enough of that love or sympathy towards
children. Children know or feel at once whether the adult who is standing
before them or who is with them is full of true sympathy or not. They also
know if the teacher has chosen his profession only in order to earn a living ;
if so, it would have been better had he become a clerk or entered some other
profession. This statement has been made to the writer by male inspectors
in many countries (less in Great Britain). Among women teachers, the percentage of those who are teachers because it is a vocation for them is higher
than among men teachers. Perhaps two-thirds of women teachers are
born teachers, and two-thirds of men teachers would be better occupied
behind some desk. But Great Britain is here, as in so many cases, rather
an exception. We must be fair to teachers, for are there many professions
in which the work has been chosen as a vocation ? Cizek, with many modern
educationists, is for the woman teacher at least as far as young children
are concerned.

Security. The small child produces in absolute security. The question
is often asked if Cizek allows rubbers. Of course he does. He allows
everything. But although or perhaps just because his pupils may use a
rubber, they hardly ever have one. Again, that remoteness from life of the
old school : because the rubber—or whatever it was—was forbidden, many

children felt an ardent desire to use one. If one watches young children drawing, one feels the absolute security of their production. Every stroke is certain. There is no hesitation, no uncertainty. The teacher who robs the child of this feeling of absolute security commits a crime. The teacher's task is to preserve it as long as possible. Again, the parallel with language. How much has been destroyed by the old school in some countries in robbing a child of his precious security in his " Altersmundart " ?

Significance. I lately had a wonderful experience. After drawing and painting for an hour, I discussed with a dozen children from three to seven their pictures ; that means we discussed them together. I had finished when six-year-old Susan started sobbing. When I asked her why she cried, she said : " But you have not criticised my picture." Needless to say, I had done it, but I did not know that Susan was outside when I discussed and praised her picture.

Susan was a shy child, but when she did not get "significance" or thought she had not, she asked for it, and in the presence of a great number of adults. How strong must have been her need of appreciation, recognition ! By the way, are we adults different ? How badly do we need significance in our profession, in our social position, after a speech, etc. ! We only camouflage it carefully and so prove even stronger that we urgently need it.

We should give significance to the child and to the work he creates. That does not mean boundless praise. A *lukewarm atmosphere* is the right one for a child. Cold, negative criticism is deadly, but extravagant praising

is not without danger.   In presence of a miracle of beauty in a child's
work one feels sometimes one must shout : " It is marvellous what you have
done.   That's as beautiful as van Gogh or Gauguin."   But one uses more
modest words.   It should be restrained praise, giving the child the feeling
that it is quite natural for him to have done such a good picture.   Still,
if a teacher is rather inclined to take for granted everything good the child
does, the danger is greater that he may give too little than too much appreciation.   I remember a teacher in my school who on principle never praised.
And he thought it was a wise economic pedagogy.   Did he know how hungry
we were for one word of appreciation ?   Of course he knew.   But he did
not want to give to our work significance.   He had no love for children.
I was born in 1894, but I shall remember to my last day what an old teacher
(not old in his heart) told me when I was hardly seven.   It was only one
sentence of praise, but it gave full value to what I had tried to do.

When we defend the child against the adult (an Austrian journalist once
said : " Where there are stronger ones, I am always for the weaker "),
against a society which still so often has not sufficient regard for the child,
when we defend his personality, we believe we fulfil a sacred duty.
But so much as we fight for the personality of the child, so much we defend
the *personality of the teacher*.   The stronger his personality the better the
results.   Therefore Mr. Smith should have a Mr. Smith class, and Mrs.
Jones a Mrs. Jones class.   But both can learn from Cizek.

" Now, if I do not have to correct or to draw for my children, nor to
criticise their work, at least negatively, for what am I paid ? " a teacher
once asked me.   My answer, a little over-simplified, was : " Just for that."
But I must expand that.

The main task of a teacher is to guide the child on his way, of course
the child's way.   That means, first, that the teacher must learn to know his
children.   The old schoolmaster had forty or fifty children in front of him
who were just numbers.   The old school used that ugly term "pupil material."
(Just like " men material," " soldier material," in certain countries.)
The teacher was a commander (and a bad one), the director of a prison.
(What a parallel between prison and some of the old schools !)   The intelligent teacher must individualise, and in order to be able to do that he must
learn to know his pupils.   To be a teacher means to do quite a lot of
exploring.   For already children of two are different in character.   It may
be weeks and months before a child is discovered.   This is one important
function of the teacher : *to discover his pupils*.

And next the task is to deal with that child according to the child's
personality.   And he will, paradoxically as it may at first sound, *help as*

little as possible. The question arises whether the adult should or can help at all. We believe in the indirect method. Sometimes a word will be sufficient, a look, a nod.

I once was allowed to experiment with a group of seven-year-old girls in a Liverpool school. As all the children were particularly interested in games, our subject was " games," and most of the girls did pictures of netball. The work was proceeding happily and I was walking amongst the children (there is no reason for a desk in a real art room), when suddenly one girl came up to me saying, " I have started drawing a girl playing, but I don't know how to put the arms." She did not say, " Please, draw the arms for me," but she probably meant that. I looked at her for a moment and replied something like : " But, Mary, surely you know it. I am quite sure you do." The girl turned round, went to her easel and continued her figure. Why did she ask me, indirectly, for help ? Or rather, what did she really want ? Perhaps she wanted to show off ; perhaps she was a little lazy ; perhaps she wanted to try it on with the stranger ; perhaps —and I think that would be the best explanation in most cases—she wanted some *encouragement,* just as young people need some push in exams, when a nod would be sufficient to encourage them to give a right answer. It is then that the examiner fails, not the students. I gave that little push with a few simple words. In other cases it might be more difficult. I remember a boy in Cizek's class who said, " I don't know how to draw a horse." Cizek's reply was, " If I wanted to draw a horse, I would know how to do it. But I don't want ; you want it. So you must draw it." That would be sufficient for many children, but not for all. What then ? Once Cizek had to send a boy into the street to see what a horse looked like. But this was rather the last resort. The boy went down, came back and drew his horse. What is right for Peter may be wrong for Paul. To individualise is the recipe.

Now, all this is much *more exhausting than the old scheme.* It is superstitious to think that Cizek's "method" makes life more comfortable for the teacher. Almost the opposite is true. Cizek himself after one and a half or two hours of work with his children was exhausted, and that after fifty years of practical experience.

It was one of the tragic misunderstandings of the school reform after 1918 in Central Europe that a number of teachers accepted it because they thought, " Oh, that's fine. We shall have less to do. Life in school will be jolly comfortable for us." School reform partly collapsed because of that selfishly wrong and wishful thinking of lazy teachers.

The child is the centre of the art room (or school), not the teacher, head, or inspector. Around this child the room should be built up and the " lesson." This demands a high *morale of the teacher*. He must be able to remain in the background. Not geographically, of course. He must be capable of disappearing (not literally). What has been said of good governments—the less heard or seen of them, the better—applies to the teacher also. He needs *tact*. Have all teachers innate tact ? There is no other kind of tact. Have they knowledge, presence of mind, personality, and courage, not mere superiority based on physical strength and external authority ?

Now what about *discipline* ? In an art room (and, again, in every decent schoolroom) there is a wonderful kind of discipline, the discipline of work. That presupposes that the children are interested in their work. If they are not, all shouting is useless. It is a commonplace that the healthy child who " has nothing to do " becomes mischievous. I hope he does.

There should be a kind of beehive humming in a real art room. That is a sign that the children feel happy. I don't like schools where one hears only the master's voice. Of course, there are children who would not say a word for two hours, but most are inclined to have, occasionally, a few friendly words with their neighbour. Why not ? We adults cannot keep quiet for long.

Cizek has no marks and no " means of discipline," and I have visited many schools in many countries, but I have not found a school where there was more intense work and *truer* discipline than in Cizek's school.

The Cizek children were not even compelled to come regularly. If they missed school, no letter from the parents was required or a reason for their staying away. And there was no report in which it was said " often absent." There was no report at all, except for those very few who wanted one. And yet there was no playing truant in the Cizek school. Oh it school would be more intelligently run ! Why tell a child " You must . . ." or, " Be careful, next autumn you will go to school, and there . . ." ?

No, the child should be told : " If you are very fortunate and when you will give your best, you will perhaps be admitted to school. It is a privilege. And if you are lucky, you may be allowed to stay there." That old principle : *Never say you must, but you are allowed*. Do you remember the story of the fence painting in Mark Twain's " Tom Sawyer " ? This is pedagogy (and statecraft) in a nutshell. But do all teachers apply the story ?

I was once in a poor (almost slum) school in Stoke—by no means typical, as they have excellent modern school buildings. It was in June or

July and the teacher in a class of fifty-four said to me : " My children are very sad to-day." I asked the reason. " To-morrow holidays begin." I told her that this spoke more for her school than anything else. I was reminded of the Vienna schools after 1918 when the school reform was introduced. The number of children playing truant sank rapidly, even the number of children who fell ill. Children were unhappy when kept away by illness ; they wanted to go to school. They stayed, voluntarily, at school beyond the legal school-leaving age. So school *can* be a place where children are happy, where they can play and work and hardly notice a difference between either, a place which they like and love. And that is precisely what at least the art room should be.

What about the " *difficult* " child, the child who, for instance, does not want a subject with which the other twenty-eight children are quite satisfied? Or the child who does not want to draw, but would like to paint, whereas all the other children are quite happy with drawing ? Is the teacher supposed to say, " What is good for all the others is good for you too " ? Even if he has to devote more time to this one " obstinate " child than to the rest of the class, he should not force the one child. Democracy does not only mean rule of the majority, but the right of the minority. And sympathetic understanding of the outsider will bear fruit.

What about the untalented child ? " *There is no stupid boy.*" There is a different amount of creativeness in the children, and children may be different in different media. It is old schools' superstition that a child who does not want to draw is lost for art. He may be excellent in painting or modelling.

Cizek once was asked what his method was. Although he does not like the word method, he replied, " *The moment decides the method.*" Children are different every day, just as we are. The weather plays a rôle ; outside events, things perhaps we shall never know, influence the children. The teacher must adapt himself to the changing personality of his children, and not the children to his.

In a good art class (and class in general) a kind of *class feeling* will arise. It is one of the reasons why we have schools and why individual education— as it was usual in former times—has disadvantages. We want the children to educate each other, to influence each other. There is nothing against Mary helping Eileen, showing her, explaining to her, *criticising* her. Of course, the latter can go too far. Children are sometimes cruel. In the discussion in the previously mentioned Liverpool school I had to stop the harsh criticism of some children. It went too far. In Cambridge one of the boys, Michael, three years old, was far from being very productive ; but while

he refused to paint, he went to the other working children and said to them,
" I bet you can't make a motor-boat." "Look at hers. It's crooked."
(It was recorded by the editor of " Child Education," who was sitting near
the children.) Now, Michael's criticising faculty was highly developed, but
this kind of criticism is not to be encouraged. But healthy, perhaps hard,
criticism by children may sometimes be encouraged. The adult's criticism
has to remain charitable, and always positive.

There are great temptations for the teacher in any case. He knows so
much more than his children. He has so much more experience, and so
on. Again, a high morale is necessary. The teacher must be able to restrain
himself and to learn from the children,—the Socratic method. And we
must learn to wait.

Of course, the teacher has the best intentions. He only wants to
accelerate the progress. He thinks he does something good in making
the children grow quicker. In our terrific civilisation the teacher should
rather slow down the too rapid growth. The tremendous danger is that
our civilisation hunts the children through their childhood and youth.
This does not make for their happiness. The slower the child matures,
the better—for himself and for his nation. Do apples from hot-houses
taste better, do flowers from hot-houses smell better, than fruits and flowers
grown in the garden ? Our civilisation threatens to become a hot-house
and tinned-food civilisation. But in hot-houses and in tins certain vitamins
get lost.

It is a blessing that there are still children. I do not want to be misunderstood. I do not preach Peter Pan. That is a charming story, but
life means growing and maturing. Children have to become adults—we
may regret it, but cannot help it. Only they should become it slowly, not
too quickly. In terms of Child Art this means : They should pass through
the different stages slowly.

Kees Boeke called his school in Holland a " working centre." This
is what every school, or at least every art room, should be. Cizek said :
" School has a sublime mission : to commit suicide." That has to be taken
with a grain of salt, naturally, but there is truth in it. The teacher must
make his pupils his *co-workers*. School is a community of pupils and teacher,
and the teacher is only *primus inter pares*. The old-fashioned schoolmaster may be shocked. But can there be anything finer than being one
of them in the art room, just a little older ?

And what about *parents* ? Some parents have a bad influence. (I
am speaking here only of Child Art.) What to do against it ? Goethe
said, " If we had educated parents we would not need education." But

not all parents are educated or have the right attitude towards Child Art. Yet something can be done. We must not forget that most parents went to schools which they did not always particularly like. Not all parents want their children to have a better school than they had themselves. Some may make the opposite mistake : they want a school in everything different from their own. (Not everything could have been wrong with the old school.) Enlightenment of parents is necessary.

Cizek's parents often fetch their children from his school, and they come ten or fifteen minutes early. So they are invited to be present at the discussion of the works. The parents stand in the background and are not permitted to say a single word. But they learn a lot. Then special parents' meetings can be arranged, so that a kind of co-operation between them and the teacher is formed which makes it impossible for the homes to destroy what the school has built up. For instance, in school the child is encouraged to create from imagination, and at home he is told to copy. If there exists co-operation between parents and teacher, it will less frequently happen that the child comes to school already spoiled.

Now, what to do with the child who is already spoilt—by his parents or in a previous school ? The task is not easy. But the teacher must do his best. Even Cizek gets spoilt children and he can do nothing but try, and with great travail, to guide them back to themselves. Sometimes he is successful—not always. Sometimes change of medium is a remedy. (To give the child a medium which he has never tried before.)

The teacher has to *inspire*. " Ce qu'il nous faut, c'est plus d'enthousiasm," said the great Belgian poet Emile Verhaeren in Vienna before the Great War. It is a bad teacher who cannot inspire. He should not be a teacher.

Should the teacher ask the child about his pictures ? We must beware of leading questions. We must not forget that a child often does not answer as he thinks, but as he believes the teacher would like him to answer. That is a kind of child's tact of heart, and has nothing to do with lying. Therefore we must ask very carefully, full of tact, or, better, we must try to make the child reveal himself, if we ourselves cannot decipher his work, in his conversation with us or with other children. Again, we must individualise. Some children can be asked without any hesitation, others not.

The real teacher in an art room is the *medium*. Now, should technique be taught ? No. The child should experiment himself, and struggle with the difficulties of a certain medium. That does not perhaps sound economical. " How much quicker if I show the child." But it is the healthier process. There is no harm in an occasional word, and certainly not in the little help by other children. But the adult must remain in the background.

Cizek often spoke to teachers—to teachers of many countries—usually against the ordinary school. It was amazing—or perhaps it was not—how his words against the school and " teachers factories " (the training colleges) were always warmly applauded by the teachers. I will quote a few sentences from a " Lecture " to teachers, soon after the last war, and published by Francesca M. Wilson :

" Education is growth and self-fulfilment. I teach children Art by not teaching at all in the accepted sense, but by letting the children teach themselves. I beseech teachers to free the schools from the schoolmaster. Make your schools into something else—make them into gardens, where flowers may grow as they grow in the garden of God. The teacher ought to learn to hover like an invisible spirit over his pupils, always ready to encourage, but never to press or force."

Never to press ! That means never urge them too much to finish their work in a given time. Nobody would or could compel a class to run a certain distance in exactly the same time. But in art (and in examinations) we do it. Peter may need forty minutes, Tommy only thirty, and Mary sixty. One of my children in Cambridge needed an hour twice (on two different days) to make one picture, whereas another girl of the same age did two pictures in one hour.

I tried to retain every word Cizek said in all those years from 1924 to 1938. I shall quote what he said about teacher and school as faithfully as it is humanly possible.

" School forms man as state wants him. Every state needs its men, and this kind of man is educated by the school, or at least it used to be so. Children are the most flexible material.

" I don't touch a child's work, because that would be forgery.

" I influence only through my presence. Of course, I influence him as every man influences. If I look at a pupil, I influence. This kind of influence I cannot exclude. If I could, a dead art would originate. But art must live : it is a result of life, and lives on for ever ; it radiates.

" I leave it to educationists how my principles can be applied to the common school.

" I divide the children who come here into two groups, one from four to nine,[1] and one from ten to fourteen, exceptionally to fifteen. These two groups produce independently of each other. I divide the children not according to their age, but according to their work. If a child of over

---

[1] But there are sometimes children of two and three in his class.

ten, for instance, still works entirely from imagination, he belongs to the
first class.   On the other hand, young children who work from appearance
go to the second group.

" I don't feel myself a teacher here, but a human being.

" School disregards or disregarded that a child produces according to
eternal laws and has his own handwriting.

" School should let the child produce from imagination as long as the
child is capable of imaginative production.

" An unspoilt child once asked me what a meadow looks like. I answered:
' Lie down in a meadow and close your eyes.'

" It is easier than many teachers think.   Habit becomes a pedagogic
means of furthering creative powers.   I can accustom a child to some form
of activity.   And by this means many difficulties disappear.

" Every young child is creative.   The degree only varies.   The teacher
must set a less creative child a task which forces him to create forms and
ever-varying forms, so that the child gets accustomed to create forms, but
not to copy.   This is the most difficult task.   The teacher must renounce
everything here.   He must be nothing, the child everything.   If he cannot
restrain himself, and if his desires and fancies become evident, the tragedy
is there at once.   The child is influenced, and, what is most important,
the conception of the child is lost, and in its place the conception of the
teacher appears, which is merely executed by the child.   With me, the
teacher must be the humblest and most modest person, who sees one of
God's miracles, but not the pupil, in a child.

" I ask a child : ' From where did you get that bird ? '   The child
replies : ' The teacher drew it on the blackboard. We had to draw it.'
I am helpless.   I ask another child : ' From where is this zigzag tree ?
Does a tree grow like that ? '   The answer : ' No, but the teacher drew it
on the blackboard.'   The children copy adults' drawings.   I try to remove
those things.   It is an enormous task.   One must try to lead the children
to where they begin to think for themselves.

" Child Art is sacred.   If it is destroyed, eternal values are destroyed.
And if it is covered by foreign layers, the natural growth of the child is
made impossible.   The task is to let the child grow naturally, but not arbi-
trarily.   Teachers misunderstood my saying : ' Let the children grow,
develop, and mature.'   They thought it meant : We let the children do
what they want to do, and we march up and down doing nothing.   To let
children grow means to let them grow according to their eternal innate
laws.   But in order to do that I must know these laws.   If there is a mis-
understanding of ' Do what you like to do,' nonsense may result.

" The wonderful logic of the child is often ruined by a spoiled logic of the adult. And wrong education cripples the child spiritually. The child thinks quite simply and logically. For instance, once a girl drew a house—a rectangle and a triangle—and asked me : ' Is that right ? ' I answered : ' Of course.' But the child continued : ' The teacher said it is wrong if one makes it so.' ' Why ? ' I asked. ' He said that the roof must always project, otherwise the rain-water will run down along the wall of the house.' But suddenly the child began to laugh. I asked why she laughed. ' Because it cannot rain in a picture.' How logical a child is !

" In a book teachers are told that they should enlighten the children about the physical qualities of what they draw. That is absolutely wrong. The author confuses physics with art. Art is what is well formed. If the roof looks well and is well formed, even if it does not project, it is art. If it is physically correct but badly formed, it is not art. If a child wants to draw a roof without projecting, I don't mind, because physics do not count here. What counts here is art. It does not rain here. But I hear almost daily things like this : A child tells me : ' I got a bad mark in drawing because I drew a horse with a rider on it, and one sees both legs.' I replied : ' But that is right ! ' ' Of course it is right,' the child says. ' Man has two legs, but our Miss says that I am not allowed to do more than one leg because one does not see the other one.' This is illogical. The child draws both legs because he knows there are two.

" *In art there should be no enlightenment.* Art is like love or religion. If there is enlightenment, love and religion are gone. There should be enlightenment in art only about what looks well or bad. If a ' wrong ' drawing looks well, I am happy, and I don't test it by physics or natural science. And further, what adults call ' wrong ' in Child Art is the most beautiful and most precious. There are no mistakes ; they are logically valuable and necessary lines of thought. They are necessary for the child. And no child should be forced to skip these stages. He should go thoroughly through them. He should not enter a new stage before the previous one is finished. Only a child who has completed all the early stages has a good basis for his whole life. If we have children with such a healthy basis, we shall get good art. These stages before puberty are the most valuable for man. What comes after puberty is in some way influenced.

" The child must learn to read as an adult reads. He must do everything like an adult. Now he must even draw as an adult. This is wrong. If the child is allowed to do everything as he likes to do it and is adequate to him, then we should have ethical, moral people. But we have people covered with layers of things which were not adequate to the child, with things he was forced to learn. It is the terror of school. But it could be different. If children were allowed to go through all their early stages, we should get different adults and not superficial ones.

" The art teaching in the ordinary school goes on till puberty and ' Volkskunst.' The further development is a matter of the art school.

" Children produce by realising themselves. They need this realisation of their ego. A child who is not given the opportunity to build himself up spiritually is not complete. He lacks something. The common school often does not form the child. There the child learns the three R's of the adults, and that means there is no self-realisation. The adults usually demand that the child works according to their standards. They usually do not allow the child to create out of himself. Thus the child is deprived of something. Many teachers just rush their children and do not care what comes after."

The teacher should not be too dignified. He must afford to be able to say, " I don't know." How dear such an honest, sincere teacher would become to his pupils ! They have an infallible instinct for an adult's and superior's defects. The reverse danger is that a teacher becomes the laughing-stock of a class, but this is much smaller. If he is so unfortunate, it is his fault. He is certainly not a born teacher. And no authority based on sheer force will make him a good one. Cizek never had to punish a child in his life.

One could sum up the whole question of teacher and Child Art in two sentences. *Not into the child, but from the child. And do not first ask yourself, What is it ? but How is it ?*

" No one can solve the child's problem for him," says *Dr. Susan Isaacs.* " Teaching is an art, not a science " (*Aldous Huxley,* " Ends and Means "). " Education is atmosphere as well as instruction . . ." (*Sir Richard Livingstone,* " The Future in Education "). Too much emphasis was laid on instruction in the past. " True teaching is concerned with the amount of interest evoked, the amount of curiosity and self-effort aroused, and not only with the mass of factual knowledge acquired " (*William Johnstone,* " Child Art to Man Art "). " Teaching teachers is the real difficulty " (*Eric Gill,* " Last Essays "). But true teachers, like artists, are born.

From one of them, a woman teacher who does marvellous work with her evacuated children in beautiful Devon, I received last summer a letter from which I quote only one paragraph : " It is so wonderful here, the trees are such a rich green, and the sun shines, and we go paddling in the river. And we have picnics, and cook our dinner over a bonfire. *Why do some people choose dull jobs, when they could be paid for playing with children ?* "

CHAPTER VI

THE MEDIA

IT has been said already that the technique or medium is the master in an art class. Which media are possible ? At least fifteen. The old schools usually knew only two media : drawing and painting. But one must be aware of exaggerating. For most small children three or four media are quite sufficient. Further, it is certainly not advisable to confuse children with too many media at the same time. If the whole class works in one medium at the same time it is an advantage. But without force.

Perhaps some will be disappointed that for many small children a *soft* pencil and *rough* paper (cheap kitchen, sugar, packing paper) are the given media. As to the size of the paper : Cizek, like many other reformers, has often been misunderstood. Of course, he always preached large-size paper, but one should use one's own judgment. Again, individualising is necessary. What would be quite a nice size for Mary may be of terrifying dimensions to Rachel, and if white paper she may really be afraid to cover it. As a rule the paper should not be too small, but it would be wrong to *force* three-year-old children to work at a huge easel. The reason why some children leave large empty spaces is that the size of the paper is too big for them. There can be a tactful training to use larger paper. As a beginning, with two- to four-year-old children, 15 by 12 inches is quite good. Those who want it may use easels at once. Cizek would give easels to those younger children who wanted them. The others get framed metal blocks in which there is always a fresh sheet of paper. This leads to the question : Should it be a book or loose leaves ? A book with many leaves is embarrassing for a young child, and not interesting enough. The exchange of paper has the advantage that the child begins every new drawing afresh and with new joy. A small child easily tires if he is given several leaves together. When the drawing is done, a new paper is introduced. In this way he has always a tidy paper.

Some young children will not like drawing. He or she will prefer *painting without drawing first*. Why not ? The old type of school regarded painting as a kind of reward for careful drawing when some of the children were really exhausted and all their eagerness gone. But some children have such a sense of colour that they want painting without initial drawing. They should be given brushes, not too small ones, and paints at once. The others get brushes and paints when they have finished their drawing.

Paints. Water-colour is too difficult for many small children. Powder colour and poster paints (cheaply bought at the ironmonger's) are the right colours. And bright colours should be used.

It is a superstition that British children, because of the climate, should be given subdued colours. They have a birthright for strong, shining colours just as other children. Small children should not be asked to mix their colours. They should not be given too many colours. This would confuse them. They should get three or four strong colours (red, blue, yellow, and perhaps green) in little pots, and everything ready before they begin. If the tools are prepared while they wait, it diminishes their interest. In some cases it is advisable to give the class first one colour, then another. But, again, we must individualise. Some children would prefer to have all the colours at their disposal at once.

There are a few children who do not like painting but are quite satisfied with their drawing. Why not leave the drawing unspoilt? This would happen if they were forced to paint. Some children will be happier with charcoal than with pencil.

Sometimes the whole class will be invited to paint at once, except those who do want to draw first. But as primitive man first drew, so for many children drawing first and painting afterwards is the natural technique. There is no place for the decadent pale mauve in a class of young children. Purple is different.

In order to make children draw the figures large, the following " trick " is used by Cizek.   He tells them to draw the head (or hat) in a way that it reaches the upper line, and the feet so that they touch the bottom line. Children should be encouraged to draw in large size.   It is not good enough if children are given the margins of newspapers.   If children have difficulty with white paper (the " dead " white), they should be given dark paper. And in rare cases of really dull children even black paper may be used. It will " draw out " from them everything.   In such a case bright crayons may be useful, but as a rule painting is better than crayoning (which is a mixture of drawing and painting).   If children want crayons, they may be given them, but they should not neglect painting for crayoning.

If there is a blackboard round the wall, it is an excellent opportunity to let children work with chalk.   The disadvantage is that nothing remains of their work unless it is photographed by an ambitious teacher.   But what is important is not the result, but the work itself.   Blackboards have the further advantage that they invite co-operation.   As a rule, children are individualists and want to work alone, but they should be encouraged, never forced, to work together.

The drawings or paintings should always be signed by the children. It is often a means of filling nicely the space.   Further, it gives them " significance," and makes them happy, and is very useful for the teacher. He knows later who has done the work.   The teacher or child should always add age and date.   It goes without saying that all the works are kept by the teacher as documents, as material for studies, for comparison with other children's work and with their own at different ages, and for exhibition. They provide an excellent education for parents and others.   There is no law which compels the teacher to let children have " their " works.   If they are accustomed from the beginning to the idea that everything done in school belongs to the school, they would not mind that they are not allowed to keep it, but would feel rather proud that their works are collected.   If they have the pictures, they would be destroyed or lost.   If children want to make a present of their works to parents or uncles, they can produce them at home.

Next to drawing and painting comes modelling in *clay*.   It is one of the most creative media, and pottery is one of the oldest arts.   Clay is cheap, and all children like to model.   But it is not in the " spirit " of this material if the whole is done.   Rather should the different parts be " added," be " built up," each part made separately, the trunk separately, the legs, arms, head.   Clay has one disadvantage, it falls into pieces if it is not baked. But this does not matter so much because, as we said before, the actual process of making is so valuable, and not the result.   In general, one should not ask children to do too huge modellings in clay. The objection of some teachers and parents that it makes too much mess can be met by providing children with a rimmed metal plate or, if that is not possible, with old newspapers.

Harder than clay and still softer than stone is another excellent material, *plaster of Paris*. But this is much more difficult to use than clay, and not many children will be capable of carving plaster. The best plan is to give them a block of it, perhaps ten inches long and three to four inches square, and, if no other knife is available, an ordinary penknife. The process is just the opposite of clay. There the different parts are added and put together, with plaster of Paris as little as possible should be removed from the block. One should still " feel " in the accomplished work the block itself. A plate will prevent mess in the art room.

One of the most excellent media and especially for young children— but older ones like it also—is *paper tearing* and *paper cutting*. Young children should be given sheets of brightly coloured paper, which they should tear—but not cut with scissors—because the direct contact between fingers and material is so valuable. The pieces are arranged and pasted on some material. There are children who " cannot draw," but make very good paper cuttings. The older ones will use scissors. In both cases no drawing should be done first.

Some children—and adults as well—have such a highly developed sense for the rhythm or contrast between black and white that they prefer *silhouettes* to any coloured picture. There was a time in Europe, about 140 years ago, when practically everybody cut silhouettes. It would be wonderful if that old technique could be revived—and through children. The revival of another old craft has been accomplished in a Slovakian village. There the beautiful design of old ceramics had been forgotten. In a school they had the brilliant idea to let children do ceramics. And so the old patterns were reborn.

One of the advantages of paper cutting and genuine silhouettes is that they encourage representation in only two dimensions. Further, this material (as Cizek, who first used it with children, has pointed out) is immensely educative ; it is a training for the co-operation of the sense of form and imagination. It also helps the irresolute pupils in having to cut out with their scissors without any drawing. Paper cuttings are even farther from nature than pictures. " The city dweller," says Cizek. " who is influenced by models and has lost the capacity of ' thinking ' in a material, has lost the capacity to appreciate the forms of the tool, and wants to replace it by nature." But paper cutting compels one to " think in the material."

Paper cuttings invite co-operation between a group of children. They can do friezes or parts of the same subject. That needs discussion or planning between those (not too many) who will work together. Cizek tells of a girl who had lost all confidence in drawing but who through paper cutting found her way back to drawing. I heard the same of a Wiltshire boy who through modelling returned to drawing.

It is good education if children are sometimes encouraged to make *pen drawings*, be it without pencil drawing first or simply the execution of a pencil drawing.

Children from six onwards should be given *lino*. For most of them lino cutting is sheer joy, and one should never underrate the importance of joy in their work. Again, if they cut without initial drawing, the better. And they should sign the prints with their name ; it gives them the feeling of being an artist.

Wood cutting is more difficult than lino cutting, and *wood carving* even more difficult than wood cutting. To work in wood is certainly beyond the powers of younger children, except in rare cases. But *potato prints* are within the capacity of even quite small children. I saw a group of happy potato printers in Mrs. Eccott's St. Pancras Juvenile Art Class.

Many girls are fond of *embroidery work* and *fillet work*. There were girls who disliked drawing and painting but were happy with embroidery. One girl had no use for any technique until Cizek suggested to her to arrange differently coloured pieces of wool. They were sewn on canvas, and a beautiful " picture " resulted.

Children are no artisans. Cizek does not ask children under fourteen to make cabinets. Not even book binding is done by his pupils. But if they find scraps of metal and pieces of wood or cardboard in the class, they construct ships ; but they are their own ships, and not copies of " Queen Mary " or " Normandie." Boys like to build sky-scrapers out of waste material. Some children of twelve are capable of doing etchings in zinc, but these are rather exceptional cases.

The expressiveness of children through their fingers should be encouraged by all means : this is a strong reason why they should be allowed to carve *puppets* or *marionettes*. What an opportunity for co-operation if a class produces its own marionette or puppet show ! And how much healthier this is than a visit to poor films.

There has been, so far, no word said about one of the most popular techniques in English schools, *pattern making*. I do not think that children should make only patterns. And there are two kinds of patterns, creative ones and just mechanical ones. If rightly "dosed," patterns can be extremely useful in a country with a very old textile industry.

In the L.C.C. Exhibition, 1938, the design of a ten-year-old boy was exhibited which was bought by a manufacturer for new fabrics. He had found the child's work fresher and more beautiful than that of most adult artists. Unfortunately, the fabric made after the design was sold much more expensively than the usual fabric.

No medium should be overdone. Strange as it may sound, there is a danger if a child becomes too skilful in one medium. It may tempt him to copy himself, to get manneristic (and this applies also to the adult artist). The child, like the adult artist, should always fight with difficulties.

Dorothy E. M. Gardner speaks of the " material which gives an outlet for power." We must not forget that much aggression is construction, and a difficult medium " absorbs."

CHAPTER VII

ART

WE have dealt until now with different aspects of *Child* Art. But Child Art is also *Art*. There are probably hundreds of definitions of art, and each one describes correctly one facet of art. For our purpose it should suffice if we say that art is expression. Child Art is expression.

The reason why so many adults stand hopeless before real infantile art is the same as why they often have no approach to modern art, or rather never had. Contemporaries seldom have an understanding of the art created in their own time. It is partly laziness, partly the fear of being wrong, and partly defence against something new, or simply the eternal conflict between old and young. This is equally true of music and literature and of adult painting as of Child Art. How was Van Gogh treated a generation or less ago? And to-day? In thousands of homes there are reproductions of his paintings. Contemporaries should be careful.

It cannot be denied that some modern painters do what the French call " épater le bourgeois." (The word is not used in a political sense.) There is probably no harm in " teasing the good citizen," but it has little to do with art. Although some modern painters are just teasers, they may all be forgiven because of those who are not. The danger is great that contemporaries would make the wrong selection. They have very often done so in the past.

" Look how natural that apple is ; just like a real apple." People who speak so—and one can meet them at every exhibition—make the mistake of mixing art with nature. These are two different spheres. The painter who only depicts and repeats nature, and maybe with utmost skill and talent, is not an artist. Art is more than the copying of nature. Photographers can do that much better.

But we must avoid the opposite mistake. Because something has no connection with nature, and does not show the slightest skill, it is not therefore art.

What is art ? Everybody feels it standing before a picture, just as when one hears music. One is touched. One probably cannot describe one's feelings and even less give the reasons for them. But there is suddenly some contact with another human soul given by a tune, a picture, or a statue which speaks to us, often through the centuries. It comes with a message from one human being to another. The revelation of a human soul, that is

art. Of course, one can only understand that for which one has sympathy. Without love no work of art can be enjoyed or understood. Criticism is not enough. And intellect is not enough. I doubt if one can get a contact with art through the intellect alone.

No work of art has been produced by sheer intellect, or to use a German expression, " auf kaltem Weg." One of the reasons why art has such a strange appeal is because its origin is in strange, mysterious regions. It is good that there is mystery about creation, the urge of creation. We have it from great painters and poets, musicians and sculptors. They had to do it. Perhaps it was only in the first few seconds and then the intellect came in ; it was not reason or intellect that called it forth, but something beyond. Call it the unconscious or the subconscious, it makes no difference. The *execution* may be a matter almost entirely of reason and skill. The conception was mysterious. About this mysterious process of begetting art, nobody has written finer or better words than the great Austrian Rainer Maria Rilke in his " Letters to a Young Poet."

And from the same mysterious spheres comes Child Art ; therefore it appeals to those who have that which responds to it.

And what about those who do not have it ? Is Beethoven or Mozart or Purcell no genius because to some people he means nothing ? Is the colour of a flower non-existent because a man stands before it who is colour-blind ?

We should not endeavour too much to discover the origin of creation.

The wings of butterflies lose their beauty if we try to "discover" their colours in a scientific way.

One sometimes hears or reads that the English are an inartistic race. Therefore English children are said not to have the artistic heritage of Continental children. It is true that the Reformation has been misunderstood, and much was destroyed at the time of the Reformation, not only the heads of all the statues but one in the Lady Chapel of Ely Cathedral. The misunderstood Industrial Revolution has done more harm than destroying part of the lovely English landscape. The creative spirit of the British has been endangered by this mechanisation of life. But the creative basis is there. England, at one time, was leading in art. This is obvious in her illuminations, lettering, wood and metal work, or in her cathedrals and churches ; also in her landscape painters, unfortunately not well represented in Continental museums, as Professor Bodkin so rightly complains. England had and has a most valuable foundation, its Celtic heritage to which it is probable most if not all European Art goes back. So there is no reason for the superstition that the English or British child is handicapped with regard to creative capacity.

One often hears the opinion expressed, and by absolutely sincere people : " If only someone would explain Art to me ! " Explanation may *add* to the joy but it cannot create appreciation of art. And it is extremely difficult to describe with words colours and forms. Can one describe or explain music by words ? " Painting with me is but another word for feeling," said Constable.

I wonder if past generations had more appreciation for art because they were less consumers and more producers. Whoever produces, and it makes no difference what, has a kind of brotherly feeling or instinct for another producer. It is not enough to deal with or to buy art as the Manus of New Guinea do, mentioned in a previous chapter. We must produce ourselves.

As Child Art became almost fashionable—a danger—some painters suddenly discovered that they too could draw and paint like children. If an early Italian produced primitive art it was the genuine thing ; but if a modern painter imitates the child, and often quite successfully and with great skill, then there is something wrong. It is at least as far from real art as the child who wants to draw or paint like an adult.

CHAPTER VIII

THE AIMS OF CHILD ART

THE normal child wants to produce. If he has no chance to produce, he destroys, which is the negative form of producing—like love and hatred. The child has a birthright to produce. It makes him happy, to use his hands. The old school hardly knew that the child had a hand, which was as important as his brains. If a child has no possibility of using his tender fingers which are made for shaping, forming, creating, he may lose his creative power. This creative power, this urge to produce something, is there from the beginning. But like every human organ, if it is not used, it deteriorates.

The Industrial Revolution transformed the majority of people in industrialised countries from producers into consumers. But culture means producing. And a nation which consists only or overwhelmingly of pure consumers will lose its culture. The machine cannot be destroyed. The Luddites were wrong. It is not the machine, it is our wrong use of the machine. If we become masters of the machine, it would be liberation for mankind from slavery, it would mean more time, more beauty, more happiness in life. But during the last decades the machine became our master, and out of that arose unemployment, social unrest, and probably even war. The inventions cannot be undone. Only we should rightly use them. That means in practical terms the reduction of working hours. The problem is not How can it be done ? For an imperfect beginning was made a generation ago, yes, but it was a beginning. It was the eight-hour day, which is universally appreciated now, except in war-time. Owing to new inventions we must come to a seven- or perhaps six-hour day after this war. It is the only solution of the unemployment problem. Of course, there cannot be a six-hour day in one great industrial nation and an eight- or nine-hour day in another one ; this would make competition intolerable. But after this war with co-operation and a reasonable world organisation we may look for a six- or seven-hour day in industry. Immediately the question arises, What will millions of workers do with their leisure time ? Will it be only cinemas, football coupons, listening to mechanised music ? We hope not. Yet, if the eight hours of leisure daily are not in some part used for productive purposes, we shall perish as Ancient Rome did, who only supplied " panem et circenses " for the masses, " dole and cinema " as the Bishop of Chichester has so well translated it. Modern democracy cannot survive if the masses are only poor consumers.   They may, or many of them, be compelled to do monotonous jobs, such as in conveyor-belt factories. But this would be one more reason for productiveness in their leisure time.

Does this mean that adults should be amateurs or dilettanti in some art or craft ?   There is certainly no harm if they are, but primarily it means that adults, if they were encouraged to use their innate creative capacity in childhood, would preserve some productive power after puberty, or at least the capacity of creative thinking.   Very few of Cizek's pupils became artists, but most if not all his children became men and women with creative initiative whatever profession they chose.

Manufacturers when questioned why some of the articles they produce are so ugly invariably reply that they supply the demands of the consumer. It may be doubtful if the general public really desire to buy trash, but just buy what is cheap and offered to them.   But even if we concede that the consumers as a whole have bad taste, there is only one way to improve their taste and to make them immune against bad products, and this is not by talking about " art in industry " or " education for better taste," but by being creative from their earliest childhood.   It is only then that they will refuse to buy mass products without any good standards.   All this does not mean that machine products are necessarily bad.   There are very good ones, and we cannot go back, to any large extent, to handwork.

The worker who was encouraged when a child to produce genuine drawings, paintings, modellings, or paper cuts, and began it, if possible, already in the nursery school to the time when he left school, will be a better man even at a machine, and certainly in his leisure time, and will also be a better consumer.

The average child of two when set on sand begins to mould and form, and when given paper and pencil will scribble.   The child wants to use his fingers and his imagination, just like the primitive who wanted to express himself.   If the child is deprived of an opportunity to express himself, to " speak out," he may turn neurotic.

They use Child Art in *Child Guidance Clinics* not only as a test but almost as a cure.   The children " abreact " through painting or drawing.   There was a boy of thirteen in Cizek's school who for months did the most horrific drawings of skeletons and other morbid subjects.   Afterwards it became known that his father was a lunatic.   Had Cizek not encouraged that boy to get rid of his heritage, it would have badly affected him.   After a time the child produced quite normal drawings.   Cizek, of course, did not " cure " that child by Child Art, but the outlet helped him   A mother in the Midlands told me about her boy of seven who reported to her for weeks

every morning the terrifying dream he had. There was absolute sincerity between mother and child. The mother with her right instinct asked her boy if he would not like to draw the bogey man and the other unpleasant things he dreamt of. After a time the dreams ceased.

It has been suggested that the purely imaginative working of the children may endanger their sense for reality and may make them day-dreamers. It is much better if they "speak out" what they dream.

Another objection is that children may lose later the capacity of doing accurate drawing which is necessary in various professions. I once went with Professor Boyd of Glasgow University to a technical college at Clyde Bank where boys and girls of fifteen and sixteen had a geometrical drawing lesson. I asked the master if he thought that his pupils would be better in geometrical drawing if they had had a chance to do creative work until they were thirteen or fourteen. The answer was definitely in the affirmative.

Child Art helps to make, or rather to keep, children happy. Man is only happy if he can produce—no matter what it is. At least in the art room children should enjoy themselves. Needless to add, in a good school they would enjoy every subject and every lesson. But for the old school, joy in learning was a contradiction in terms.

Thanks to Cizek and others we can now read many things from children's works. It is quite natural that a child's drawing, not influenced by adults, reveals as much as if not more than his handwriting or language. To learn to know the child's type, his mental age, fears, etc., is another aim of Child Art. But the analysing or psycho-analysing of children's works should not be the first consideration. The work of a child is primarily a work of art.

Tests can be made with children's works, but tests are not the main object of children's drawings. There is a danger in all tests.

I could imagine that in the future in teachers' training colleges one hour per week might be devoted to the " reading " of children's works. We are, to-day, only at the beginning of this new science. Cizek has opened a door. Others will come and explore further.

And some will perhaps retrace through Child Art prehistoric events. In " reading " primitive art we learn to understand Child Art better. Why not also the reverse ?

But these are side-issues. The main purpose of Child Art is the development of a full personality. Children who have done Art and Crafts from their earliest years as long as they had some creative power become richer personalities. As a rule, such children are better in other subjects in school as well, because they are accustomed to express themselves freely ; they are more sincere, and remain so. They are not afraid of speaking out. I said Art *and* Crafts, because, as *R. R. Tomlinson* pointed out, " Art and Handwork should never have been separated in view of the inseparable relation between design and craft."

Young children who are inclined to do geometrical patterns are often those who seek protection behind some fence. Free Child Art means free life instead of seclusion and sheltered life—which is not real. Handling of material means contact with life. Fighting or overcoming difficulties is a preparation for life. Copying from adults will certainly not educate for independent working and thinking later on. We are only God's creatures if we are productive.

Child Art certainly has *not the aim to produce artists*. This is beyond its scope. Artists, like teachers, are born. We have to accept them as a gift from God.

" The principal aim of Child Art," said Cizek, " is that the creative power develops and influences right through life."

There are teachers who think that one can teach appreciation of art. Good old and modern pictures are shown and explained to the pupils. The best way to art is to produce. Only when the creative capacity has gone, appreciation of art may take its place—as second or third best.

Miss Marion Richardson wrote in the Annual Report of the London County Council, 1936 : " There is no more certain way of understanding painting than by trying to paint sincerely.   In the light of their own struggle with the artist's problem the boys and girls begin to understand pictures, fine pictures of the kind that are now bought by schools.   They begin to be able to choose between the real and the sham because their own work, to themselves unmistakably sincere or otherwise, is giving them the touch-stone.   But will this touchstone help them to understand other forms of art ? Already there are signs that it will.   Real understanding, which alone is worthy of being called good taste, is not to be looked for during school years, but the best hope of good taste becoming more general among us lies in the growth of a generation who, while yet young, have gained some internal standard by which to measure art, some glimpse of the relation of art to man's spiritual sense.   On such a foundation the special training that is needed for the full appreciation of any particular branch of art, whether pottery, sculpture, embroidery, or architecture, will not be given in vain."

To this statement I should only like to add that children should not be shown pictures of adults too early.   They usually are not interested or, what is worse, they might be tempted to copy them—consciously or uncon-sciously.

Schools in most countries have neglected the *emotional* side in education. *Prof. John MacMurray* : " The emotional life is not simply a part or an aspect of human life, it is the core and essence.   To neglect this side of a child's training or to fail in it, is to fail completely in the primary business of education."

We suffer from a lack of *imagination*.   Perhaps there would not have been war if we had possessed more imaginative people.   *Herbert Read* suspects " that much, if not all, of the misery in the world to-day is due to the suppression of imagination and feeling in the child. . . ."

Once a children's doctor told Cizek that since he encouraged his little patients in hospital to draw and paint their bodily health improved. " Free drawing has therapeutic value," states *Dr. Ruth Griffiths*.

CHAPTER IX

CHILD ART AND PUBERTY

" ABOUT little children's paintings we know a good deal," wrote *Clive Bell*. " Their art is conceptual : that is to say, they try to render their notions of things and not what they see. They put the accent on what concerns them most. So much we understand : what we do not understand is why these little savages devise quite naturally combinations of line and colour, shapes and patterns, of enchanting prettiness, immeasurably superior to anything they are likely to admire in later life. Something happens to them between the ages of twelve and eighteen. *What happens ?* "

One has traced the origin of Child Art to the fact that the child, like the primitive, cannot express his feelings by words, his language being not sufficiently expressive. It follows that the spoken language becomes richer and richer, the graphic language of most children deteriorates or is reduced to writing, which is nothing but petrified pictorial language. *Karl Bühler*, who repeatedly points to the parallel of language and art, says : " Language has first spoilt drawing, and then swallowed it up completely " (" The Mental Development of the Child "). But he and *Hildegard Hetzer* (" The Symbolic Representation in Early Childhood " : Vienna, 1926) draw attention to the fact that the child stops his spontaneous drawing when he loses his joy in fairy-tales. He feels ashamed of both because he enters the stage of more realistic world-conception. Most adults remain at the stage of ten- to eleven-year-old children in their drawings.

In other words, the awakening intellect destroys the joy in the unconscious creating of early childhood. Most teachers know this. The children suddenly discover mistakes in their drawings, they declare that they cannot draw any more, they become self-critical, whereas before they were not critical at all, or only as far as other children's works were concerned. They say : " I can't draw, I know it. I don't want to draw or paint any more."

What are the reasons for the awakening of the intellect and of self-criticism ? Is there a connection with the beginning of puberty ? There is one strong argument for this explanation. Primitives have no puberty in our sense, and therefore no break in their production. *Margaret Mead* in her book " The Coming of Age in Samoa " relates out of personal experience that with the primitives " adolescence is not necessarily a time of stress and strain, but that cultural conditions make it so. . . . The stress

is in our civilisation, not in the physical changes through which our children pass."

But why have primitives no puberty in our sense ? Because they take it naturally, while we did not acknowledge until recently the existence of puberty. The old school refused to acknowledge it, as so many other facts which are of primary importance to the child. Peasant children suffer much less or not at all from the " stress and strain " of puberty, and seldom have any break in their production.

In 1921 Cizek dealt with the problem of puberty in a lecture to teachers. Francesca Wilson in her booklet " A Lecture by Professor Cizek " quotes him in this way : " People make a great mistake in thinking of Child Art merely as a step to adult art. It is a thing in itself, quite shut off and iso-lated, following its own laws and not the laws of the grown-up people. Once its blossoming-time is over, it will never come again. The crisis in a child's life usually comes about fourteen—this is the time of the awakening intellect. A child then often becomes so critical of his own work that he is completely paralysed and unable to continue creative work. Until then he has worked entirely out of feeling, unselfconsciously, spontaneously, pressed on by some urge within him. Of course, there is no reason why the Intellect should be a hindrance to Creation ; it ought to be a help. But quite often it is not. The teacher ought to try to help the child to get over this crisis. Too much pressure should be guarded against—the child cannot stand too great an inrush of knowledge. His personality may disappear altogether under the multitude of outside ideas and influences.   In any case, the great break, the caesura, comes at this period, and after that you have either the art of the adult or no more creative epoch at all."

Where some teachers may disagree with Cizek is the *time* of the crisis : " about fourteen."   They will put the age earlier.   And some will regard the time after puberty as the crisis, especially with girls.   As a matter of fact, more girls than boys preserve their creative capacity until or immediately after puberty.   There are cases where the creative power stops for a while and then reappears.

People exist, besides the primitives, who scarcely have any puberty crisis in our sense—the great artists.

I often had discussions with Cizek about the puberty problem.   He was *not* of the opinion that puberty in itself is to be blamed for the vanishing creative power of most children, but its misuse, and especially our over-intellectual school system.   This is how he explained it : " The child starts with symbols.   These symbols are more and more enriched by experience and knowledge.   The symbols come nearer and nearer to nature, and get influenced by adults, until at last Child Art stops.   It is an accident that at this time, as a rule, puberty begins.   The real reason for the end of creativeness is the fact that the child gets away from symbols and imitates nature.   The crisis begins.   Child takes nature for art and copies nature.   Thus Child Art and art in general stops.   It is an extremely difficult task to bridge over the crisis and to help the production of the child to another level."

The question as to whether imaginative work of the child must stop at or before puberty is the foremost question which occupies teachers and parents when they deal with Child Art.   I have given no lecture on Child Art in Great Britain where this question was not raised.   In June 1938 I wrote to Cizek about this fact and mentioned also that at the moment I touched the adolescence problem, and tried to point out that with most children the creative capacity lessens and often vanishes when they enter the stage of puberty, I felt a kind of resistance among my audience.   I felt, they did not want to face the fact that in the majority of thirteen and fourteen-year-olds Child Art has come to an end.   Or perhaps they even asked : What is the good of Child Art if it stops at puberty ?   This is what Cizek replied a short time before this war : " The two problems which arouse special interest amongst your audiences, the real infant work and the further development of ' Gestaltung ' (creating) after adolescence, are the most interesting problems with which I have been associated for more than fifty years and I like to hear that English teachers are also interested in these two problems. I know that English art is burdened by tradition, and I see this tradition even in many English children's drawings, but I take it as a proof of the common sense of English people that they are interested in the two problems mentioned. The work of a very young child can only be compared with the genial work of the great Masters.

" As far as the continuation of creation is concerned, i.e. after adolescence or even after eleven years, there is no uncertainty for me. The creative dies out only owing to the unfavourable influence of three factors : parents, school, and environment (civilisation). The three most important reasons for creation are : (1) the creative instinct, (2) the instinct to set in order, and (3) the imitative instinct. If the child is wrongly influenced, the imitative instinct will conquer the other two ; that is the fate of the creative capacity of most children if they are not rightly guided or if they are tempted. But when the child grows up strongly and is guided according to his individuality, he grows in an organic development provided that he possesses the necessary heritage and vitality. But even if not so gifted, it is possible to maintain the straight direction of creation, but on condition that the children are encouraged already when they are very young to work creatively, and not encouraged to copy. With right guidance the child can be further developed after twelve, thirteen, or fourteen years ; then of course the creative study of nature should take place.

" But all these problems nowadays are almost impossible to solve because of school and because of teachers who have insufficient understanding and training. As you have seen yourself with me, I had to fight the whole time."

One thing one draws from this letter : Cizek blames the bad influence of adults for the diminishing of the creative capacity. It is consistent with his general attitude. He has always defended the child against the adult. He has always regarded our civilisation as hostile or at least dangerous to the child. The factors mentioned by Cizek play their important part, with some children perhaps a decisive one. But I still believe that Cizek underrates—consciously or unconsciously—the purely biological factor of puberty in our civilisation. Would it not be strange if a child during this evolutionary and revolutionary period—a time in which mind and body are in an upheaval and during which " puberty suicide " is known—would produce anything remarkable or could remain creative ? Cizek repeatedly pointed out that there is no break with primitives.

I believe that the strongest argument for the theory that in our civilisation the biological factor is the main reason for the vanishing of creative activity of children is the fact that out of thousands of boys and girls who went to Cizek since 1897, only very few retained their creative power after puberty. I do not refer to those five or ten who eventually became artists, always understood not encouraged by Cizek. But even if Cizek did not succeed in preserving the creativeness in any considerable number of his pupils after adolescence, although he often had them from their earliest childhood, was not then the biological factor decisive ?

Whatever the reason for the disappearance of creativeness, the fact itself cannot be denied.

There is another explanation for the break. *Britsch-Kornmann* say that " children's drawings are ' archaic ' in the true sense, and thus eternally young as every genuinely early production. When the child grows out of this mental attitude, when he seeks and finds the contact with the life of the adults and their pictures, he cannot furthermore draw like a child. . . . Instead of the pure picture of an early stage, a more or less dilettantish little picture is made. Thus exactly that which was *only* of value in the child's work gets lost. In its place comes a more or less skilful representation of nature without artistic features. . . . Do the creative powers really dry up which the juvenile possessed and exercised when a child ? There are certainly cases where the powerfully awakening intellect absorbs all vitality and the productive forces get stunted. But they must not be stunted. . . . During childhood ' picture ' and representation are one. The powers of seeing and reflecting balance each other. There is yet no conflict between the imagined and shaped ' picture ' and the ' image.' This mental attitude of the child is the same as in all early cultures, the Egyptian, and the early Greek culture, e.g. when picture and image were one. . . . The basic problem of the puberty crisis in drawing is the problem of the separation of image and picture. The child is still living in the unity of picture and representation as in earlier cultures. . . . The separation would have been successful and no unsolved conflict would have arisen if no artistic aim in drawing had been set, but only technical and scientific tasks had been given. . . . The conflict of the puberty crisis is to a large extent the reaction of the art crisis in our time which is nothing but the conflict between picture and representation.

" Perspective drawing has bad artistic consequences, because it is a substitute for real artistic value. The immense importance given to perspective in art teaching needs a thorough revision."

How can creative Child Art be continued without the surrogate of perspective and without mannerism ? Kornmann believes in the possibility of greater differentiation. And he suggests beginning with new crafts. Cizek too recommends a change of medium. Two cliffs endanger creative drawing, the same which are also fatal to great art: naturalism and mannerism. " The artistic production of the adolescent is frustrated by the false ideal of unshaped naturalism."

We said in Chapter III that the ideal way goes straight to pure " Gestalten "—forming and shaping. I have seen excellent work by adolescents, by boys and more frequently by girls, but I still maintain it is the exception.

Exceptional teachers may be exceptionally successful. There were exhibitions of adolescent art of outstanding level. Mr. Weidmann, the director of the unique international collection of Child Art in the Pestalozzianum in Zurich, has some perfect adolescent art. He also believes in a change of medium as a means to prevent the too early stoppage of creativeness. There was an excellent exhibition of adolescent art held in London in 1940. I have also seen fine pictures done by girls of fifteen and sixteen painted under Miss Marion Richardson's guidance. At Eton College I saw a group of twenty boys from fourteen to sixteen painting entirely from imagination, a small percentage for such a big school. Langford Grove School for Girls is a school in which outstanding adolescent art is produced. Perhaps there is a way out? " We have endeavoured to keep artistic consideration before the pupils at an age when sensibility and spontaneous expression are often crushed in their trying to acquire realistic technique," wrote the Art Master of Ilkley Grammar School for Boys.

But if there is no way out for the great majority? If there is no means of preventing the termination of creative work in the realm of drawing and painting at the age of puberty, must we regret it? *Charlotte Bühler* has pointed out that the different activities of man reach their highest degree of fulfilment at different ages. As, for instance, most people are at their best in sports between twenty and twenty-four, that is relatively very young, whereas mental capacities reach their maximum development often between fifty and sixty. Is it not possible that most of us do our best work in art before puberty? Artistic creativeness may disappear in one sphere to reappear perhaps in a quite different sphere. It cannot be entirely lost.

Cizek advises creative nature study when the imaginative power has vanished. It is one of the many misunderstandings of his ideas that Cizek is against all art lessons. When the imagination ceases, *but only then*, not earlier, drawing lessons—of course not dull ones—are rightly commenced.

One idea we should give up. That growing must necessarily be a progress. Is the finished flower more beautiful than the bud? How many buds never become fruit?

Opinions about Child Art and puberty are divided. Perhaps each one sees only one side, one facet of the truth. Perhaps there will be discoveries in this sphere in a not too distant future, and made in Anglo-Saxon countries with their genuine understanding for Youth. But I still believe that it is significant that Cizek never had pupils between fifteen and eighteen. However, I agree with Miss *Nan Youngman* (" New Era," February, 1943) that the fact that puberty was a barrier which Cizek met is no reason why others should not try to proceed beyond it.

Harold H. Holden, A.R.C.A., Director of Art Education, Birmingham College of Arts and Crafts, kindly supplied me with information about *Catterson Smith*, who worked there a generation ago :

" The most important feature of Mr. Catterson Smith's methods is systematic memory training and the practice of drawing with closed eyes. The exercises in memory drawing are of two kinds ; the first, for which there is a preparation by deliberate observation, and the second, which calls upon impressions already existing in the mind.

" In the first type, the object to be drawn is shown for a time, is then removed or covered, and a drawing made from memory. . . . In the second type, the unprepared memory drawings are usually made in response to a suggestion from the teacher, intended to awaken some phase of memory picturing. The subjects are always such as are within the range of the student's experience and which are likely to appeal to his imagination.

" The practice of eye-shut drawing is a preliminary stage. Given his subject, the student tries to see it clearly in his mind's eye. In this effort he closes his eyes to isolate his attention from the distraction of visible objects. When his picturing appears complete, he attempts to follow with his pencil on paper the forms of the conception on which his attention is fixed. The whole value of this is in the effort to focus which it induces, and not in the resultant tracing, though this may be a very interesting manifestation indeed. The student is not encouraged to regard it as a performance in itself. These shut-eye drawings, however, often have a spirit and sensitiveness which may not be recaptured in the ensuing stage with eyes open. This is because the student then encounters difficulties of technique and lack of knowledge, and because in his former detachment from these considerations there crept in subconscious qualities which do not always reappear in the more deliberate phase of his drawing. That they should have been evoked, however, shows the value of this means. Continued training in these methods has proved that the precious quality of emotional feeling can be gradually controlled and brought into the later drawings made with the eyes open." This method is still applied to 12–15 year old pupils.

CHAPTER X

QUESTIONS

IT is a nice and democratic British habit to ask questions after lectures. I was asked at least five hundred different questions after my lectures in 1934, 1935, and from 1938 until the present time. I am giving you here some of those I consider of more general interest.

(1) *Can others get the same results as Cizek ?* (New Education Fellowship, Glasgow.)

Cizek, undoubtedly, has an easier task. He is a genius and the discoverer of Child Art. The average teacher cannot possibly have his experience. He may have had no training, or a bad training, or a training much too short in Child Art, and often he may find a rigid curriculum, or insufficient space in the art room—if there should be one—and the small amount of time devoted to arts and crafts too great handicaps. Still, he has one thing in common with Cizek—the child.

(2) *What number of children had Cizek in his classes ?* (New Education Fellowship, Glasgow.)

The average number of children in Cizek's classes was twenty-five. There are classes in Great Britain and other countries of fifty children. To do Child Art in an overcrowded class is a very difficult task. But one can attain something even with a class of fifty-four. I have seen it. The ideal number is around twenty-five. Thirty-five are too many and fifteen too few.

(3) *Do any of Cizek's children " survive " fourteen (as creative artists) ?* (New Education Fellowship, Glasgow.)

Very few.

(4) *Could drawings help children who are weak to write and express ideas ?* (New Education Fellowship, Glasgow.)

Certainly.

(5) *Is the child conscious of any conflict previous to adolescence ?* (New Education Fellowship, Glasgow.)

Some children are.

(6) *Do children ever want to learn perspective ?* (New Education Fellowship, Glasgow.)

Very few young children.

(7) *What shall we think of the method in some schools, where a model is set up and children have to draw that model, the teacher helping ?* (New Education Fellowship, Glasgow.)

With young children it is wrong.

(8) *Would Cizek have models for clay modelling?* (Streatham Hill Training College.)

There are no objects in Cizek's classes.

(9) *Does Cizek paint himself?* (Thistley Hough School, Stoke-on-Trent.)

Cizek was a painter, but so far as I know he has not touched a brush in the last thirty years. There are enough artists, he says, perhaps too many. It is more important that children should create.

(10) *Are visitors allowed to see children at work?* (Thistley Hough School, Stoke-on-Trent.)

Yes. The children, if they are really interested in their work, will hardly notice a tactful visitor.

(11) *Do the Cizek children do pottery?* (Thistley Hough School, Stoke-on-Trent.)

Some do.

(12) *Have they examinations?* (Thistley Hough School, Stoke-on-Trent.)

No.

(13) *Is there punishment for disobedience?* (Thistley Hough School, Stoke-on-Trent.)

No. But what is disobedience? There are no commands. The teacher and pupils are co-workers.

(14) *Was Cizek's school independent?* (Abbotsholme School.)

Thank God, yes.

(15) *How young does Cizek take his pupils?* (Abbotsholme School.)

He is happiest when he gets children of two or three. Then he is sure that they are unspoiled by adults. Usually the children are six years old, and he keeps them until fourteen. If a child enters his Juvenile Art Class only at nine or ten, his task is much more difficult. Then he has to counteract the influence of adults ; then he has to do all he can to guide the child back to himself.

(16) *When a child is too skilful, the medium is changed—why?* (Chesterfield.)

It does not very often happen that a child will become too skilful in one medium. But if he does, there is the danger that he will produce automatically. (It happens with adult artists too !)

(17) *Do children of all years work together?* (Manchester University.)

The children are divided into two groups, one up to ten, and the other from ten to fourteen. It sometimes happens that a child of eight is in the

older group and vice versa. There are advantages in having children not quite of the same age together. (Of course there are boys and girls.) There is some kind of co-operation, although children are great individualists and want to work alone. Still, a friendly talk with the neighbour, a visit to the friend on the other side of the class, inspecting his work, indeed the whole atmosphere in the room with its gentle beehive humming,—all these are helpful to creative work. It is a room where children like to be.

(18) *Did Cizek ever find very young children scared of expressing themselves ?* (Manchester University.)

Very rarely.

(19) *Have the primary schools adopted Cizek's ideas in Vienna ?* (Manchester University.)

Yes.

(20) *Can parents' influence be counteracted ?* (Course in Kent.)

It should be in many cases, but it is no easy task. First of all the teacher should try to make the parents see the work of their children with right eyes. They very often will only want skill, repetition, copying. Discussion with parents, exhibitions of children's work, but not only the "best" ones, visits to the art class, might be helpful in preventing parents from influencing their children in a wrong way.

(21) *If a child of seven produced work of a child of ten, is there something the matter with him ? Do children not progress at different rates ?* (St. George's Training College, Liverpool.)

The precocious child should not be encouraged. There is no reason for a mother to be proud of her seven-year-old child who produced like the ten-year-old child of her neighbour.

(22) *Infants splash colour and do no more. Is that right?* (Edge Hill Training College, Ormskirk.)

"Playing" with colours as a beginning is all right. But it should not go on for too long. Perhaps the child wants to draw. To cover a huge paper with colours for a long time, and doing nothing else, should not be encouraged.

(23) *Does Cizek ever connect poetry with art?* (Edge Hill Training College, Ormskirk.)

He suggested to thirteen- and fourteen-year-old girls to keep a diary with text and pictures.

(24) *Is there any definite teaching of colour?* (New Education Fellowship, Liverpool.)

No. Children have their own harmony of colours, and it is sometimes better than ours. What would happen if primitives were "taught" colours?

(25) *Does Cizek tackle design as a separate subject?* (Birkenhead Training College.)

No.

(26) *Should children always be allowed to paint what they like?* (Bournville Art Club.)

At five years of age some children will already need the suggestion of a subject, others not. Individualise.

(27) *Supposing a child of seven years old wanted to draw Peter Pan and the Crocodile but had no knowledge of crocodiles, how should one deal with the situation?* (Bournville Art Club.)

The teacher or mother should talk about the crocodile to the child.

(28) *Are young children not to have any pictures in their story-books?* (Bournville Art Club.)

As far as possible, their own pictures or pictures by other children. This is the ideal. Next to that come pictures by real artists, but not sugary, cheap pictures. The primitive picture is better than the sophisticated one.

(29) *All children should be encouraged to use large paper. If a child naturally draws small, should he be allowed to do so?* (Bournville Art Club.)

There can be no general rule so far as the size is concerned. But the tendency should be towards the bigger size—without forcing a child to use too large paper. Individualise.

(30) *Should one child imitate another ?* (Bournville Art Club.)

No. But some children are more imitative than creative. The teachers' and parents' task, however, is to encourage the creative side, whatever its strength. If a child in school permanently copies from his neighbour— why not separate them tactfully, or suggest a different subject or medium to the imitative child ?

(31) *Children are also very creative in other arts, e.g. music. Should they be encouraged in the same way ?* (Bournville Art Club.)

There were schools in Vienna (not with Cizek) where seven-year-old children actually produced their own melodies. And to Cizek for years groups of American music teachers came who wanted to study his " method " because they thought they could also use it to a certain extent in music.

(32) *If a child does a painting which is unintelligible to an adult, should one ask the child for an explanation ?* (Bournville Art Club.)

Not by leading questions ! Some children never should be asked. Some children will answer in a way which they think would please the adult. It is the child's courtesy (and certainly not lying). So we would only hear from the child what we want to hear. Very young children will often be quite incapable of explaining what they mean in their drawing. The reason why they draw may be that they cannot " tell " by words. If possible, we should have a talk about the drawings with the child. But most of the conversation should be done by the child. Indirect method !

(33) *Could you give a comparison of two children at fourteen years of age— one who had opportunities of self-expression in art classes from three years upwards, and another who had ordinary art instruction at an elementary school ?* (Bournville Art Club.)

One must only look at what a fourteen-year-old child produced a generation ago and what he often produces now. In the L.C.C. exhibition 1938 hung drawings of autumn leaves and cubes, executed by poor children thirty years ago, and next to those " pictures " were exhibited the beautiful works now done from imagination. The effect was devastating.

(34) *At what age should a child go to the cinema ?* (Bournville Art Club.)

As late as possible. And almost the same applies to the theatre. The ideal is that the child should produce his own plays. In Cizek's classes were puppet and marionette shows. Everything was done and executed by the children themselves.

(35) *What kind of toys ?* (Bournville Art Club.)

Simple, not sophisticated ones which are bought by adults because *they* like them. The ideal toy for a young child is a piece of wood. It is king and queen, mountain and boat, man and animal for the child, because of his enormous imaginative power.

(36) *Isn't it a fact that children cling to the plain old toy and ignore the lovely new one ? They go back to the old favourite.* (Bournville Art Club.)

The normal child prefers simplicity to sophistication.

(37) *Would not suppliers risk a long period of failure and people refuse to buy the more artistically designed wrappings until educated to their standard ?* (Bournville Art Club.)

When the first milk bar was opened by Dick Sheppard in Fleet Street in London in 1934 or 1935 it was said that the English people would not drink milk. The milk bar would be bound to be a failure. After a year or so there were 400 milk bars in London, and they were a very good paying proposition. Education works sometimes quicker than one dares to hope. I do not believe that people *want* bad things, bad products, bad wrappings, bad posters, bad advertisements, bad newspapers, and bad films. And I do not think that all manufacturers and traders have bad taste. Some have very good taste. But some are just lazy and make no effort to understand what good taste is, and also they believe that ugly things are cheaper. This is not necessarily true, and certainly not in the long run.

(38) *Were other subjects taught at Cizek's school ?* (Course at Walthamstow.)

No. But art was not " taught " either.

(39) *Is coloured chalk used by young children ?* (Course at Walthamstow.)

White chalk on blackboards is excellent. If children prefer highly coloured chalks, there is no objection. But for many children the enormous contrast already between black and white " tears " out of them everything which is in them.

(40) *What brushes ?* (Course at Walthamstow.)

Different ones, but not too thin ones.

(41) *Would a child come back to a half-finished picture ?* (Course at Walthamstow.)

If a child has not finished his picture in one period, he will usually finish it the next time. Children have a different " tempo." If a child occasionally hesitates to finish a picture, he should be encouraged to finish.

(42) *At what age do children use plaster of Paris ?* (Course at Walthamstow.)

Hardly before nine.

(43) *How much time was given to art in Cizek's school ?* (Course at Walthamstow.)

The children under ten came once or twice per week on free afternoons for one and a half hours each time ; the older children came once or twice for two hours each time.

(44) *In the picture of the fish pond, did the boy turn the paper round ?* (Course at Walthamstow.)

Yes.

(45) *Should children be allowed to trace ?* (Course at Walthamstow.)

Never.

(46) *Some children of five paint a picture and then proceed to cover it up with a mass of colour. What should be done ?* (Course at Walthamstow.)

They should be tactfully stopped. Perhaps we act here from the purely adult's point of view who hates to have a good picture destroyed. But I do not think any harm is done if a child is, tactfully, prevented from destroying what he has accomplished. It may be his sheer joy of going on using colours. If he is given a new paper, he will make another picture.

(47) *Does Cizek allow paper cutting and modelling as freely as other work ?* (Course at Walthamstow.)

Yes.

(48) *How long do the children work to make these pictures ?* (Course at Walthamstow.)

It varies considerably. But it has educational value if the class is encouraged to finish a picture in more or less the same time. We must not, however, forget that the tempo of children is different just as children of the same age run or swim a certain distance in different times. In some classes a child easily did two quite excellent pictures in one period, and another child needed two periods for one picture. Individualise.

(49) *Should ten or twelve colours be given to a child under six ?* (Course at Walthamstow.)

No. The child, by the way, will hardly ask for so many colours.

(50) *What about the introduction of writing ?* (Course at Walthamstow.)

The old or intellectual school started writing too soon. The Eastern nations, who begin with painting or drawing and after that with writing, are right. Miss Marion Richardson's great contribution is her way of introducing writing.

(51) *How much space does a child get ?* (Course at Walthamstow.)

Very much. In old schools the child usually had not space enough. In the art room the horizontal table is right. If they work on easels, they should have much space. Their whole body should work.

(52) *Instead of a knowledge of technique should a teacher rather have a knowledge of child psychology ?* (Course at Walthamstow.)

Both.   Every teacher should have a relation to art, which does not mean that he must be an artist himself (or a composer or a poet).

(53) *What happens to the work of the children ?   Is it not a shame if they may not keep it ?*   (Course at Walthamstow.)

Most of them will feel proud if their work is kept.   If they realise from the beginning that all their work done in school belongs to the school, they will not bother.

(54) *If a picture in history is shown, would not this be an outside influence ?* (Course at Walthamstow.)

Yes ; but it can be made quite clear to the children that it is a different sphere, as a photograph is different from a picture.   The ideal, again, would be if the children would make their own pictures.

(55) *Did Cizek's children pay ?*   (Course at Walthamstow.)

The poor children paid nothing, the wealthier ones a little fee, but all got the material free.

(56) *Are children really satisfied with their own work when they fail to produce photographic or realistic work ?*   (Erith.)

Young children are very happy with their unrealistic work.   It is the adult who is often unhappy, but the adult should refrain from imposing his standards upon the child.

(57) *I told Scriptural stories and the children drew the pictures of saints in modern trousers.   Was this right ?*   (Erith.)

Certainly.

(58) *Will the intelligent child produce better work than the dull child ?* (Course in Kent.)

One cannot generalise.   Often children who are weak in intellectual subjects are excellent in arts or crafts.   Their hand is better than their head.

(59) *If Cizek encourages children to fill blank spaces, is this not influencing them ?*   (Newcastle University.)

A picture is not only something mysterious, but also something very real :   the filling of a certain space.   A child may out of laziness or forgetfulness leave empty spaces.   Why not encourage him in these cases to fill the space ?   The child often only needs to be reminded.   (In certain cases the empty space may have an artistic meaning.)

(60) *Are we getting worse by growing older ?*   (Newcastle University.)

There can hardly be any doubt which is stronger, more genuine, more beautiful, in one word, more artistic, the work of the four- or five-year-old (Cizek would say the two- and three-year-old) or the fifteen-year-old child. Still, we cannot eternally remain small children.   But what Cizek fought for during his whole life was to make people, and especially teachers, see the immense beauty in the so-called clumsy, stupid works of small children. There is nothing stronger on earth, he said repeatedly.

(61) *Can the savage in the child be subdued ?* (Newcastle University.)

It should not. The child should be a savage as long as possible. With our terrible civilisation he becomes civilised too soon in any case.

(62) *How many schools are going to be allowed to teach art in this way ?* (Newcastle University.)

As many as possible.

(63) *Do any children prefer to draw from objects and not mainly from memory-imagination ?* (Durham University.)

It is rare that young children want to draw from objects.

(64) *Are children ever encouraged to base imaginative drawings on a concrete object before the child ?* (Durham University.)

Young children never.

(65) *Is it often difficult to get children to make figures large enough ?* (Leeds Pedagogical Society.)

Usually not.

(66) *Why is the circle in the fish-pond right ?* (Wrexham.)

Because it is a " grown " circle. How horrible would be a geometrically correct circle !

(67) *Does Cizek agree with drawing in ink ?* (St. Mary's Training College, Bangor.)

Yes, occasionally, for educational purposes.

(68) *Why is the head so large in proportion to the body in young children's drawings ?* (St. Mary's Training College, Bangor.)

Because it is more important than the body.

(69) *Are they allowed to use various media in a class or do they all work with the same medium ?* (St. Mary's Training College, Bangor.)

They are allowed to use various media at the same time, but the tendency is that as many as wish should use the same medium. That helps. It fosters a " class spirit." But there are bound to be outsiders, and especially after ten or eleven it would be wrong to expect a great majority to be fond of the same medium or subject.

(70) *Does Cizek tell the children to draw something which they have actually seen ?* (St. Mary's Training College, Bangor.)

Both seen and not seen. He definitely tells them sometimes about things which they never have seen or heard of, and he asks them to make a drawing or picture of them. The purpose is to get purely imaginative work.

(71) *Is it not wrong to isolate art from the rest of the school work ?* (St. Mary's Training College, Bangor.)

It is. The ideal would be schools where art and crafts penetrate all subjects.

(72) *Why do we pay great attention to the reproduction of the real thing in school ?* (St. Mary's Training College, Bangor.)

I do not know. Perhaps out of a feeling that children must be prepared for an adult world as quickly as possible.

(73) *When the child sees a crocodile and afterwards draws it, is it not reproduction ?* (St. Mary's Training College, Bangor.)

To a certain extent. It means drawing from memory, but there is or can still be a great amount of imagination.

(74) *Does the child represent himself in his drawing ?* (St. Mary's Training College, Bangor.)

Very often—consciously and unconsciously.

(75) *Is there a solution to the difficulty that the adult must judge child's art by adult standards ?* (Bangor University.)

A difficult problem. But no modern teacher would judge the essay of an eight-year-old by an adult one or even fourteen-year old's standard. Our concept is wrong. We must try to see through children's eyes.

(76) *How is it possible for a child to preserve his freshness if constantly surrounded by picture-books, cinemas, etc. ?* (Bangor Normal College of Wales.)

It is difficult, and therefore we do not always get the kind of Child Art we should like to get. We would get it if the child was less spoilt by adult and over-intellectual civilisation.

(77) *How can a child's drawing be perfect ?* (Bangor Normal College of Wales.)

It is perfect if it is adequate to his age, uninfluenced by adults, not a copy, and genuine.

(78) *If the child's work is perfect, where does the teacher come in ?* (Bangor Normal College of Wales.)

Firstly, not every child's work is perfect. So the teacher can and should encourage the child to produce perfectly. Secondly, even with perfect works of a child there is plenty of scope to guide that child *his* way. The temptations are great.

(79) *Explain why it is not desirable for a child to tend towards naturalism.* (Bangor Normal College of Wales.)

It is a preconceived idea, and one highly treasured by some people, that naturalism is the perfection of art. It is rather a decline. The child wants to be creative. With our civilisation he will be naturalistic anyway very soon. But the teacher or school has to fight against the child becoming an adult too quickly—a " hopeless " adult, as an Austrian once said. On the other hand, it would be wrong to keep the child artificially at an early stage. Again, organic growth !

(80) *Has Cizek come across children who prefer to copy rather than create ? If so, what policy does he adopt ?* (Bangor Normal College of Wales.)

He sometimes gets children whose copying tendency or instinct is greater than their creative. He tries his best to strengthen the latter—not always successfully. Sometimes change of medium is a help. There are media where it is much more difficult to copy. Modelling, for instance, compared with drawing.

(81) *Is object drawing allowed ? If it is allowed, at what stage ?* (Bangor Normal College of Wales.)

There was never an object in Cizek's classes. But objects are allowed when the creative faculty has vanished.

(82) *Should a teacher be dissatisfied when two children of the same age show different abilities ?* (Bangor Normal College of Wales.)

No. Is he dissatisfied if they show different abilities in history, mathematics, or games ?

(83) *Should a young child's imagination be controlled and brought into contact with things around him ?* (Bangor Normal College of Wales.)

No.

(84) *Should a camera be given to a child ?* (Anglesey.)

Not too early.

(85) *Do the children only work under Cizek's supervision, or do they work at home ?* (Hull Education Society.)

Both ; but home work is entirely voluntary.

(86) *Should English children be guided in their choice of colours ?* (Hull Education Society.)

No. They have, like other children, when not spoilt, an innate harmony of colours.

(87) *If children's work is shown in school, will the other children copy it ?* (Hull Education Society.)

In Cizek's school the walls are full of children's pictures. Most children hardly notice them, so concentrated are they on their own work. Generally they will only be conscious that the room is gay, and that bright pictures are displayed on the walls. The danger that children copy those pictures or are much influenced by them is not great. There are, of course, copiers among children (less than among adults), but a very strange subject and a different medium will help in many cases. As a rule, children are so absorbed in their work that they hardly know what happens or is displayed around them. I once watched five- and six-year-old girls painting at a double easel. The one hardly knew what the other did. They were so interested in their own pictures.

(88) *What is the objection to teaching a child the little tricks of perspective to enable him to express himself better ?* (Dundee Teachers' Meeting.)

The young child has no use for right perspective. It does not help him. Imagine the introduction of " right " perspective or naturalism in ancient Egyptian drawings ! When the naturalism of later Greece was introduced in Egyptian Art, it was ruined. We must wait.

(89) *Why should we not give the children the cumulative experience of what artists have discovered through the ages ?* (Dundee Teachers' Meeting.)

First, can any human being learn from the experiences of his ancestors ? Must he not go through them himself ? And is not the way the most important ? Should we " spare " the flower the trouble of slow growth ? The child should not be given ready-made things or knowledge. He should acquire as far as possible everything himself. The collective heritage of mankind is within himself. We should not accelerate the process.

(90) *Should not Art enter into everything the child does ?* (Dundee Teachers' Meeting.)

It could.

(91) *How can we account for a girl who did only black-and-white drawings ?* (Dundee Teachers' Meeting.)

Some children—like some adults—have such a sense for the black-and-white rhythm that they don't need colours. Some adults feel black and white like music. (Farleigh's wood engravings in Bernard Shaw's " The Adventures of the Black Girl in Her Search for God " would be a modern example.)

(92) *Is it not good to copy the great artists and so closely study their technique ?* (St. Trinnean's School, Edinburgh.)

It is certainly not good for young children.

(93) *Should we not use pale shades ? Nature has pale shades.* (St. Trinnean's School, Edinburgh.)

Art is not nature. Art is not a representation of nature. Children do not copy nature. As strong, courageous creatures they have a birthright for bright colours. The brightest colours are just right. No normal healthy young child will choose pale colours. The adult usually supplies them.

(94) *Why do poor children often work better than wealthy children ?* (St. Trinnean's School, Edinburgh.)

They are often less spoilt, and less over-fed. They see less and less is done for them.

(95) *Sometimes young children are content, when working at easels, merely to splash paint on. Are easels right for young children ?* (Montessori Society, Edinburgh.)

It depends. For some children easels are too big. They get frightened. They would be much happier if they could work on the floor.

(96) *If children continue to splash paint as above, would Cizek give them some suggestions for a picture ?* (Montessori Society, Edinburgh.)

Certainly. He would not let it go on indefinitely.

(97) *Do the children criticise their own drawings ?* (Montessori Society, Edinburgh.)

To a certain extent, but more generally those of their friends.

(98) *When a young girl was asked, " How do you draw ? " She replied, " I think and think and then I draw my think." Are children often conscious of thinking in a creative way before they begin to draw ?* (St. Leonard's School, St. Andrews.)

Some are.

(99) *Are there any schools in other countries run on these lines ?* (St. Leonard's School, St. Andrews.)

Yes, especially in Great Britain and America.

(100) *Are the children taught perspective or do they find out about it for themselves ?* (St. Leonard's School, St. Andrews.)

The word " perspective " is unknown in Cizek's school. The children themselves develop it gradually.

(101) *Do children of seven begin too late ?* (Ministers' Daughters' College, Edinburgh.)

They should begin earlier, as early as possible. Eighteen months would be right. But seven, anyway, is better than eight or ten or never.

(102) *Do children work at home ?* (Ministers' Daughters' College, Edinburgh.)

Many children do some drawings, paintings, and sometimes even modellings at home, but quite voluntarily. They usually bring their private efforts to Cizek, who speaks about them, and, if it is genuine work, sometimes keeps it.

(103) *Do the children regard their work as a recreation ?* (Ministers' Daughters' College, Edinburgh.)

C.A.—6

Small children make no distinction between work and play. And work done with love amounts almost to recreation also for older children.

(104) *Is there competition in Cizek's class?* (Ministers' Daughters' College, Edinburgh.)

Hardly in the usual sense. There are no marks, no reports.

(105) *Are the Cizek children modest?* (Ministers' Daughters' College, Edinburgh.)

The true artist and the genuine child artist are both modest.

(106) *Do they get as much time as they want?* (Ministers' Daughters' College, Edinburgh.)

Certainly. Nobody pushes them.

(107) *At what age ought a child to stop drawing houses with beds, etc., showing through the house?* (New Education Fellowship, Kilmarnock.)

It is normal with young children to draw " transparent." The ancient Egyptians did it. Most children will stop doing it about eight.

(108) *Larger size is not popular among children. How to overcome?* (New Education Fellowship, Kilmarnock.)

Gradually.

(109) *Pastels and crayons as media?* (New Education Fellowship, Kilmarnock.)

Cizek does not very much encourage them. But they can be used if the children want.

(110) *Referring to the space between the narrow sky and ground, should we have the same type of picture after eight as under five years old, that is, should the child make the same mistake? If he does, we shall be criticized by the powers above.* (Nursery and Infants' Teachers' Course, Matlock.)

First, there is no mistake in a young child's picture, unless it is influenced by adults. The narrow sky is a kind of ceiling. Young children have no use for the horizon. Secondly, there is a great difference between the work of a normal child after eight and before five, but the narrow sky may occur with some children even after eight, and we should be grateful. Are there really " powers above " which have no use for real Child Art? I thought they welcomed it. Exhibitions organised by the authorities seem to prove it.

(111) *Will children of their own accord study pictures of adults for information?* (Nursery and Infants' Teachers' Course, Matlock.)

Young children seldom.

(112) *If it is true that appreciation of colour is natural, why do we get disharmonies later on?* (Nursery and Infants' Teachers' Course, Matlock.)

Because of misunderstood civilisation. Primitives do not show this decline, unless wrongly influenced by civilisation.

(113) *What shall we do with a child who can think of nothing to draw?* (Dundee Training College.)

Tell him an exciting story.

(114) *Shall children be given the best of materials?* (Dundee Training College.)

Simple, not sophisticated material, which is often inexpensive.

(115) *Should wrong colours be corrected in a young child's work?* (Dundee Training College.)

There are no " wrong " colours in a young child's work. And a correction of a young child's work is rather a corruption or, as Cizek says, a forgery.

(116) *Will neurotic children's geometric pattern, or formal drawing, change in time under Cizek?* (London University Institute of Education.)

The geometric pattern and formal drawing of the neurotic child is a desire for protection. Working in Cizek's sense may gradually change the neurotic child.

(117) *If a child prefers design—pattern making—should we leave him with it?* (London University Institute of Education.)

Children should not be encouraged to make only patterns.

(118) *Do children and grown-ups like the same picture? And what do children like best?* (London University Institute of Education.)

Sometimes they have the same predilection. As a rule, most children like a story in the picture.

(119) *Can children paint to-morrow what they draw to-day?* (London University Institute of Education.)

Why not, if there was no time to paint the picture to-day?

(120) *Does it not make a big difference where children live?* (London University Institute of Education.)

There is a difference between city and country children, and Cizek was always longing for peasant children. But we should not overrate the influence of environment with young children, as far as Child Art is concerned.

(121) *Will the children ever ask Cizek to help them?* (London University Institute of Education.)

Seldom. They know he would not do it, at least not directly.

(122) *Should children be told not to leave a space between sea and sky?* (London University Institute of Education.)

It would be very wrong. This empty space between the child's narrow sky and the sea is something quite different from leaving empty spaces, for instance, one half of the picture.

(123) *Any general difference between boys' and girls' work?* (London University Institute of Education.)

Not with young children.

(124) *Are the children shown anything during an art lesson?* (Course in Essex.)

Nothing.

(125) *What kind of children go to Cizek's school, why do they go, and what are they aiming at?* (Course in Essex.)

Regular schoolchildren of both sexes, some before school-entering age, and both rich and poor, but more poor children. They go because they like it. They hardly have an aim.

(126) *Are the children ever colour-blind because they paint green leaves red?* (Course in Essex.)

Five to eight per cent. of *male* adults have a distorted sense of colour, which is not always colour-blindness. Among women the percentage is much smaller. But the percentage of girls who use " wrong " colours is certainly not smaller than that of boys. The " wrong " colours of primitives have nothing to do with colour-blindness.

(127) *Do they model, paint, weave, etc., at the same time in the same room?* (Course in Essex.)

Yes, especially those over ten. And thus is underlined the workroom atmosphere. There is nothing resembling the musty and dull atmosphere of some schoolrooms.

(128) *Should a child's memory be stimulated by putting an object for a few minutes before children of twelve to fourteen?* (Parallel Course in Essex.)

Cizek has never used the three-minutes method. Catterson-Smith at the Birmingham Art College a generation ago used the following method : The youngsters (boys over thirteen) were allowed, for instance, to draw a horse or cart in the street from nature. Then he asked them to make the same drawing with closed eyes. A number of drawings of both kinds are still to be seen in the Birmingham Art College. Needless to add, the drawings made with eyes closed are much more alive.

(129) *What do you understand by a young child?* (Parallel Course in Essex.)

Roughly, a child before puberty. In some cases the child with sufficient imaginative power.

(130) *Child Guidance Clinics find that delinquents only draw patterns, and cannot do creative picture work. Why?* (Parallel Course in Essex.)

Protection behind a fence, fear.

(131) *Is our task not harder than that of Cizek because we have to stimulate the powers of imagination in our children ?*   (Parallel Course in Essex.)

Is the English child really less imaginative than the Continental child ?

(132) *If a child of four and a half years only draws a ring for a long period, should we leave him ?*   (Parallel Course in Essex.)

Rather encourage a change after a while.

(133) *Did the child put in the house only to fill the picture ?*   (Parallel Course in Essex.)

Probably.   The same thing happened with the blue door in the Punch and Judy picture of Jill.

(134) *Do the children turn their papers round ?*   (referring to the fish-pond).   (Parallel Course in Essex.)

Usually.

(135) *My children of eight years do not draw houses upside-down.   Why ?* (Parallel Course in Essex.)

Perhaps they are already influenced by adults.

(136) *My children of six years prefer to do original drawings.   Is it then necessary to suggest a subject ?*   (Parallel Course in Essex.)

Generally not.   But at certain times a common subject, naturally one in which they are really interested, may be suggested for educational purposes.   Those children who absolutely wish to do their own drawing should be allowed to do so.

(137) *Are stencils ever used ?*   (Parallel Course in Essex.)

I do not ever remember their being used.

(138) *Should the children be encouraged to sketch drawings first ?*   (Parallel Course in Essex.)

With big pictures it is often done.   With lino cuttings it occurs, but Cizek prefers to encourage direct work on the lino.

(139) *Does the creative period with country children last longer than with town children ?*   (Parallel Course in Essex.)

Yes ;   and rural teachers in countries where there are still peasants point out that the break in creative art is very slight or scarcely perceptible.

(140) *What is to take the place of Child Art when at adolescence the creative power has gone ?*   (Parallel Course in Essex.)

Creative nature study, crafts, as far as possible.

(141) *Is the conviction that most children cannot draw after adolescence a great influence in child's work ?*   (Parallel Course in Essex.)

Children live in the present.   They know very little about the break in their production.

(142) *Why music, occasionally, during art lessons ?   Is there not a danger of outside influence and distraction ?*   (Parallel Course in Essex.)

Rather the opposite.   Cizek believes that the rhythm of music helps the rhythm of work.

(143) *Should children be put into groups according to ability or according to age ?*   (Course in Wiltshire.)

According to ability and mental age as far as possible.   Modern schools do it.

(144) *Is it usual to discuss how compositions are to be set out on paper before work begins ?*   (Course in Wiltshire.)

Often there is a discussion before the children start to do the common subject.   If there is a room to be drawn, Cizek will not hesitate to ask : What do you think about it, where is the window, where is the door, the table, etc.?

(145) *Should we go back to primitive art ?*   (Course in Wiltshire.)
We cannot.

(146) *Could the principles of Child Art be applied to all subjects ?*   (Course in Wiltshire.)

Yes, to a certain extent.

(147) *How are young children in Cizek's class taken ?   Do they have a talk first ?*   (Barnsley Nursery School Association.)

They are more or less taken as they come.   Once a mother brought her seven-year-old girl to Cizek, saying, " The teacher told me to bring her to you.   I do not think she is any good at drawing.   But here she is."   Cizek asked the mother politely to withdraw.   Then he went with the child to the large classroom, and gave her paper and pencil, saying in a friendly tone : " Now sit down, and draw just what you would really like to draw."   He left the girl, and after half an hour the most marvellous drawing was done.

(148) *If a child repeats the same picture several times, should another subject be suggested ?*   (Streatham Hill Training College.)
Yes.

(149) *When a child has little imagination, should a subject be suggested ?*   (Streatham Hill Training College.)
Yes.

(150) *If a child of seven wants to start again, should she be allowed to do so ?*   (Streatham Hill Training College.)
Why not ?

(151) *Should children be allowed to colour outlined drawings in magazines, etc.?*   (Rachel MacMillan Training College.)

They should be discouraged from doing so, although some children like it very much. They should produce their own drawings.

(152) *When children begin to make lino cuts, etc., should they be helped with the use of tools?* (Rachel MacMillan Training College.)

They should experiment and acquire their own technique. This process is healthier than the mere being shown.

(153) *When should children be introduced to great pictures?* (Rachel MacMillan Training College.)

Not too soon.

(154) *Should children be encouraged to make their own illustrations to stories, etc.?* (Rachel MacMillan Training College.)

Yes.

(155) *If a child gets so wrapped up in his medium and goes on working at it after it is really finished, should one stop him before he has spoilt his work?*

Yes, tactfully. (Rachel MacMillan Training College.)

(156) *How can children illustrate a story of things they have never seen?* (Rachel MacMillan Training College.)

Because of their stupendous imagination.

(157) *Should one give children books illustrated by other children?* (Rachel MacMillan Training College.)

Yes, and books illustrated by themselves.

(158) *Surely one cannot leave out design altogether, as it is a link between art and craft?* (Rachel MacMillan Training College.)

But one should not begin too soon.

(159) *Does a child draw entirely from his imagination?* (Rachel MacMillan Training College.)

The small child, yes. Later imagination gets weaker.

(160) *Should children be allowed to continue with morbid subjects?* (Rachel MacMillan Training College.)

By all means, as long as they want them.

(161) *Why do we give the child a subject at all? Doesn't it limit the child?* (Rachel MacMillan Training College.)

For the young child a subject may be a help, a suggestion ; for the older child the subject may have educational value. But the subjects must always be of interest to the child.

(162) *Is it wrong to compare the children's drawings with the children?* (Rachel MacMillan Training College.)

It is right.

(163) *Doesn't a child draw from his own experience and not from imagination?* (Rachel MacMillan Training College.)

From both.   The younger child more from imagination, the older more from experience.   The stages overlap.   All growing is transitional.

(164) *Do children have moods or are they always able to draw ?*   (Rachel MacMillan Training College.)

Like grown-ups they have moods, but perhaps less often.   Still, they are influenced by outside factors (weather, events).   Those factors may be something unknown to us.   It may occur that a class which did marvellous work one day will be quite different the next.   But often it is not the class, but that we have, unconsciously, altered the atmosphere.

(165) *Is the Cizek method a poor preparation for a world of facts, as it is self-expression ?*   (Rhyl.)

It is a superstition that we must prepare the child as soon as possible for the adult world.   Elizabeth Rotten once said :" It is not the child who should be adapted to the environment, but the world to the child."   This is perhaps a little too idealistic, although essentially true, and not to be realised in our civilisation.   But we do not make the child better fitted for the world or stronger for it if we deprive him artificially of his childhood.

(166) *Does the child's particular emotions affect his skill in execution ? If the answer is Yes, is it cruel to be critical ?*   (Rhyl.)

The child is emotional, fortunately.   His emotions influence him. Negative criticism is cruel—for most children.

(167) *It seems teachers of Art are going to have easier work in school ?* (Rhyl.)

Rather the opposite.   It would be a tragic misunderstanding to think that Cizek's " method " is easier than the old one.

(168) *We cannot all have Cizeks in our school.*   (Rhyl.)

But every teacher could learn from Cizek.

(169) *Are arts and crafts the most important subjects taught in school ?* (Shottin.)

Cizek would say so.

(170) *Is not pictorial expression an escape from town ugliness and therefore of less value to the country child ?   The natural beauty of the country child's surroundings seems to me to take away the urge to invent on paper a better world.*   (Trowbridge.)

There is some truth in it, although we should not overrate the difference between country and town child.   There are differences, but there is always the eternal child.

(171) *Are there not two different approaches to pictorial art—that represented by Egyptian bas-reliefs and the other represented by the cave-drawings and modern attempts to capture movement ?   In the first the primary emotion is*

the recording of ideas and may lead to colour designs and arrangements (sym-bolical, not attempting to represent nature). In the second, the primary emotion is capture of something seen and may lead to economy of line and caricature. (Trowbridge.)

Both can be traced in children's work.

(172) *After adolescence should instruction in perspective and composition be given?* (Trinity College, Carmarthen.)

Yes, gradually.

(173) *How assess marks in drawing?* (Trinity College, Carmarthen.)

No marks. The kind of reports that some British schools have could be a guidance.

(174) *Does this philosophy only apply to children under adolescent age?* (Trinity College, Carmarthen.)

I am glad to hear the word philosophy. Because behind the new conception of Child Art lies a whole philosophy. Yes, mainly ; or could be applied—with certain limitations—after adolescence also, but this is even more difficult. Puberty, as a rule, is the great caesura.

(175) *Is it possible to preserve naturalness and also avoid imitation?* (Trinity College, Carmarthen.)

It is. Dürer is an example. But it does not occur too often.

(176) *Are children influenced by magazines? How are we going to stop it?* (Trinity College, Carmarthen.)

They are influenced, and the more imitative they are, the more they are influenced. It is difficult, but to make children produce out of their own imagination will help to make them immune to a certain extent against bad pictures.

(177) *Suppose a child is so interested in his work that he wants to continue after the lesson. Should we let him?* (Trinity College, Carmarthen.)

Of course.

(178) *Why will children produce different work with different teachers, even if all teachers are trained by the same master?* (St. Mary's School, Hampstead.)

Because of the personality of the teacher, which will influence, unconsciously, most children.

(179) *How far does Cizek interpret children's paintings?* (St. Mary's School, Hampstead.)

He is careful not to read too much into them.

(180) *Do children not ask advice which they have no intention of taking?* (St. Mary's School, Hampstead.)

It sometimes happens.

(181) *Should we accept pictures from children without asking for a comment on them ?* (Alexandra College, Dublin.)

Very often.

(182) *Isn't there in certain schools, almost unconsciously, a certain definite style ?* (Alexandra College, Dublin.)

Yes, the influence of a strong teacher personality.

(183) *Did Cizek ever attempt to let children paint in time to music ?* (Alexandra College, Dublin.)

He did it rather often. He found that the rhythm of music helps them in their rhythm of work. There is a gramophone in the class—the gift of an English lady—and he has records of really good music, and, not always, but often, there is music. Sometimes the children ask for it. There is a piano in the adjoining room, and any child who wishes is allowed to play there for a while. All this has nothing to do with translating music into colours or lines. Another Austrian, *Professor Rainer*, has done that with his adolescents in a secondary school in Vienna. But this is a different matter. And only highly musical and artistic teachers with long experience in both spheres should attempt it, and even then it is an experiment which could certainly not be made with every child.

(184) *What about using the left hand ?* (Alexandra College, Dublin.)

Of course, left-handers should be allowed and encouraged to use the left hand. The number of left-handers in schools increases, probably the result of the freedom to work with the left hand if wanted. The old school in many countries, out of sheer stupidity, regarded left-handedness as almost a moral defect.

(185) *May a child have a ruler ?* (Alexandra College, Dublin.)

If he wants it, yes. Ruskin : " Famous draughtsmen, as far as my experiences go, can draw every line except a straight line."

(186) *Does discussion of, say, " an elephant " not give a visual image ?* (Alexandra College, Dublin.)

This is partly its purpose.

(187) *Does Cizek ever paint for the children ?* (Nursery School Association Summer School, Bromley.)

Never.

(188) *Are children much influenced in their work by pictures in the home, the cinema, theatre, etc. ?* (Nursery School Association Summer School, Bromley.)

Unfortunately, yes.

(189) *Was Cizek's work introduced into Germany ?* (Nursery School Association Summer School, Bromley.)

To a certain extent.

(190) *If a child draws an orange sky or purple trees, is it because he thinks it is prettier done in this way ?* (Godolphin School, Salisbury.)

Yes.

(191) *In a hundred years' time, do you think young children will still draw Egyptian eyes ?* (Godolphin School, Salisbury.)

I hope so.

(192) *If older girls draw purple trees, is there something wrong ?* (Godolphin School, Salisbury.)

Possibly. In rare cases it may be sincere.

(193) *Has every child talent ?* (Godolphin School, Salisbury.)

Yes, in some medium.

(194) *If boys always draw war machines, what should one do ?* (Course at Newport, I.O.W.)

Certainly not stop them.

(195) *Why are there no marks in Cizek's classes ?* (Course at Chelmsford.)

Because a good teacher can do without marks.

(196) *Why do " free " schools produce brilliant pupils and dunderheads ?* (Course at Chelmsford.)

They do not produce them ; they get them—like other schools.

(197) *People have tended to take Child Art as a diversion. Has it been taken seriously enough ?* (Course at Chelmsford.)

Many people take Child Art very seriously, and especially in countries like Great Britain and America, I suppose because of their innate love and respect for children. But there are still people everywhere who do not take the child seriously. How can we then expect them to take Child Art seriously ?

(198) *Do adults draw themselves unconsciously ?* (Course at Chelmsford.)

To a certain extent. It has been stated that great artists, in portraits, unconsciously portray themselves. Leonardo da Vinci's " Gioconda " is also Leonardo's portrait.

(199) *Are the clay models done in one lesson ?* (Course at Chelmsford.)

As a rule, yes.

(200) *Does Cizek teach children after fourteen years?* (Course at Chelmsford.)

No.

(201) *Do the children ever criticise their own work ? (A child was found crying over her own work, aged under ten.)* (Mount School, York.)

Rather an exception with young children.

(202) *Would they be given green paint or should they be allowed to mix ?*
(W.E.A., Vaughan College, Leicester.)

Younger children should be given the ready-made colours.

(203) *Why is intellect fatal to art ?*   (Dartington Hall.)

Because intellect in art is the sin.

(204) *If a child is asked to draw a dragon and has never been told what a dragon is, should he be given any concrete information in reply to any questions raised by the child ?*   (Dartington Hall.)

Of course information should be given.

(205) *In developing Child Art exclusively as an expression of the child's imagination, will a gulf be created between the world of imagination and the world of reality ?*   (Dartington Hall.)

No.   The child goes through the world with open eyes, and the process of growing is a transitional process.

(206) *With reference to a slide of a drawing by a child coming from a cultured home, was it not possible that the child had absorbed this culture unconsciously and that, therefore, it was expressed in the drawing ?*   (Dartington Hall.)

Precisely.

(207) *A child has an innate sense of rhythm which is often destroyed. What can be done to develop this rhythm and keep it ?*   (Dartington Hall.)

Let him be creative as long as possible.

(208) *A small child's sense of rhythm is often spoilt by the method of education and only restored sometimes with a very great deal of trouble.   Does the Cizek school prevent this destruction ?*   (Dartington Hall.)

Very often.

(209) *Most present-day teachers have not had the right kind of education in their childhood—therefore, must there be three generations of teachers before a good one can be produced ?*   (Dartington Hall.)

We cannot wait so long.   Teachers with bad education, if good-hearted, will do their best to spare the children their own bad education.   The present system in England to build up good education, beginning with nursery schools, is the right one.   First the foundation and then the superstructure.   But in the meantime, much can be done and is done in the later stages.   Life is a process of gradual change.   There should be no break between young and old (the tragic misconception of all revolutionaries).

(210) *What about camera clubs in schools ?*   (Dartington Hall.)

Not too early.

(211) *How far is it possible for a teacher to control his own innate taste*

and, therefore, not influence the taste or artistic development of the pupils ? (Dartington Hall.)

It is possible, provided the teacher can remain in the background.

(212) *Should children be shown photographs of art through the ages as they correspond with their own artistic development ?* (Dartington Hall.)

For young children it would not be without danger. They should not produce consciously or do it because " the ancient Egyptians did it."

(213) *Were the few children who ultimately became artists the only children who wished to become artists ?* (Dartington Hall.)

Yes.

(214) *Would Cizek encourage all the other children to go on with handwork —perhaps in the form of masonry, needlework, etc. ?* (Dartington Hall.)

Certainly.

(215) *Didn't the children resent their course finishing at the age of puberty ?* (Dartington Hall.)

Some would have liked to go on. But they knew from the beginning that they could only be at the school until they were fourteen.

(216) *Does civilisation as it is in Europe defeat Cizek in that no further development is possible after the age of puberty ?* (Dartington Hall.)

Cizek blames our overwhelming civilisation.

(217) *At what age is the most exciting art produced ?* (St. Mary's School, Godalming.)

It depends upon personal preferences. Cizek thinks at three or four.

(218) *What should we give to a nine-year-old child who is already corrupt, if he only wants to copy ?* (Bedford Training College.)

Change of medium. In nine cases out of ten it will work.

(219) *What is the attitude towards neatness in drawing or painting ?* (Middlesbrough Froebel Society.)

Not neatness, but clarity is the quality of genuine infantile art.

(220) *Would Cizek be distressed if he told the children an exciting story and they did not respond ?* (Middlesbrough Froebel Society.)

No. I was thrilled with my Glasgow nursery children who did not draw my story.

(221) *Is it an advantage to ask children to draw or paint immediately after hearing a story ?* (Middlesbrough Froebel Society.)

It often is. They should start working when they are quite under the impression of the story.

(222) *How long would it take an eleven-year-old child who had been wrongly taught to recover her freedom ?* (Middlesbrough Froebel Society.)

It depends. Some can never recover.

(223) *Do children who develop individuality in art have better taste in colour, clothes, houses, etc., when they grow up ?*   (Philosophical Society, Scarborough.)
Certainly.

(224) *Why do some children do such small drawings ?   Should we give larger paper to encourage them to draw larger ?* (Philosophical Society, Scarborough.)
Some children are shy, or have not sufficient confidence.   They should be gradually encouraged to use a larger size.

(225) *Are the best examples only chosen for exhibiting ?*   (Philosophical Society, Scarborough.)
In exhibitions mostly average work should be shown.

(226) *Is there no use for copying from nature ?*   (Leeds Training College.)
Not as long as children can produce from imagination.

(227) *Is there such a thing as imagination ?*   (Leeds Training College.)
Yes, blind children prove it.

(228) *If children are given more guidance while young, will they retain their creative powers longer ?*   (Leeds Training College.)
If right guidance is given.

(229) *Would a mother be as helpful as a teacher ?*   (Leeds Training College.)
She could be.

(230) *Is the creative part of art interfered with by the examination system ?* (Leeds Training College.)
Often it is.   But an understanding teacher can succeed to a certain extent even with the present examination system.

(231) *If a young child is allowed to create in his own way, will he when older reach a stage of right proportions ?*   (Leeds Training College.)
Yes.

(232) *Must people be trained to appreciate beauty of art created by children unspoiled by instruction ?*   (Leeds Training College.)
Many people need to be educated.

(233) *Should we have exhibitions of children's work, and if so, should we include both good and poor ?*   (Leeds Training College.)
Both ; but we must be careful not to hurt the producers of poor quality.

(234) *Is it best to tell the child what colours it should use ?*   (Leeds Training College.)
We should leave it as far as possible to the child.   He will do it much better as a rule.

(235) *What if an animal is drawn with six legs, should we correct the drawing ?*   (Leeds Training College.)
We should be happy about it.

(236) *If an individual child had a picture to draw, would the picture have to be topical ?* (Leeds Training College.)

Not necessarily.

(237) *Should the best drawings be shown to the rest of the class ?* (Leeds Training College.)

Rather all drawings.

(238) *Will children pick up perspective naturally ?* (Leeds Training College.)

What they need, certainly.

(239) *Does it happen that a class may copy one child and a fashion be set ?* (Leeds Training College.)

Yes, occasionally. There are stronger and weaker children. The teacher must try to make the weaker ones do creative work and not to copy.

(240) *Do all children have human beings as their first and favourite subject ?* (Leeds Training College.)

Almost without exception, and probably because the human figure is the most important.

(241) *Does a child lose interest in his drawing immediately he has finished it ?* (Leeds Training College.)

Usually, and in common with great artists.

(242) *If a child hasn't a chance to work freely and then has an opportunity, does he have to work through a series of stages then, or has he lost something ?* (Leeds Training College.)

Sometimes it may somehow be possible to repeat those earlier stages.

(243) *In doing cut-paper work, is it necessary to draw outline first ?* (Leeds Training College.)

No.

(244) *Can we do much for the child's art if he is influenced by films ?* (Leeds Training College.)

Bad films may have a bad influence. Change of medium may be a help.

(245) *Should young children be taught what are discords and harmonies ?* (Leeds Training College.)

Certainly not.

(246) *Do Education officials try to rush the idea of perspective too quickly ?* (Great Ayton, Yorks.)

Some do.

(247) *Do the boys and girls have mixed classes in Cizek's school ?* (Great Ayton, Yorks.)

Yes.

(248) *What can one do when bound by limits of time-table ?* (Southlands College.)

Try to change the time-table. Teachers are powerful in Great Britain.

(249) *Can one estimate the advancement of art among the primitives by comparison with Child Art ?* (Solihull School.)

Yes.

(250) *A child of six drew always in correct perspective. Would he have been taught deliberately or did he find it out himself ?* (Saffron Walden Training College.)

In rare cases he may have found it out himself.

(251) *Can nothing be done to prevent loss of genius at adolescence as long as education only deals with the intellect ?* (Woodbrooke College, Birmingham.)

Hardly. And the question arises if even change of intellectual education can counteract the influence of civilisation.

(252) *At what age does one cease to be criminal in presenting a model to a child ?* (Woodbrooke College, Birmingham.)

When the child begins to be incapable of drawing from imagination.

(253) *How can one counteract the influence of bad art in home and general surroundings ?* (Woodbrooke College, Birmingham.)

By adult education.

(254) *Should one try to influence taste at all in children ?* (Woodbrooke College, Birmingham.)

Not directly.

(255) *Can anything be done to purify the bad taste of adults ?* (Woodbrooke College, Birmingham.)

Through education. By showing them better things. In Stoke-on-Trent Museum excellent and poor pottery are exhibited side by side.

(256) *Can the creative desire not come out in craft in later years ?* (Kingsmead College, Birmingham.)

Yes, it can.

(257) *How can this method be used in helping aborigines, native peoples ?* (Kingsmead College, Birmingham.)

It is done in parts of West Africa.

(258) *Is not the child only partly creative ? Is half perception ?* (George Cadbury Hall, Birmingham.)

Yes ; but with the young child most is creativeness.

(259) *Do not young children copy unconsciously the work seen around them, rather than create ?* (Aberystwyth University.)

There is a certain influence of environment, but most is innate in the young child.

(260) *Why is it so important that the child should create ? Is it to make the child happy ?* (Aberystwyth University.)

Only partly. The main reason is to have productive men and women.

(261) *Why are all the figures in children's works facing left ?* (Aberystwyth University.)

Consequence of right-hand drawing.

(262) *What is one to do with a child who puts six arms ?* (Birmingham University.)

Be grateful. The adult is not allowed to interfere. But Mary's neighbour will perhaps point out to Mary, who did six arms : " You stupid thing, man has only four arms." (The questioner did not see the point.)

(263) *When the children discuss a subject, does Cizek try to find a common subject ?* (Belfast.)

Mostly.

(264) *Do many children start things they do not finish ?* (Sheffield Central Library.)

Not very often.

(265) *Does Cizek impose his personality on the children ?* (Ilford.)

A serious objection. He does his best not to, but there is a strong influence, especially on the less strong ones. But I do not think that this influence is necessarily bad.

(266) *Does a child get subdued colours if he wants them ?* (Cambridge.)

A young child will hardly ask for subdued colours.

(267) *Does Cizek talk to the whole class or only to the individual child ?* (Brighton.)

Both.

(268) *Do Cizek's pupils want to paint models ?* (Bristol University.)

Hardly ever (*or* seldom).

(269) *Why are the girls generally less humorous in their work than the boys ?* (Badminton School.)

Perhaps because they are more gentle in general.

(270) *Does the method of teaching children to write when young spoil their creativeness ?* (Ripon Training College.)

It may if they are taught writing too early.

(271) *What about students who have been brought up on imitative work and have to teach creative art ?* (Ripon Training College.)

Study of primitive art and Child Art may help.

(272) *Can an adult understand a drawing from a child's point of view ?* (Warley Woods Adult Institute, Smethwick.)

He should try.

C.A.—7

(273) *If a child brings a drawing for our approval, shall we praise it even if we do not like it ?* (Warley Woods Adult Institute, Smethwick.)

Certainly not. But there is something good in every child's work, and that should be praised.

(274) *Should children have opportunity every day ? (I know a little boy who does much for a fortnight, then there comes a lull.)* (Nursery School Association Summer School, Cambridge.)

It is different with different children. For some daily to do Child Art may prove too much.

(275) *Should the third dimension be suggested to them ?* (Nursery School Association Summer School, Cambridge.)

Never.

(276) *Should a child be trained in observation ?* (Rochdale.)

Not too early as far as art goes.

(277) *How do we make use of accident in Child Art ?* (Bradford Education Society.)

We should not overrate the occurrence of " accidents."

(278) *Is the short time the children spend at Cizek's school enough to counteract the bad influence from outside ?* (Keighley Girls Grammar School.)

Not always.

(279) *Why do young children paint the left leg and right arm blue and vice versa ?* (Kintore Way Nursery School, Rede Hall, Burstow, near Horley, Surrey.)

Because of the child's sense of symmetry.

(280) *One child may demand most of the attention of the teacher to the detriment of the rest of the class. Is this right ?* (Kintore Way Nursery School, Rede Hall, Burstow, near Horley, Surrey.)

It would not be detrimental to the rest of the class if the teacher uses even such an occasion for the benefit of the whole class.

(281) *Is getting rid of inhibitions the chief aim of Child Art ?* (Kintore Way Nursery School, Rede Hall, Burstow, near Horley, Surrey.)

It is one of the aims. For some people it may be the chief aim.

(282) *Does the child get rid of fears by putting them into pictures ? Does it not perpetuate them ?* (Kintore Way Nursery School, Rede Hall, Burstow, near Horley, Surrey.)

" Speaking out " is always better than keeping something to yourself.

(283) *Why do children like bright colours ?* (Hinckley Grammar School.)

Because they are strong and bold.

(284) *Would it be correct to sit at table where children are modelling and*

create something yourself? (Honor Oak Nursery School, Birch Grove House, Haywards Heath, Sussex.)

It would be dangerous, especially for less creative children.

(285) *Why is paper tearing better than paper cutting?* (Honor Oak Nursery School, Birch Grove House, Haywards Heath, Sussex.)

Not because scissors are dangerous (children are much more intelligent than we think they are), but because of the priceless value of direct contact between fingers and material.

(286) *Should one make a child change from left- to right-hand drawing?* (Honor Oak Nursery School, Birch Grove House, Haywards Heath, Sussex.)

It would be dangerous, and might have bad consequences, for instance on the child's language.

(287) *How treat a person who says, " Oh, but that's not art!"?* (Percival Guildhouse, Rugby.)

Try to open his eyes.

(288) *How teach a child who does not want to draw or paint?* (Percival Guildhouse, Rugby.)

Encourage him to work in another medium.

(289) *Does " walking around " a classroom disturb certain children?* (Merthyr Tydfil.)

It depends on the kind of walking.

(290) *If we have a group of forty children, should we arrange that one group does painting while the other does modelling?* (Merthyr Tydfil.)

In many cases an excellent way.

(291) *What of chalk on blackboard?* (Merthyr Tydfil.)

For many children white chalk is ideal. But some will prefer coloured chalk.

(292) *Has not the child a great pride in his possessions?* (Merthyr Tydfil.)

Yes ; but if he knows from the beginning that the work belongs to the school, he will not mind. If he wants to possess a picture, he may do it at home.

(293) *Children draw aeroplanes, bombs, etc., not because they want to get rid of something, but because they are interested in them.* (Merthyr Tydfil.)

Quite so. But by drawing and painting bombed houses or ships, they gradually get rid of them. So we ought not to prevent them doing war pictures.

(294) *How does Cizek correct work?* (Merthyr Tydfil.)

By tactful conversation.

(295) *Is there any use for a blackboard in an art room?* (Kendal.)

Certainly.   For the children to draw on it, or for displaying their work after a " lesson."

(296) *If a child does a morbid drawing, may the rest of the class see it ?* (Kendal.)

Why not ?

(297) *If a child is drawing a house and its perspective is all wrong, would you interfere ?*   (Appleby.)

There is nothing " wrong " in a young child's work.

(298) *Talking about " love, security, and significance," are you not showing that love by helping the child ?*   (Appleby.)

Helping, yes, but indirectly.

(299) *Early impressions are lasting ; why should we allow wrong impressions to be left uncorrected ?*   (Appleby.)

The impressions are not wrong, but are according to age.   We should not accelerate the process of growing.

(300) *To educate is to change children's conceptions, and if this is so, ought we not to correct their wrong conception of form and colour ?*   (Appleby.)

" To educate " comes from the Latin and means " to lead, to guide, to bring up, to train, to bring out, to develop," and not " to change."   To cultivate a flower is not to put in another root in the place of the one you find.

(301) *What would you do with a class of children that had been spoilt ?* (Diocesan Training College, Fishponds, Bristol.)

Try to guide them back ; if not successful—change of medium.

(302) *When would you know a child needs white or dark paper ?*   (Board of Education Course, Bristol.)

From the child himself.   There should be papers of different colour in the room.

(303) *How would you grade intelligence from drawings ?*   (S. Katherine's Training College, Keswick.)

Florence Goodenough has written a book about it, " Measurement of Intelligence by Drawing."   But Child Art, primarily, is not an opportunity for tests.

(304) *Does the child depict the period in which he lives ?*   (Course in Tredegar.)

Children are a product of their time to a certain degree.   In spite of the " eternal child " of all ages, the period may be traced in children's works.

(305) *When a child is born an artist can it be seen in the work of the child ?* (College of the Venerable Bede, Durham.)

Not with certainty.   Puberty is the crisis.

CHAPTER XI

OBJECTIONS

EARLY in 1938 the " Listener " reproduced Children's Drawings and Paintings and a month-long controversy in Letters to the Editor followed. The supporters of Child Art tried to convince those who saw only clumsiness and mistakes in the pictures. I do not think that many of those who lacked appreciation of Child Art changed their minds.

In the autumn of 1938 the " Schoolmaster," the weekly journal of the National Union of Teachers, published an article by *Charles T. Smith*, " The New Approach in Art Teaching : To Be or Not to Be ? " which culminated in the following statement :

" If the theory and practice of the ' new ' art teaching can be derived from a fundamental principle of education which is accepted as being sound, the teaching is justified ; otherwise, it stands condemned. Now, I am not going to deny that the aim of education and the function of schooling can be defined in many different ways, mostly acceptable because supplementary to each other. But I do deny that any two definitions can both be sound, however plausibly stated, if in effect they are mutually destructive. For instance, a teacher might subscribe to the handing-on-the-torch idea of education—that it should seek to train a child to adjust himself to the present state of civilisation and fit him for contributing to its further advancement—the purpose of schooling then being to ensure that he has the right equipment, that is, sufficient skill, knowledge, and clearness of vision to be able to act without repeating the errors and crudities which man committed when less mature, less competent, and less enlightened. This view of education, not without bearing on the matter in hand, regards the child as having *possibilities*—nothing more—which have to be discovered and trained ; that though these possibilities may be distinctive to him, they will not be original or have any real value until they have been developed along the line of growth to which they belong and until they pass beyond the stage to which the technique and knowledge of to-day have already taken them. The child is therefore always in a state of tutelage, and his efforts are to be taken seriously only for purposes of correction and further instruction. He has no illumined state of mind lit by an inner light of an effective candle-power, only a childish state of mind gaining in incandescence from the illumination around."

There followed a number of replies, some defending Mr. Smith's views, some opposing them. I should like to repeat the essential points in these letters, because they seem to me to be typical of what was and still is in the minds of many teachers.

Frank Hoyland maintained " that there is something to be said for allowing the child to interpret the world of his experience in his own way, unhampered by the sophistication of the adult. . . . The quality of a child's perception is very different from that of an adult. To force him, therefore, as the old object-drawing lesson did, to accept an adult perception of objects, which he is incapable of reconciling with his own, is unsound and simply teaches him to draw by rule-of-thumb. With the older child it is different. His perception approximates more to that of the adult. . . . The actual age at which the child is ready for this formal instruction varies, of course, with the individual. An intelligent child may be ready at ten, the majority between twelve and thirteen. . . ."

" The following letter from a *London Headmaster* gives a widely held view," commented the " Schoolmaster." In his letter, " Enquirer " stated :

" ' The children love it ' is hardly satisfying. Of course they do. What normally active child would not welcome the opportunity to revel with brush and colours, large spaces of paper to cover and ' go as you please ' ? As an infant's ' occupation ' it has much to recommend it, but is the child to remain artistically an infant for the remaining years of its school life ? And here, in the minds of many, lies the gravest objection to the ' new approach to art.' There appears, to the unbiased eye, no progress from the work of tots of three or four to that of girls of fifteen or sixteen or even instructors in art schools. . . ."

Then came a contribution from *George E. Mackley*, defending the new approach :

" The value of art is not to be measured by the degree to which its makers ' foreshorten ' or use ' perspective ' or refrain from violating ' every canon of art.' . . . Nor is the history of art to be regarded . . . as a steady progression from the work of the ignorant, primitive man through the Renaissance and on to a culminating point in, perhaps, the realism of a nineteenth-century academician. Art is not like science. It is not cumulative. . . . It is quite possible for an ancient work by an uncivilised artist to be as artistically significant as a later work in which the artist's sensory and emotional experience is dressed up in perspective and foreshortening and which is bristling with canons of art. . . . The history of art is the story of the violating of canons. . . . As one who is a painter as well as a teacher I can assure Mr. Smith that the achievements of the modern child

in these fields have meant the overcoming of difficulties far greater than those met with by children of, say, thirty years ago. . . . Yet the modern work, because of its spontaneity and looseness of handling, appears to a layman's eye easy to do. Nothing could be further from the truth. Nor is it easy to teach. Very skilful teaching is required, but it differs from the teaching of previous years in that it serves the needs of the children as those needs arise, . . . children must live as children before they can function as adults. To cope with this task a teacher must have an understanding of children and constant experience of the nature of artistic expression as well as a knowledge of technique. He must, moreover, have sufficient knowledge of art as a whole to be able to differentiate between the spurious and the genuine, for even in children's art all is not gold that glitters. . . . In the junior school it has, I am convinced, been a magnificent success, but in the senior work there is something lacking. . . . I believe that there is normally, after the age of about twelve, an increasing interest in the appearance of things, a more critical and analytical interest. . . . It is also accompanied by a desire to do things in the ' proper ' way, that is, as adults would do them. In short, there is, as the *Board of Education Handbook* suggests, a gradual adoption of adult standards. . . . The ' new art ' appears not to recognise this tendency, but to foster artistic Peter Pans who will not grow up. The half-grown-up stage may not be a graceful one artistically or physically, but it must not be ignored and cannot be avoided. Its needs must be served and its problems met."

F. W. Burrows, A.R.C.A., formerly H.M. Inspector of Art, in the next letter, made two important statements :

" Can it be agreed that the main aim of teaching art to children should be individual artistic expression ? If so, surely the new methods have come nearer to the achievement of that end than did any of the earlier methods. . . . Where the teacher has no sensitivity to art and is blindly following a recipe for teaching art in accordance with the new methods, then the failure is probably more obvious than under the old formalised system. . . ."

" A Further Contribution to the Controversy " came from *J. Morrison Townley :*

" I agree it is unwise to stem the flow of the creative stream, but surely we can help to clear away the weeds. We can discuss the child's work with him, and venture to make suggestions. By observation of objects and children around him, their relationships to their backgrounds, I have tried to lead children to notice their own faults in accuracy of drawing, placing, proportion, perspective (but don't use the term), and have seen their faces light up with pleasure on finding how to improve their work. Is this uneducational ? . . ."

Gladys Corbyn, A.T.D., wrote this to the " Schoolmaster " :

" When ' new art ' is carried to an extreme there is a tendency to allow the child continually to draw on his own resources. Now, a child's experience is, except in a few unusual cases, very slight. Is it in any way helping in his education to allow him to work always from within the limits of that experience, never teaching him to see and discover new facts for himself ? If that were good, there would be no mental growth. In the infant school, where a child's ability to express himself by the spoken or written word is practically nil, art should be perfectly free. For in picture making the child finds a means of expression that is easy to him. . . . In the junior school a little more control over his work should be exercised. By control I do not mean the correction of technical faults. I mean just making the child stick to the point. For example, if he is making a picture of Robin Hood and his Outlaws, he should not put in his sister's kitten ! . . . As ' compositions,' unhampered by grammar, on the lessons he has learnt, picture making is invaluable. There is no harm in teaching drawing—by degrees —in a senior school. Slowly. Carefully. For at that age children become critical, and their art will do them most good if they can achieve satisfactory results. . . ."

In his final comments *Charles T. Smith* summed up :

" I will say quite definitely that I believe the New Approach advocates actually have a case, but not the case they seem to think they have. Cizek proved it in his practice when he trained his young pupils to do masterly work in a masterly way ; unfortunately the case was lost in the theorising of his followers, and when teachers were encouraged to believe that, without his genius, skill, and labour, they could do work which his practice would fortify."

The danger does exist that Cizek simply is copied. How far the mis-understanding can go I have experienced in an *Austrian* village school, where, when I entered, the children traced paper cutting from Cizek's class with tracing paper. When I asked the teacher what his children were doing, he replied : " I work according to Cizek's methods." And he meant it. It was a very exceptional case, but if it could happen in Cizek's own country. . . .

In America Cizek's ideas were enthusiastically welcomed. The number of Americans who came to Vienna between 1920 and 1930 only in order to see Cizek and his children ran into thousands. A serious problem was raised by an American, *A. Philip McMahon*, in " Parnassus." the College Art Association's publication :

" Like most movements that have met an initially hostile reception and then enjoyed a world-wide popularity, this one is a logical development in more ways than one. If the romantic notion is true that art is primarily significant as a release and embodiment of emotional pressure in the artist, and if the more spontaneous, primitive, and unsophisticated, the better the art, then of course very young human beings should be the greatest of artists because they fulfil the romantic views as to the psychological basis of art and its most desirable characteristics. If art is important as psychothera-peutics and not as a significant symbol of the best that cultural maturity can produce, the production of genuine art stops some time before adoles-cence, and persists only in rare cases when the artist's psychological pattern has been permanently retarded, that is, when it is persistently infantile. Again, if the psychotherapeutic function of art is successful, the disease that causes art having been cured by homœopathic treatment in its early stages, art will in normal individuals cease almost completely when the psychic strains of infancy have been balanced in the mature adult. . . . On the other hand, if few important artists have been developed after a start of this sort, the romantic, popular theory of art automatically brings about its own extinction. . . ."

When I showed Cizek this American statement, he said this : " I began as an artist. I did not want to teach children. For this reason I founded the Juvenile Art Class, where I tried to create a sort of refuge for the

children.   My activity in the Juvenile Art Class consists in working with
the children as an artist, and not as a teacher.   What is the aim of the
Juvenile Art Class ?   From the beginning it was an artistical aim.   I
intended to discover the roots of art.   This was in the 'eighties, when art
was in decay and imitative.   I gave to the ordinary school a definite aim,
too, art education of the people.   I said in the 'nineties that one understands art only as far as one has worked it out.   I wanted that children in
the schools should work out what they need for a better understanding of
art.   My aim was also the forming of new customers of good taste.   That
is a practical aim.   What is said about romanticism in the article is not
clear.   Everything connected with the natural growing of child work is
quite clear.

   " I wanted to create a ' soil ' for art.   This kind of soil they had in
ancient Greece.   We have not this soil because our people became industrialised and too intellectual.   There is nothing romantic about my aims."

   While I was giving a course in Wiltshire in the spring of 1939 I received
the following letter from a head teacher which seems to me so significant
for the honest attitude of the British teacher who is sympathetic to the
" new approach " but has his serious doubts, that I will quote it at full
length :

                                                        " *May* 31*st*, 1939.

   " Because I am most anxious that the children of my school shall gain
a lasting love of the beautiful, and skill and joy in expressing themselves
with pencil, brush, and other media, I am writing to disclose to you my
reactions to your last lecture, not only in the hope of receiving correction
and enlightenment for myself, but also because I believe that some of my
friends are similarly exercised in their own minds with regard to various of
the things you then said.

   ' I cannot draw at all myself.   I feel that I am in exactly the same
plight as some of my pupils whose figure drawing is grotesque and mis-
shapen, and who are obviously disappointed with their results.   They
know what they want to draw, but they simply cannot do it.   The legs
refuse to be legs, the face will not come like the face they want.   Do you
suggest that my accomplished young art teacher should refrain from giving
that guidance which would make those refractory legs look like legs, or
that dead face to live ?   I think that in my own case, if such appropriate
guidance had been given to me as a boy, I should at least be able to draw
my wife (after Rembrandt !).   Should the art teacher attempt to bridge
the gulf between observation and execution ?

" Then am I correct in thinking that you suggested that a child should acquire technique in various media mainly by the process of unaided trial and error ?   If that be so, how many of our pupils will make much progress before they leave school at fourteen years ?   As one who likes to think that he is a craftsman, though of limited skill in one direction, I believe that the little I can do was acquired : (*a*) by watching a highly skilled craftsman at work when I was very young ; (*b*) by patient instruction later on at the hands of a master in the craft.   But for these, I wonder whether my interest would have been awakened, my fingers ever gained any facility, my nerves acquired any ' instinctive ' response to the media in which I work.   Am I wrong in thinking that the art and craft department of a school should provide such conditions for our pupils, or are we to shut them off from the accumulated knowledge and transmitted skill of the past, start them at zero, and leave them to get only as far as personal experiment will carry them ?

" In your lecture you said that you were averse to children ' growing up.'   I am almost entirely in sympathy with this attitude and I would prolong school days by several years if I could.   But the horrible fact is that our youthful charges go out into a very drab world of mill and factory at the age of fourteen, and after leaving us there is often little or nothing in their lives to prolong and develop their interest and skill in things of the spirit, i.e. their artistic education ceases.   Because of that, is it not our privilege and duty judiciously to foster and stimulate those processes of development, which under better conditions would proceed more slowly ?

" May I now return to the pictures which you showed of children's work in clay and plaster.   As you said, they were really lovely examples of medieval art as regards conception and workmanship.   But should we rest satisfied with productions of that nature in the year 1939 ?   Presumably work of that character was the best that could be produced in, say, 1400, maybe because (*a*) the standard of anatomical knowledge and observation was then low, (*b*) technique in these media lagged in sympathy with (*a*), but later centuries have seen great advances in these directions with such resultant as the statue at Whitehall which you mentioned.   My point is this—should we not assist our children to reach a standard compatible with that of the present age ?   With you, we all accept the recapitulatory theory that the child passes through the same stages of development as the human race, and we endeavour to make the best use of those natural phases of evolution in the individual pupil, but is it in his interest that he should linger in its early stages ?   Is he best able to enjoy life, express his inner self and appreciate what later centuries have produced of the good and beautiful, if personally he is five hundred years behind in his own developments ?

"All this leads me to ask why you suggested, (*a*) almost the total exclusion of beautiful pictures from the child's environment and the substitution in their place of pictures drawn by children ; (*b*) the drastic reduction in the number of beautifully illustrated books which the child should possess ? The reason which I think you gave was the risk the child ran of being over-influenced by them. Should not our watchword be the words of the Apostle, ' Whatsoever things are pure, good, lovely, and true—think on these things,' i.e. surround him with them ?. Subconsciously will they not become part of his thought, life, and mould his standards of taste, if he is allowed to grow up in their silent but eloquent presence, always granted their selection be judicious and their character appropriate ?

"One of your slides, as you pointed out, showed very definitely the influence of Burne-Jones upon the youthful artist, and you told of the steps taken to eradicate that influence in order to throw the child back on her own resources of idiom and subject. This is a minor point, but I found it very provocative, so I would ask, was it sound psychologically ? Youth and childhood, of course, are the time of hero worship and hero imitation. Such imitation applied to art would seem to (*a*) give inspiration, (*b*) stimulate exact observation, (*c*) direct the mind and taste into worthy channels, (*d*) lead the hero worshipper into the adoption for the time being of a certain idiom and technique. Are not these four things mainly to the good ? In the acquisition of a good prose style, it is customary to set the adolescent to imitate standard authors such as Addison, Johnson, or Stevenson, the object of such exercises being that the child's methods of thought and expression shall take on something of the excellence of such universally approved stylists. Is not a similar process desirable in the case of art also ? Further, as in youth one's object of imitation soon changes as one's mind grows and one's literary taste changes and as the cumulative result of these early ' loves ' becomes a personal individual style embodying certain features of each—so in art, should not one's ultimate style and technique incorporate the influences of a number of great masters ?

Yours sincerely."

I shall try to repeat what I then replied in my course: The "accomplished young art teacher," of course, should not refrain from giving guidance, but he should not give it too soon ; his help should be an indirect help as long as possible.   Yes, a young child should acquire technique mainly by himself.   He will learn as much of a medium and technique as he will need.

If so much must be pressed into the curriculum of what the children should have later, because the children leave school at fourteen, there is only one answer : the school-leaving age should be raised, and crafts would play a very important part after fourteen.

I am not so sure that our head master acquired his skill as a craftsman " by watching highly skilled craftsmen at work when he was very young," rather than by using his fingers in early childhood.   " Patient instruction " has its place, but, it must be said again : Not too early !   The old school was too early in many ways—perhaps out of a fear that children would remain too long in their state of " imperfectness " and be handicapped later.   We all agree now that it is not sensible to give a young child " modern," sophisticated toys.   We cannot *begin* with the " accumulated knowledge and transmitted skill of the past."

I do not think that I said or wished to say that I was averse to children growing up.   Perhaps I had asked : Is the world of the adults so happy, is the life of adults so harmonious and perfect that we should do all in our power to rush children through their early stages, and make them adults as soon as possible ?   There are nations where children are no longer children, and it is a sad thing.   Of course, I am not against " growing up."   That would be wrong romanticism and sentimentality.   I am for *slow* growing, natural, " organic growth," to use Goethe's word.   School (and family) should not be a hot-house.   What I have seen in British schools seems to prove that one realises here, as a whole, the value of a long childhood and youth.

If the fourteen-year-old " goes out into a very drab world of mill and factory " I can only say that there are jobs which simply have not to be done by young people who have just left school with its sheltered life.   We must realise that it is a terrible waste—if not something worse—to force fourteen- and fifteen-year-old boys to stay at conveyor belts in peace-time, and young girls in little underground " cells " with artificial light and no ventilation in order to check mechanically the bills which rush in from the sales department.   Again and again it is misconceived industrial revolution. We and our Youth became slaves of machines instead of their masters.

The head master himself answers the question, " Is it not our privilege and duty judiciously to foster and stimulate those processes of development ? " by the concluding sentence, " which under better conditions would proceed more slowly."

The normal young child always will be "a little savage." Our mis-directed civilisation takes care that this state does not last too long. In this we do not need to assist our children ; we should do all in our power to slow down the rapid absorption of misunderstood mechanical civilisation.

Beautiful pictures, of course, but not too early ! They may in many cases not lead to imitation by young children, but will simply make no impression upon them. An experience in Vienna illustrates this, in no connection at all with Cizek. A group of boys from eleven to twelve was shown round the big Art Museum (as rich as the National Gallery or the Louvre) by a very artistic teacher, who pointed out to the boys the beauty of Titian, Rembrandt, Brueghel, etc. After two hours of inspection he assembled the boys at the door of the Museum and asked them to tell him frankly what they liked best. He expected to hear that one special Giorgione or Vandyke had aroused their special admiration, but a bright boy shouted : " It was jolly fine how the corridors were waxed so that we could slide on them."

The parallel between " the acquisition of a good prose style " by imita-ing standard authors and the imitation of great masters in the realm of art is interesting, but is there any reason for imitation before adolescence or, better, as long as there is sufficient imaginative and creative power in the child ?

The last part of the letter seems to indicate that the writer is concerned with making artists out of young people. It cannot be said often enough that the ordinary school—some may even include the art college—has nothing to do with the production of artists. It has nothing to do with that one out of a thousand who is a born artist. He will go his way. All school, society, or state can do, is not to make his life too miserable. School has to deal with the 999 out of 1,000 who will not become artists but who should become productive men and women whatever their profession will be. And they should work imaginatively as long as possible, should express themselves and in a medium suitable for them. They should use their hands, which are just as much a gift of God as their brains. There must have been something wrong with the old " art teaching " if so few adults are capable of producing in any medium whatever, and when, as so often, their taste is so bad. They had the innate foundation, but school did not encourage creativeness, it did not pierce through the layers with which originally very artistic souls were covered from the time of the industrial revolution. Much is now done, but more could be done.

It may be difficult especially for the more elderly and conscientious teacher who passed through a school and training college, where, as a rule, creativeness was far from being encouraged, or even allowed, to go the new way. He should not do it against his conviction. But if a teacher (or parent) believes that there is something immortal in Cizek's ideas and worth while following, then he should not be afraid to try, and according to his personality. The children will help him. And they will thank him.

For decades Cizek has been furiously fought, now some carry his ideas to excess. They are so afraid of influencing children that they tend to think tactful guidance is crippling children's souls. This fear is, of course, far less dangerous than the other extreme of frustrating children and crushing or endangering their creativeness.

After a lecture some teachers made the following objections :

1. Why the emphasis on filling space ? If what the child does is " perfect," then why not let him leave empty space if he wants to ?

2. You say the child may be " too lazy " to finish the picture : in that case your task is to find out why he is lazy.

3. First you say " Leave the child alone," then you say " Tell him to fill up space."

Here are some answers and comments by *Margaret E. Isherwood.*

" Leave the child alone *in essentials* ; don't try to teach him how to draw, but encourage him to use his materials, inner and outer, to best advantage. Some teachers in their anxiety not to impose themselves, fall over backwards into negative passivity.

" The word ' perfect ' seems to be somewhat misleading. People get the idea that you mean that everything the child does is so right, so ' perfect ' that there is no room for development in any aspect of his work.

" What is in fact the point about Child Art ? Not, as the conventional teacher has thought hitherto—that the child should learn how to draw things and draw them correctly—but that he may grow in understanding of himself and the world around by ' making the inner outer ' (Froebel).

" In my school we were given marks for drawing, the marks depending on how accurately and neatly we had made a copy of the tree or the deck-chair or the cylinder. The dominant emotion connected with drawing was therefore fear of the teacher's rebuke for carelessness or inaccuracy. The dominant emotion in true child art should be joy in revelation. ' How wonderful the world is.' ' I see and I can make.' Therefore only a teacher who is himself experiencing this sense of wonder and delight can possibly be a teacher of art. A dull clod as art teacher (or indeed as any teacher) is a contradiction in terms. All the ' training ' in the world will never make anything of such a one."

CHAPTER XII

CIZEK—"LESSONS"

In this chapter I have attempted, as far as possible verbatim, to render some of what Cizek said to his classes during a number of " lessons." Also some of the sayings of the children during the lessons from November 1935 to June 1937. What is impossible to render is the gentle voice of Cizek, his kind face, bending over little heads ; and indeed all that charm of his whole attitude towards " his " children. Neither is it possible to reproduce the whole symphony of noises that filled the Juvenile Art Classes —that cheerful atmosphere of laughter and intense work, of chattering and concentrated production. It gives only a faint notion of all the life in that enchanted place.

Cizek never spoke down to the children, but although they often did not understand the words which he used, they certainly felt what he meant.

In the class between the ages of ten and fourteen he said very little. There he treated and spoke to each pupil individually. In the class under ten he spoke both individually and to the class as a whole. What I have given in this chapter relates only to those children under ten years of age. There is, however, one exception—which is indicated—when his words to the ten- to fourteen-year-old ones are related (16th January, 1937).

30th November, 1935

Cizek : What nice things would you like to do to-day ? Think about it and tell me ! *Child :* I shall make a queen. *Child :* I shall make a gun with soldiers. *Child :* I don't know. *Child :* I shall make a doll's pram. I shall make a " Krampus." [1] *Child :* And I a Santa Claus. *Child :* I a Christ Child. *Cizek :* Christmas comes later. *Child :* I should like to make a window where Santa Claus has put something. *Cizek :* We shall take a block with the long side at the bottom. Or would you prefer it the other way round ? *Children :* No ! *Cizek :* Who wants to have

---

[1] " Krampus " and Santa Claus come to the children on the evening of December 5th. " Krampus " is the devil and Santa Claus the good bishop. It is a kind of forerunner of Christmas and a great event in children's lives in Roman Catholic countries. Santa Claus brings fruits and sweets to the good children and " Krampus " is supposed to thrash the naughty ones. Men disguised as " Krampus " and " Nicolo " (as Santa Claus is called in Austria) used to visit families with young children, and the shops, especially the sweet shops, are full of white Santa Clauses and red " Krampuses."

CIZEK STUDYING A CHILD'S DRAWING

it in this way ? (Shows a block with the long side at the bottom. All the children want it this way.) *Cizek :* We shall draw a line down the centre. This is a wall. At one side of the wall Santa Claus will stand, and on the other side—who will stand there ? The " Krampus." At the side of the paper near the window[1] we have Santa Claus, and at the side near the door we have the " Krampus." How does Santa Claus look ? *Child :* He wears a mitre. *Child :* And a long coat. *Cizek :* Yes, a long coat. But you should begin with the head. How does his head look ? *Child :* It's like a man's head. *Cizek :* What kind of head has he ? *Child :* A very funny head. *Cizek :* He has a long beard and beautiful white hair. *Child :* No, I don't believe it. *Cizek :* What has he on his head ? *Child :* A mitre. *Cizek :* Do you know what a mitre looks like ? But you can draw it better than describe it. Who can describe the mitre ? *Child :* I. *Child :* I. *Child :* I. *Child :* Like a bishop. *Child :* There is an arch and it closes down and at the top is a cross, and that is all. *Cizek :* I shan't bother you to describe it—draw it. Begin with the head, then the mitre, then the rest. Start ! But don't make the head too small !

Cizek (later) : You all must begin with the mitre near the top of the paper —as Trude did. Not in the middle ! Otherwise it would be a wee Santa Claus. *Cizek* (to one child) : You have done the head and mitre, but don't forget his eyes and eyebrows. *Cizek* (to another child) : You have given

[1] Undoubtedly some of the very young children would not know left and right.

Santa Claus a black beard like the Emperor of Abyssinia,[1] but Santa Claus has a white beard. *Cizek* (later) : Who has finished the head ? (Nearly all children put up their hands.) One child has made the beard with two lines, but that is not enough. It should be outlined to show the full size. Who has done the eyes ? (Nearly all.) *Cizek :* You say you have finished, but if I look closely, nothing is there. (Pointing to one drawing) That's good. But the beautiful white hair is missing. And I said : Make now only head and mitre. You shouldn't be in such a hurry.—What is the beard made of ? *Child :* Of hair. *Cizek :* You should draw each hair separately. Now listen. I have looked at all the drawings. Most of them are good. And now we shall go on. What comes after the head ? *Child :* The neck. *Child :* I shall do the neck. *Cizek :* What comes below the neck ? *Child :* The body and the arms. *Cizek :* We shall make these now.—What else joins the body ? *Child :* The legs. *Cizek :* The hands. First the arms, then the hands. And the hands have six fingers. *Child :* Five ! *Child :* Seven ! *Child :* Each hand has five fingers. *Cizek :* All right, five fingers. If someone makes one more—it doesn't matter. As Santa Claus gives so much away, perhaps he needs more fingers.—What do the arms do ? *Child :* Hang down. *Cizek :* You must think about it. If he carries something, he must have the hands in such a way that he can hold things. What does his hand hold ? *Child :* The sack. *Child :* In my drawing he does not hold the staff. *Child :* Mine is different. (Several children go to Cizek saying : I have finished.) *Cizek :* A crowd of children come and say they have finished. But actually they have done nothing.—Now, if Santa Claus goes to the children he puts on his best clothes. He has a long golden coat, fastened with a clasp. There are golden decorations on this clasp. *Child :* Nice patterns ! *Cizek :* Yes, decorations. Therefore he looks very fine. The coat is lined inside with red and the shirt underneath is snow-white. You see only a little of his shoes under the coat. On his shoes he has golden buckles. We shall paint them with real gold. Now do the rich decorations on his coat. (To a child who shows him his drawing) You must cover all your paper nicely. (To another child) You must make the decorations thicker. And sign with your names. In the right-hand top corner. The right side is near the door.—Don't make a few quick strokes, but cover the paper carefully. Some do it carelessly. *Child :* Do I do it carelessly ? *Cizek :* You could do it a bit more carefully. You can't paint a single line. You can only paint what is between two lines. You must have double lines. (To another child) This is too muddled.

---

[1] It was the time of the Abyssinian War and all the children were frightfully interested in the Emperor of Abyssinia.

Not careful enough. You must always be careful. (To another child) That's nice. It can be painted.—Who has done the feet ? (Nearly all.) Have you done the shoes with buckles ? You must do them, because we shall paint them with gold. (To a child) You have made a swollen and crippled foot. (To another child) That is very nicely done, but I have said you can only paint between two lines. *Child :* I can't make double lines now. *Cizek :* Oh yes, you can do it. Listen ! Those who have finished their drawing may begin painting. You get the red colour now. *Child :* I have finished. *Child :* I too. *All shout :* I too. *Cizek :* What are you going to paint red ? *Child :* The lining of the coat. *Cizek :* Paint red what should be red. (In the meantime an assistant is distributing paints and brushes.) *Cizek* (later) : Now you get the paint for skin and hands. What are you going to do now ? *Child :* Face and hands. *Cizek :* Those who have finished their work will show it here (on the board). We haven't time to-day to talk about all the pictures because it is already four o'clock. In all your tasks you should take notice of what I say. I give you tasks to teach you to think. When I say, for instance, Make the hair, a child should not be satisfied with making decorations. When I say, Now do the eyes, you should not make blots, but eyes with lids, pupils, and all the parts of the eyes. I try to guide you slowly so that your work grows slowly, but also clearly and well, not muddled. That would give me no pleasure. The next time we shall finish one side with gold and silver and begin the other side. And when I tell you then to make the hands, you must think : How do hands look ? And now we shall go home.

7th December, 1935

(On the wall hang nine Santa Clauses and nine " Krampuses " done by former pupils.) *Cizek :* These are done by former pupils and they should help you to do as well. Now I shall cover the " Krampuses " so that you can't see them. You should make quite different " Krampuses." But first we shall finish with Santa Claus. What else have you to do with Santa Claus ? *Child :* Decorations. *Cizek :* Now you get more colours : gold, silver, orange, and yellow. Much yellow. (To the assistant) A beautiful yellow ! (To a Child) Show me what you have done. Yes, you can make nice decorations. In gold, silver, and so on. And you get a nice paint now. What can you do with it ? I must ask you what you want. Not you ask me what I want. I want nothing. You must want something. Do the parts you want yellow. Quick ! We must make the " Krampus " to-day Now begin to paint. Santa Claus is tired of waiting. *Child :* But Santa Claus is not alive. *Child :* Oh yes ! *Cizek :* The first Santa

Claus was a bishop who was buried 1,500 years ago. He was Bishop of Lybia. (Blue paints and *brushes* [1] are distributed.) *Cizek :* Try to make your pictures more beautiful than those of the former pupils which you saw. You should make more beautiful things because you are younger. The young ones can always paint better than the old ones. (Later) You never bring me drawings from home. Marion has brought me one. (To a child) You should not make the head so small. Now we shall see what Trude has done. She is sitting to-day at the back of the class. (To Trude) You have not used enough red. Otherwise it is nice. Brushes must always be cleaned. And you should not use them for different colours. (To a child) You take too little of each colour. You must take a lot of each colour or it won't be nice. (To another child) You do it very well and very fully. (To another child) This isn't bad at all. (To another child) You do the white beard on the white shirt, which makes no contrast. You must make what is below dark. (To the class) You are dull. Those before you were much brighter. You are really slow. *Child :* I have finished Santa Claus. *Cizek :* I am anxious to see it. Now you can make the child who is praying. Come and look. (He leads him to a statue) This is a Santa Claus also, and here is the child who prays. Do make a boy like it. (*Cizek* covers the " Krampus " sculptures later.) Who has finished ? (Nearly all put up their hands.) *Cizek :* It is high time. *Child :* I have finished. *Cizek :* Have you done the boy ? *Child :* I hadn't enough room for the feet. And the face did not come out very well. *Cizek :* Now we shall use blue and red. (To a child) Would you like to paint with gold ? Not covering other colours, but between colours !

Cizek : We shall begin the " Krampus " on the other side of the paper. We shall draw it first. We shall draw the " Krampus " in such a way that every part is done separately. First the head, and only the head, then only the neck, then only the body, and then joined to it the legs and arms one at a time. *Child :* And then comes the tail ! *Cizek :* Yes, and in the head put the eyes, and the snout—because the devil has a snout—and then the ears. And the ears are pointed like a hedgehog's. And at the head he has horns. We shall draw everything separately. *Child :* And the tail comes too. *Cizek :* And below put the legs on separately. The legs are thick as an elephant's, and one leg has a cloven hoof. The other leg has an ordinary foot. But there are " Krampuses " who have cloven hooves on both legs. And then comes something which is very important : the whole body is covered with bristles like a brush. *Child :* And then comes the tail

[1] The smaller children get new brushes for each colour. The older ones clean their brushes themselves.

behind. *Cizek :* Really ?—Now who can tell us something ? *Child :* Me !
Cizek : All right, tell us so that all can hear. *Child :* Yes, he has a long tail.
Cizek : Right ! I quite forgot the tail. The devil has an enormous tail.
And he has it, so that he can beat children who are very bad. And that
hurts. Now begin. First the head, and then the separate parts of the
body. And not everything at one go. You can do that when you are
twenty. The whole is made up of many parts. Not one line. I wonder
who will do this. You should start at the top. Not in the middle of the
paper. And Trude will do her best now. (To a child) Now do the arms !
(To another child) But these are very thin legs—you should make thick
legs. (Later) Listen. What else has the " Krampus " besides his tongue
and horns ? *Child :* A birch. *Child :* His tongue hangs out. *Cizek :* His
eyes are gleaming. How do they gleam ? *Child :* Yellow. *Child :* Green.
Child : Red. *Cizek :* And what stands beside him ? *Child :* Santa
Claus. *Cizek :* There is something beside him on the ground. *Child :*
The hamper. *Cizek :* And what is in it ? *Child :* Sweets. *Child :* Chocolate. *Cizek :* The bad children are in it. (To Trude) You must try your
best. Santa Claus is badly done. And you should not do the " Krampus "
with a skirt but with long thick legs. (The light is switched on.) *Child :*
That's nice now that we have light on. *Child :* The Santa Claus is not nice.
He has legs the wrong way round. *Cizek :* How would you like to paint
the " Krampus " ? *Most children :* Black. *Some :* Red. *Cizek :* Do
you prefer a black or a red one ? (The children first are equally divided,
but gradually more and more choose red.) *Cizek :* Those who prefer red
will get red and the others black. Now, who wants black ? (A few children
put up their hands.) At the question : What would you like ?, some
children answer : Black and red. *Cizek :* First, all children will get red,
and who wants black will get it after the red. (Red is distributed to all
children.) After a pause. *Child :* I have finished the " Krampus."
Cizek : You must give him eyes and then hair. (To another child) Get on ;
it's all right.—The next time we shall see who has finished first. *Child :*
Perhaps I shall be the very first. I think I shall. (Cizek rings the bell.)
Cizek : Now we shall stop painting because the other class is waiting outside.
They are in a great hurry and want to rush in.

21st December, 1935

Discussion of the work. *Cizek :* This pupil has not done it all in a piece,
but as it should be, each part separately, the head, the hands, the body,
everything separately. All parts must be joined together. That is nice.
Only an adult painter can do it in one piece Children can't do it yet.

Because to-day's the last lesson before Christmas we are going to make something very nice, and something to do with Christmas. Once we made houses here with Christmas trees inside. The children from Meidling [1] did them, and did them very beautifully. They made three, four, and even five little houses. In these little houses Santa Claus came with a Christmas tree. He put it there and some children looked through the key-hole, others stood in front of the Christmas tree full of admiration, and we can look in one little house. There the Christ Child decorates the tree with angels. It was very beautiful. We will make such things to-day. A small house, for instance, with a simple roof, and inside one sees the table with the tree. You can make three, four, or five little houses like that. In each house something different is to be seen. Now be quick! First we shall draw. Then we shall outline the whole drawing, and then we shall paint. Somebody sends us Christmas cards from far away, but you are going to make your own cards. I am looking forward very much to seeing the first little house. (Cizek walks round and the children show him how much they have done.) *Cizek* (to a child): You can't draw windows and the doors, but you should only draw the four walls, the floor and the ceiling. And then comes the roof. *Child:* Shall I draw the house from inside? *Cizek:* Yes. Now the floor, and put the table on the floor. *Child:* I thought I should make the window. *Cizek:* One must see what is inside the house. I see a girl who does not make a Christmas tree but a " zigzag " tree. We don't have " zigzag " trees. I told you before that everything has to be put together out of different parts—the Christmas tree too. The trunk, the branches, the twigs, and on the twigs the needles. Everybody should do this, and not a " zigzag " tree. Only the thoughtless make a " zigzag " tree, the others know that there is a trunk, and on it are branches, and on them twigs, and on the twigs needles. This is a real Christmas tree.

Here is a child who, instead of a Christmas tree, has made a broom. (Laughs.) It must be a poor child who makes a Christmas tree out of a broom. How does the Christmas tree grow? Close your eyes and think about it! There grows a trunk, then come branches, then twigs, then needles. You must imagine how a tree grows. The branches of one tree grow high, and it has leaves instead of needles. You must imagine that. Drawing means thinking. Who cannot think cannot draw. He can only copy. (Cizek shows an artificial tree.) You will say this is not a real tree. I say it is no tree at all, it is only a thing of wood to hang candles on. It is a Christmas pyramid. A Christmas tree is something quite real which grows. *Child:* Can we make a wooden Christmas thing too? *Cizek:* You can,

[1] Suburb of Vienna.

but we want to make a Christmas tree.   One must think.   When we are older we may make wooden things.   This wooden thing here was made by a nineteen-year-old student.   (To another child) You make everything too carelessly, not accurately.   You did the head well, but not the body.   You must draw carefully.   (To another child) That's nice.   (To another child) You must put the table in the middle.   (To another child) It's good. (To another child) Your tree probably reaches the ceiling.   *Child :*   No, it reaches the other side of the house.   *Cizek :*   Why haven't any of you made a pointed roof ?   Pointed roofs are so beautiful.   Look here !   Here is a pointed roof and it is very beautiful.   If you could look inside you would see a lot of people sitting round.   They are waiting for the Christ Child.   Or for Santa Claus.   And no one is sitting here, because they do not expect a Christmas tree until next Tuesday.   But these people are like us, they are already celebrating Christmas to-day.   That means, Santa Claus comes earlier to us.   He is so busy in Vienna.   (To a child) Make Santa Claus a nice coat bulging with apples, nuts, and sweets.   *Child :*   There is no Santa Claus, only the Christ Child.   *Cizek :*   The angels are flying from house to house.   First the Christ Child is flying with the Christmas tree, and after Him the angels are flying.   They carry little parcels in their hands.   They follow the Christ Child.   (To another child) Now you do it very nicely. Quite accurately, not carelessly.   (To another child) Both trees are very beautiful.   Each one is different.   That's good.

(After a quarter of an hour he comes back from his studio.)   (To a child) That's the most beautiful tree.   (To another child) Now make another little house !   (To another child) What is this ?   *Child :*   The wind.   And there a cloud is jumping over the house.   Someone has done this in school. *Cizek :*   What is this in the air ?   *Child :*   Birds.   *Cizek :*   These are not birds.   You should not draw as they do in school.[1]   You should draw as we draw here.   Here we draw quite differently from how they draw in schools.   You should say : " After all, I do not copy what the teacher has done on the board, but what I have thought out myself."   This is not so simple.   You must think : What does a bird look like ?   Head, beak, eyes, feathers make a bird.   That's a bird.   Your bird does not fly because the wings are inside the body.   You must draw it as it sings in the branches of the trees.   Birds always look at the sun when they sing.   They always hold their heads high.   The schools are quite good, but you only learn what you need there.

(To a child) That's not a tree, that's a broom.   *Child :*   This is a tree. *Cizek :*   Where does this tree grow ?   *Child :*   On the table.   *Cizek :*   Now,

[1] Cizek means the ordinary schools to which all the children over six go.

how does a tree grow—think about it. *Child :* The tree grows out of the soil. *Cizek :* Now, there is the trunk. And on the trunk are branches, many branches, and on the branches are twigs, and on the twigs are needles, which pierce. That is the way you should do it. But you haven't made a tree. (To all children) You shouldn't draw as you draw in school, and as they want it there. These are two different things. But now finish your work.

Christmas Celebrations

We have eternal laws in our hearts. And you should follow these eternal laws. This is your supreme task. (The parents are present.) And now I should like to turn to the parents and relatives of the children. The eternal, divine laws are innate in children. Woe to parents who do not recognise these laws but who despise them. We are living in a time of decay. We are not to be blamed that we are born in this time, but our duty is the greater to care for the future and to explore the eternal laws of nature and to follow them. In front of this Christmas tree we will keep this in mind, and follow the eternal, innate laws of all mankind. We depart to-day with the promise that we shall always respect these eternal laws and that we shall always endeavour to keep them alive. The future of our people depends upon this. The Austrian people is an artistic people. The Austrians have created great things in the realms of music, science, and fine arts. The Austrian barock is famous. The barock is a Dinaric, not a Nordic accomplishment. Here in Austria immortal things have had their birth. And this eternal Austria is the Austria which mankind reveres and loves. I get samples from all over the world which show how far the confusion in the realm of art is spreading. Now, fifty years after the exploration of Child Art began, I see that the success of the whole movement is negligible. The spirit I evoked haunts me still. It seems to me it must be so, because the confusion of mankind is so great that they no longer recognise any laws in art.

The parents especially have the worst influence on children. I regret to say it here, but it is common knowledge. Every parent believes he knows best, and corrects the work of children. But the parents know nothing at all about the eternal laws of a child's development. Child Art is nothing but the natural development of the child's logic. Even when the child scribbles he thinks and creates. But we must distinguish this from the bad copying when the child merely repeats. And therefore teachers should never *infect* children with their bad examples. These bad forms are impressed upon children for ever, and they destroy for ever a normal, logical,

God-given artistic development. I beg you to help us to allow the children to follow their right way. Like angels, guard them through the greatest dangers! In this I see the co-operation of parents. I regard everything which disturbs this development as hostile. Please renounce your opposition and help us. These words are intended as a Christmas present, to guide us towards the right way to art.

11th January, 1936

(The children have brought drawings which they have done in the holidays.) *Cizek :* I am glad you brought me so many nice things. And I am glad you had so many lovely Christmas presents. We shall show our joy on paper. As spring is in the air already,[1] you probably think that we shall paint Spring. But it is too early. There will be real winter yet. *Child :* The Easter hare has not come yet. *Cizek :* It is deeply buried in the earth and fast asleep. It is very warm and cosy there. And he won't come out before March. We shall still have real nice winter, and we shall paint it as we like to have it. All the lovely games and sports which come with snow three feet deep. You can slide, throw snowballs, ski, make snowmen, skate, etc. Now we are going to draw winter pleasures. You hold the paper in this way. (Shows them the long side at the bottom.) Make a slope that you can ride down on a sledge, or ski down. Those who can walk on snowshoes can make a straight line. (Shows it with a finger.) Tobogganing can be done down hill. *Child :* We also can make snowmen. *Cizek :* When I was a small boy we made a snowman rolling down the hill from the top. So he got bigger and bigger. And we made a huge head and put it on him. But we had to find a hat for him. We found an old shabby hat and put it on. *Child :* Where were his eyes and mouth ? *Cizek :* I won't tell you. You must find out yourself in the picture. Don't tell me, but put it in the drawing. Everything you know put in the drawing. Now begin ! *Child :* May I make a snowman ? *Cizek :* Yes. But I suggest that you make the figures very big. No midget men ! Everyone should invent for himself and not look at what the neighbours have done. If anyone copies from his neighbour, it is a shame, because it means that he has no ideas. Everybody should invent something he can do himself and on a large scale. What is large ? *Child :* From the top to the bottom. *Cizek :* Yes, that is large. (To a child) What is inside here ? *Child :* This is a dung-hill from where the snowman gets his high hat. *Child* (to Cizek) : Herr Professor, Pepy copies from me ! *Cizek :* Nobody should copy. (To a child) There is so much room, and the figures are so small !

[1] The preceding days were extraordinarily warm.

So much space remains empty. Rub your figures out and make bigger ones ! (To another child) Fill the space ! Make big figures. (To all children) The space must be filled. Paper is made to be used. And the line at the top tells you to draw until you reach it. All figures must touch the top line. You will see, when we have finished, how well the figures look that reach the top line. Who has finished ? (Nobody answers) Now we are going to make the figures, and those who have finished may begin painting. (First dark blue is distributed, later red. Some get yellow, others green. Before the end :) Let us show the pictures on the board. (The pictures are put on the blackboard. The children sit down on the tables in front of the board.) As a matter of fact, not all the drawings are finished. Much remains to be done. But if we look at the pictures now, you will see many things and that will help you next time. If we look at the pictures quickly we see that some give the impression of snow and others don't. For instance, this one. On this picture there is scarcely any white. Has one the impression of snow ? *Child :* I shall make the snow. *Cizek :* Now you see there is no snow. Perhaps it is moonlight. Here two masked people come home from the ball. (To a child) Here there is more snow. Snowflakes begin to fall. *Child :* These are snowballs. *Cizek :* Aha ! snowballs. And the snowballs stay hanging in the air. *Child :* Just at the moment when they are there. *Cizek :* They usually go here and there. One should see that they are really thrown, but in your drawing they are still. —Here is much snow. One gets cold. One freezes. I hope the children get warm clothes so that they won't freeze. Here in the air a blue snowball is flying. It came too near the sky and so it was painted blue. That too gives the impression of snow, but should be done better so that one sees how the snow is thrown about.—This here does not look well because one half is blue and the other white. It looks like a flag. You can't see clearly what's going on in the blue, and in the white two specks are flying. I said : big figures ! Therefore away with these midgets.—This drawing was started quite well, but it is not carried out properly. You can't see what they are doing. If it is carried out well, you will probably see that they are skating.—Here something is flying about. That is the storm which raged amongst the angels. (The children laugh.) And here the blue sky is pouring down. I asked the child what it was, and she replied : Fircones are hanging down from the sky. The child probably meant icicles. *Child :* Yes ! *Cizek :* But it looks as if the blue colour begins to run down. The colour was frozen and now it thaws. Who did this ? *Child :* Evelyn. *Cizek :* Now Evelyn will do it so clearly that one sees at once what it is. (To another child) How is this ? Is it good ? *Child :* No. *Cizek :* Why not ?   *Child :* It needs finishing.   *Cizek :* Quite so !   Now let us be patient and wait !—Something good seems to be coming out here.   The man has got a nice green striped ski-ing costume.—Here everything is higgledy-piggledy. The man on the top is pushing his tummy out.   *Child :* He is sledging down on his tummy.   *Cizek :* He is sledging down, but he does not move.— This man is probably slipping.   It is very alive, but it can be even more beautiful, when it is finished.—I don't know what this means.   The thing is nicely drawn, and it is almost a pity it is painted.   Yes, the child drew very nicely, but the colour is rather clumsy.   The colour does not follow the neat line.—This is done by C. and very nicely.   But she cannot yet follow the line with her brush.   That's too bad.—Here everything is higgledy-piggledy.   It thunders and lightens.   A streak of lightning kills a ski-er.   He will soon be dead.—What is this here ?   *Child :* The moon. *Cizek :* Many things are happening here.   This is one of the pictures where everything happens.   There is nothing missing, except a waterfall.   *Child :* That will come too.   *Cizek :* So ?   But here the drawing is not sufficiently good to carry the colour.   This is a story-telling picture.   It starts with an idea.   The real artist has few ideas and much shaping power ; the writer has more ideas and less shaping power.—This here is story-telling in pictures. You must be satisfied next time with fewer subjects and with more working. The artist must not deal with too many things, but use a few as well as possible.   Not dozens of ideas impossible to execute.   It is impossible to do so many things at one time.—There is not enough here.—Here there is more.   It shows a nice distribution of dark and light.   The snowflakes, too, are nicely spread.   If it was carried out as well as it was planned, it would be very good.

18*th January*, 1936

Cizek (holds a block up) :   Look here !   We are going to draw to-day with a pen.   We shall do something easy.   When you are used to drawing with the pen, we shall do something more difficult.   Make a square first with your pencil.   Do you know what a square is ?   A square is something not round.   *Child :* It has four corners.   *Cizek :* Now you are going to draw some of those squares with your pencil.   Only with your pencil, not with ink.   You can draw five or six squares, very small ones, medium ones, and big ones.   And between them there will be room for more squares. But don't make them too small, or slanting, but straight ones.   Afterwards when I tell you, we shall outline them.   The squares should not touch each other, but one should be beside the other.   (Later) Show me !   (To a child) You have far too many.   Make fewer.   (To another child) You too have too

many.   (To another child) You should draw a small square.   Five squares
are enough.   Those who can't count up to five may make fewer squares.
   Now we will begin.   Inside the smallest squares you will draw a room.
What is in such a room ?   *Child :* A bed, a chest, a window.   *Cizek :*
What else ?   *Child :* A rug, a wash-stand.   *Cizek :* Now put the furniture
inside that room.   Draw with your pen what there is inside.   For instance,
a table with chairs, or a table with a chair and chest.   But only draw a
few things.   And do them nicely and straight off with the pen.   Make it
as nice as a doll's room.   Those who haven't a doll's room may make it
like a real room.   *Child :* I have put a little man in my room.   *Cizek*
(to all children) : Each room you draw should be outlined.   *Child :* I have
put a sweet little man inside.   *Cizek :* You should only outline the square
where there is furniture.   (Later) You should not shade with your pen, but
only draw the outline.   Don't make the outline thick with ink, but only
draw a line.   Or else the room will be a black hole.   (Later) Now you will
have black Indian ink, which is much more beautiful than blue ink.   Who
has finished his room ?   (Most children put up their hands.)   Now we shall
make the second room.   In the middle of this room there is a table, and on
each side of it there is a chair.   A boy sits on one chair, a girl on the other.
There is a dish on the table and there is soup in the dish.   The boy and girl
eat soup from the dishes in front of them.   On the wall above the table
there is a beautifully painted picture in a golden frame.   We are going to
do that now.
   (*Cizek* walks around and says to a child :)   Finish it carefully.   (To
another child) Think what you should put here.   (To another child) Haven't
you left too much room here ?   What are you going to do with it ?   Think
about it.   If I had a room as big as that, I would make the figures twice as
big.   Then the room would be nicely filled.   In the next square we will
put something we know about ourselves.   For instance, Santa Claus and
" Krampus."   In another square we can make the Christmas tree.   (To a
child) The playing-room is quite nice too.   But you must make these four
corners and lines.   *Child :* What shall I put into the next square ?   *Cizek :*
What is that ?   *Child :* That's a princess.   *Cizek :* Listen !   For the rest of
the rooms you must invent something yourselves, for instance nice furniture.
You could put in what you like.   *Child :* I shall make a Red Indian.
Cizek : You shouldn't make Red Indians or dwarfs, because a Red Indian
doesn't go indoors and dwarfs are best in cellars.   *Child :* I shall make an
underground.   *Cizek :* In a modern room a Red Indian does not look at
home.   Another time we shall make Red Indians.   *Child :* The next time ?
Child : I have finished my Santa Claus.   *Cizek :* You could put Mother

Day into another square.   Mother with a little child.   Or mother surrounded by many children.   Or many children rushing in through a long corridor. Now be quick.   Who has finished ?   (Most children put up their hands.) Those who are ready, come to me.

24th January, 1936

Which of you has seen a horse ?   (Most of them.)   Who hasn't seen a horse ?   (Four very small children put up their hands.)   *Cizek* (to one of them) :   You haven't seen a horse.   (Only a few now raise their hands.) Who can describe a horse ?   *Child :*   It has a long tail, then four legs, then a head.   *Children :*   It has ears.   *Cizek :*   Who else can describe a horse ? *An English child :*   It is black.   I have never seen a horse in England. *Cizek :*   Who else can describe a horse ?   *Child :*   What does that mean, describe a horse ?   *Cizek :*   It means how does a horse look ?   *Child :*   It has a bushy tail.   White horses have white tails.   Then it has a body and four legs, horseshoes like a cow, and a long head, not a round one.   *Cizek :* What has it got on its head ?   *Child :*   Hair.   And at the neck too. And ears.   *Cizek :*   What else is on its head ?   *Child :*   Eyes, mouth, nostrils, and teeth.   *Cizek :*   The horse has a long, roller-like body, and on its body four legs.   Behind the legs is the bushy tail.   Before the body comes the long neck.   The neck is thick.   On the neck the head is placed, which is—as Elizabeth has just said—long and not round.   Remember that :   not round, but long.   On the head there are ears and in front two nostrils.   Then two mouths.   *Elizabeth :*   One mouth.   *Cizek :*   I was wrong.   You must always correct me.   *Child :*   Big nostrils.   *Cizek :* Then it has a mouth for eating.   What does the horse eat ?   *Child :*   Oats. *Another child :*   Grass, sugar.   *Cizek :*   Now we know more or less how a horse looks.   What is there on the horse's feet ?   *Child :*   Hooves and horseshoes. *Cizek :*   We are going to dip the pens into the ink and we shall draw a horse. You can draw the horse in such a way that it either goes out of the window or leaves by the door.   *Child :*   My horse is jumping out of the window. *Cizek :*   How shall we draw the horses ?   *Child :*   Big.   *Another child :* From top to bottom.   *Cizek :*   Why ?   *Child :*   So as not to waste paper. *Cizek :*   If we draw the horses like flies, we learn nothing.   *Child :*   I shall draw a horse jumping.   *Cizek :*   We shall draw a line in the middle.   (Shows it, a horizontal line.)   It need not be quite straight.   It is supposed to be the floor where the horse stands.   Then the horse will reach from the floor to the ceiling.   At first we will make a standing horse.   Above this middle line you will draw horses only.   Here there come the big and the young horses.   But perhaps a second young one also.   Below the middle line we shall draw something quite different. You must save the space below. *Child:* Shall I saddle the horses? *Cizek* (to a child who has copied): Those who copy show that they know nothing. Now let us see who is ready. Who hasn't finished? (two put up their hands). Be quick! We shall wait another two minutes.

In the lower space we are going to do this. A horse. And this horse is pulling a cart. The horse will fill half the space and the cart the other half. Everybody has seen a cart. *Children:* Yes! *Cizek:* Now, I am going to tell you something. First close your eyes. Don't look at me. Think what a cart looks like. I shall think too. A cart has four wheels, not two, nor three. Who can count up to four? *Child:* Me. One, two, three, four. *Another child:* I can count up to eight. *Another child:* I can count up to a hundred. *Cizek:* You need only count up to four. Now you will put four wheels on the cart. *Child:* Should the horse draw the cart? *Cizek:* Of course. *Child:* Should there be a driver on the cart? *Cizek:* The driver can go before the horse or sit on the cart. I leave that to you. And the driver draws the horse with the bridle. In order that it does not slip. Those who have finished can show their picture on the board. You must finish it carefully. Everybody will show his picture to me first, and I shall say if it is finished. (A child comes to Cizek.) *Cizek* (to the child): The picture is not yet finished. You must make the driver. Or a young horse which is fastened to the cart and runs behind. *Cizek* (to another child): The driver may go behind and push the cart to make it go quicker. You must think about it very quickly. (To another child) Perhaps there is a dog running in front of the horse? Why did you do it so small? There is so much space here. Just think about it!

(To another child) Invent something beautiful. (To another child) You should add something else. Perhaps a driver. Or his wife. Invent something very beautiful. (To another child) Why didn't you do it on the line? Always draw the line first! (Cizek rings the bell.) Listen! All write your names on the drawings. Those who have finished, show me their work.

Cizek (at the discussion): I have told you already that many of you can't hear. Now we shall see who has really listened to me. And you should judge for yourselves who has listened the best.

The first work (by Elizabeth): Has she listened well? *Children:* Yes, yes. *Cizek:* She has made a horse above, she has drawn it rightly, and she has given it hair. A good work. *Child:* My right hand aches very much. *Cizek:* The horses look very nice. That shows we are getting on. We shouldn't be satisfied just with lines, but we should go further than that.   It is always good to do better and better instead of being satisfied with a few strokes.   Now has " Schorschi " done what was asked ?   *Child :* I don't think so.   *Child :* I have made a horse which is getting the whip from the driver.   *Cizek :* He has done a good big horse.   A long body, a long stretched head with a big mouth.   With that it can eat very much at one go.—Here we see a strange thing.   *Child :* That's a young horse. The other horse has taken the whip from the driver.   *Cizek :* Is that supposed to be a toy horse and driver ?   It is rightly thought out.—Now let us have a look at the drawings below.   They are good too.

This cart is very strange.   This cart shows the fourth or fifth stage of growing, whereas the horse represents stage one, and the wheels are just copied.   All the horses are good, although they represent the second stage. At the right stage the legs are at equal distance.   Brenda has done it very nicely.—Who likes this ? (Many put up their hands.)   Who doesn't like it ? (Child puts up his hand.)   *Cizek :* Why don't you like it ?   *Child :* Because it is decorated.   *Cizek :* You don't like it ?   It is not decorated at all.   It is nicely drawn.—Cornelia has reached a much higher stage.— Now we come to a work of T.   He has drawn the horse quite nicely.   But he has an imagination far too lively and he wants to do twenty things besides the one which is asked for.   Because of his imagination he is not able to separate one thing from the other.   Too much imagination leads to a muddle.   The work is very much alive, but it shows a stage far above his age and capacity.   He said that the other work is too decorated, but his is even more decorated.   He has not even put the legs on the body. They are barely glued on and they fall off the body.   The horse is going at such a gallop that all the legs are flying away.   It goes so quickly that it does not go at all.   The body is running away by itself.   T. should stick to one thing and do that well.   He should learn how to draw orderly, neatly, and simply.   This will be his task.

We have made these pen drawings so that we can learn to draw with confidence.   Those who draw with a pen, first must think before they draw, and later draw when they have thought things out carefully.   Not draw first and think afterwards.   That's what some do.   With pen drawing one must think very carefully.   Each stroke must be thought out.   By doing this we get used to clearness and firmness in the shaping.   That's the reason why we do it.   Willi's case is a similar one.   His mind is ahead of his hands. But he has not enough imagination. Willi must imagine certain things more fully.   He will close his eyes and will think about a certain thing and its forms.   What are forms ?   *Child :* One can imagine certain things at night.   *Cizek :* Yes, and then one isn't disturbed.

F. already tries to keep close to nature. He does not build things up, but joins forms which he can't master yet. You all try, and rightly, to build up. Some aim at joining forms, but your knowledge of forms is not yet sufficient, naturally. I should make an object as I imagine it. Not let the imagination stay at home so that the hands don't know what to do.

1st February, 1936

Again we are going to do something which will please you. Whether I am pleased or not I shall know at four o'clock. To-day you will get all the colours we have at once. Then you will get a brush and then you can paint whatever you like. (*Children :* Oh, good !) Listen ! You should make something which really pleases you. And it shouldn't be a thing you have seen in a book, for instance a fairy-tale book. And you shouldn't do what you have seen in picture-books, but you should do what you see when you close your eyes. Close your eyes. And what you see now with closed eyes . . . *Child :* I have seen beautiful things at night. *Cizek :* I see the most beautiful things at night. One sees the most interesting things at night. And you will make those things now. Begin now ! I should like to tell you only one more thing : If you have a big block like this (shows one), don't draw only below, and not only midgets, and don't leave empty space. I don't like that. That's a waste of paper. You should use all your paper. Do you understand me ? *Children :* Yes. *Cizek :* Are you quite sure ? I am afraid I shall see again and again half of the paper empty, and only a little bit used.—You should not draw first this time, but paint straight off with the brush. But first think about what you are going to do. *Child :* I shall make a tree with a horse. *Child :* I shall make a Red Indian. *Child :* I shall make a man in fairy-land. *Cizek :* Everybody make what he likes best. I am going away now. You will make what you really like.

Cizek (much later, at the discussion) : Listen. To-day you had complete freedom. It is like an acre which rests and does not grow corn ; the weeds grow, sometimes with beautiful flowers amongst them. But it is chiefly weeds. If you do this . . . *Child :* Is this a beautiful flower ? *Cizek :* Now let me talk. It is your turn when I have finished. If you do what you are told to do, it is like being in a garden. There flowers grow as they should grow. But in the other case the flowers grow wild, as in the meadow or as weeds in the field. But weeds too can be very nice, and to-day we are going to see the weeds. Beautiful flowers are dotted about between the weeds because the wind has carried flower seeds.

F. at the beginning worked very well, because the things he painted are in good contrast with his background. But later he painted the background, and now all is lost in the colours. It is like someone falling into some dye and being drowned. In order to make a thing clear we must make it different from the background. We make it stand out from the background. That's what F. always should remember. He should not let the figures be drowned in the colours, but separate them from the background.

Marion's work is beautiful. Why? Because one sees the figure and the tree clearly against the background. The background is done so well that it does not interfere with the figure and the trees. The sky is beautiful. Below the sky there is yellow air, and below the yellow air the trees and forms show up clearly. We don't know what they are, but that does not matter. It only must be beautiful. The writer always asks : What is it? The painter asks : How is it? Is it beautiful? The figure stands out well from the background.

There is something new in the next picture : The background is clearly done. Only the hair does not stand out well from the background. It is too fair and is drowned in the background.—I like Gertrud's work. Everything is clear and beautiful and stands out well from the background. And the figure is beautiful and not ordinary as ordinary people would do it, but it is something special, different. The clouds hang in the sky. The sun rises. The flowers are clear and distinct. How is it? Beautiful! I must praise Gertrud. I wish she would do at home things as beautiful as that.—Cornelia as usual has very beautiful colours. But one can't tell what things she wants to do. *Cornelia :* It is a house. *Cizek :* It is not clear enough, because the colour drowns the shape, but it is nicely formed. One feels that she enjoys the making of colours. Face and hands are very nicely and gently done.

Trude has excelled this time. She has not blurred the background with colours, but she left it so that the figures show up clearly. She has learned that here and she does it well. Trude hasn't done such a good work as to-day for a long time. Peperl is good too. He has made a door. Probably a forbidden entrance. Everything is very clear.

Marion has beautiful colours. If one looks at it one need not know what it is. Wonderful!—Grete is bold in her drawing. When she paints she is not as good by a long way as when she draws. She is not used to colours.

T., of course, has worked with great imagination. One sees here how his colours are drowned by his imagination. *Child :* Is my imagination drowned? *Cizek :* The mood of the colours is all right, but they are not alive. T. has so much temperament that one should rather expect his colours to be glowing, loud, assertive, but he shows very subdued colours. But his colours are nice. And his work is always full of ideas. He has so much imagination that he could easily make five pictures out of one.

The colours of Elizabeth's work are also beautiful. The S. children always have beautiful colours. They shape things well and the forms are made nicely.—Willi is uncertain of his forms. We don't see the separate figures clearly enough. His ideas are ahead of his age and yet they are not clear. He is satisfied with a shapeless splash.—Brenda's is very good. Again she has done some beautiful painting, just like her Madonna the last time. Her drawings are marked by a certain regular strength.

As a whole, the weeds were very eatable. And I should also like to mention to-day that Peter has done some very good work at home. The forms and the interesting things he does go far beyond the usual and show that he has made progress. Peter should make more things like that, and so should Trude.

15th February, 1936

Cizek : Let us have a few words together. We have finished the first term to-day. You have got your reports from school. But there is no mark from the Juvenile Art Class.—Those who haven't worked hard and those who haven't brought drawings with them will bring drawings full of forms and figures. *Child :* I have never brought anything with me. *Another child :* It is almost the same with me too. *Cizek :* He seems to be proud of it. Now let us see. Perhaps you have kept those things in your head and you will let them come out to-day. *Child :* I always want to go skating. *Cizek :* I have told you before that former pupils always brought work from home because there is not enough time here. This short time is not enough to show people the right way. So you must make up for it by work on your own. I don't make anybody do it, but—and now listen—those who are full of art have no rest ; they are like a volcano. But nothing happens to you. In days gone by children travelling with their mothers on the tramcars said : " Give me the ticket, please, and the pencil." And then they made beautiful drawings on the tickets. That only took four or five minutes. Now you haven't got even that much time. Take those five minutes from skating !

But here we have hardworking children also. Some often bring works from home, but others just look at them and think : " I would rather do nothing." And so I tell you : We begin the second term having made up our minds to bring at least one little sketch, even if it only takes a minute. On Sunday perhaps you will have two minutes to spare, and you should use these two minutes to notice something, and to draw with a few strokes what especially pleases you. *Child :* On a Sunday one can draw all the morning and all afternoon. *Cizek :* If you have so much time you can draw longer, but I think that those who have only a little time could find at least one or two minutes for this work, two minutes for thinking and remembering. *Child :* I always feel like drawing. *Cizek :* You should write down on a piece of paper : No day without drawing ! Then a lot of ideas will come to you. And certainly you will have so many ideas that you will not have time enough. And you will give me a happy surprise every time. When I came to Vienna fifty years ago—who can count up to fifty ? (almost all show their hands)—it was a custom in Vienna to have beautiful carnivals. Do you know what a carnival is ? *Children :* Yes ! No ! *Cizek :* It's better if you don't. You will then draw it the better. For these processions there were cars pulled by horses. Two horses were put to the cars. They were decorated with ribbons, hundreds of ribbons. And the horses were very proud because of them. And the cars were decorated with silk paper. The whips were decorated with rushes. Then there came a car with a baker who was as thick as a barrel. He held in his hands a " Kipferl " and a " Bretzel." [1] The latter was so big that I could hardly hold it with my hands. The people in the streets shouted for joy. So beautiful were the cars. Now you are going to make such beautiful cars. First two horses, then a car. The car will be wonderfully decorated. The wheels also will be decorated. Now begin. To-day we shall draw, and the next time the most beautiful colours will be ready for you.

(*Cizek* shows for a minute the works of twelve- to fourteen-year-old pupils who had done this subject before. Then the works are put away.) *Cizek :* When you have drawn the horses and the car, then you should begin to decorate them. You must put the horses together out of separate parts, not make them at once, or they will turn out bad. The larger you draw the more you can put in. (After a quarter of an hour) Many things are still missing, ribbons, rushes, flowers, confetti.

22nd February, 1936

I have been looking forward very much all the week to our painting. The colours will be distributed now. What is not finished in the drawing will be put in with the brush. First we shall paint what you want yellow. You can paint whatever you like yellow. If you get another colour and you don't like the yellow, you can paint over it. On Monday the children from Meidling come and they sing a song : " Who comes from the hill ? " or

---

[1] Special rolls.

" There rattles a mill." The whole class sings it quietly. Nobody chatters and all work the song into their drawing. . . . At the discussion of the work : *Cizek :* Now we shall see what you have done. There is an enormous wealth of material. Some have done so much that there is a real muddle. T. has done so much that one can't understand it. The colours are very nice— embroidery could almost be made out of them. But T. lacks one thing. Who knows what it is ? *Child :* It is all scrappy. *Cizek :* So it is. No form is completed or rounded. The horse is made up of a hundred pieces, as if it had swallowed a bullet and this had exploded inside. From the point of view of painting it is quite nice. He has a gift for colours, but he would be better if he could make things more of a piece. For instance, the head should not be in a thousand parts, but in a finished line. That's what he should learn and he should surprise me with it. Then I should be happy.—Now, Peperl is our old friend. *Child :* Aren't I a good friend of yours ? *Cizek :* You are also my friend, but my young friend. Now, our old friend's father had a horse. *Child :* And Peperl still has a hedgehog. *Cizek :* Yes, the hedgehog is always there. Peperl, because he has been here longest, can paint everything and express everything he imagines. And as well as this he has many ideas which are often bad.

This work is done by Trude. She copies Peperl's horse because she knows that Peperl knows horses well. Her colours are nice. These colours, even when one does not know what they mean, are very beautiful. But when she decorates the cap she should leave the outline clear or else the cap is broken up into many bits.—Elizabeth has so much imagination that she could make ten pictures out of one. This is an animal. *Elizabeth :* That's the roof of the car. *Cizek :* Excuse me, I did not recognise it. But it does not matter. The whole picture is very nice.—Susi is a new pupil. She has to struggle with the form. So far she has only muddled patches from which no shape comes. But these patches are very interesting. The way the whole is arranged makes a good impression. If it had shaping as well, it would be perfect.—F. is in a stage where he leaves the abstract for the concrete. He makes one mistake. He tries to do things that only a grown-up can make. He tries to make them with his small powers instead of staying at his own stage. He begins already upon anatomy— which is beyond him, of course. He wants to say with his inadequate means what only grown-ups can say. He must beware of that. The other pupils do what is within their power. One should not try to paint as a grown-up does.

The work of Gertrud is as beautiful as always. She too possesses great powers, but they do not lead to confusion.—Bruna also makes certain things she does not understand yet. One should only do what one understands, and in a way one knows. This spot here is beautiful. The colours occur in patches. It is almost "counterpoint" work, I should say. She makes shift by taking a brush and daubing the paint without any thought. She should, as Gertrud, want to form with every stroke.

Martha has worked with eggs and spinach. That's very good to eat, but not so nice to look at. You should not make men to look like flowers nor as men in picture-books. You should not look at picture-books, at models, at copies. There (points to his forehead) you should look! The best things, the real things are there. But you look at things which are not meant for you. They are often done by artists who care nothing for children, who have no time for them at all. No picture-books! *Child :* Can't you have picture-books without copying from them ? *Cizek :* Trude works very hard without sweets.[1] But her paintings are not sugary, and that's the nice thing. And her work has nothing to do with a picture-book. You are all of an age when you are the happiest human beings, when you have the most splendid forms, something the grown-ups can never have.

Marion has made the figure all of a piece. Although she is so small she aims at real creation. Everything is complete, and her ideas are great, not sugary. She is strong and yet not without imagination. It does not matter that one doesn't recognise the horses here. (To Evelyn) The drawing here was quite nice, but the colours have ruined the whole thing. Those with a strong drawing sense have the colour against them.—Until S. had that muddle, everything was all right. Now it is all broken up. All the charm is lost. She will probably ask : How should I have done it ? My answer is : Keep the big forms.

As a whole the works are very alive. I see clearly where some pupils tried to make forms and did them clearly, and others, where the imagination was not enough, became tired. Some of you have done good drawings to-day, and I am glad about it. Many of you are getting on. But some waste the time of youth. Things you do not do when you are young are never done again for the rest of your life. Time is short. Use that time well !

29th *February*, 1936

Cizek : The last time Brenda was not here. So she does not know what happened. We made a very nice carnival. *Child :* Lately I saw a carnival. It was very gay. *Cizek :* We shall talk about it later. *Child :* I went to the Punch and Judy show the day before yesterday. *Cizek :* Now, the

[1] She was a very poor child and Cizek often gave her sweets.

last time we used the expression picture-book, I warned you not to look at so many picture-books. Why? *Child:* Because one copies from them. But I don't copy from picture-books. Can I look at picture-books? *Cizek:* We won't look at picture-books at all. They are for the older ones, for the twelve- to fourteen-years-old. There are no picture-books for you except the ones you make yourselves. Look inside yourselves—there are the most beautiful picture-books. Those don't hurt you, but help you, and it is those kind of picture-books we are going to make to-day. We shall begin at once with one story, afterwards with several stories. We shall bind them and make a picture-book. You will look at it and show it to others. And you will keep it until one day when you are fathers and mothers you can show it to your children. The picture-books you buy are made by painters who know nothing of children, but you will make proper picture-books to look at and to keep. Now let us begin. One always begins with A. Which words begin with A? *Child:* Apple. Ape. *Cizek:* We shall draw an apple. What can one draw with an apple? Do you know? *Child:* An apple tree with a little man climbing it and throwing down the apples. One falls on his head. *Cizek:* All right! We shall first draw an apple tree, and then boys come and climb the tree. Girls are standing below, holding out their aprons. And the boys throw the apples in them. But listen! We shall first draw this apple tree with apples on it—beautiful apples, and then the boy who has climbed the tree. And he throws the apples down. Two or three children are standing below who catch the apples. That is what we are going to do to-day. And until the next time you will think how the story goes on. Every child will think about it. Now let us begin with the apple tree. We shall start in the middle or left or rather towards the right. And so big that the tree reaches the top line and grows out of the ground. We shall make a big tree so that we can draw the leaves very plainly and clearly. And everything in the right order, the apples too. We shall first draw, and then outline with pen and Indian ink, and then afterwards paint with beautiful colours. Out of the trunk grow branches and out of the branches twigs. (Later) Martha has made a dog also. Where there are children there are always dogs. *Martha:* That's a hare. *Cizek:* Hares are like dogs.

(During the discussion) On the whole you worked quite well. We have started a fairy-tale. It should go on. We shall make it up ourselves, everyone on his own. *Child:* I have made up something already. *Other children:* Me too! *Cizek:* The next time you will all tell me what you are doing on your second sheet of paper, so that each one has a different and more beautiful picture-book than the other.

Now we shall have a look at the work.—I am surprised that Trude did so little. The tree is beautiful, but the rest is too hasty. She will think at home how she will go on.—Now comes a very lively gentleman. His task was to do a fairy-tale about an apple tree. First he made a house. He always likes to let his thoughts wander, and his imagination is so alive that when he talks about an apple tree he thinks about five houses. He will try not to do this, but to make . . . *Child :* I know already what I shall make the next time. *Cizek :* We shall see that the next time. You can make some sketches. All of you can make some sketches for the second picture. Make something up ! For instance, an apple may fall on the earth, and then a gnome grows out of it or a man ; or you go on with the story yourselves. I leave it to you.—T. did the boy climbing the tree very nicely. And here he seems to see a nest . . . *Child :* Only when the apple falls on his head. *Cizek :* What does he have on his head ? *Child :* He has concussion of the brain and reels around. *Cizek :* So T. paints a concussion of the brain. I would rather that he had drawn the apples and the leaves better. But they seem to be ruined as after a hailstorm. If the wind blows, everything will fall down. As I said before, everything should be in simple, well-thought-out lines. Then they will be nice.

Marion started with a muddle and drew everything higgledy-piggledy, but later she found herself and began to draw the tree nicely. The figures too are beautiful. Everything is in keeping with her age. She does not get ahead of her age, but is satisfied with working within her stage.—Evelyn begins by coming out of the muddle and she has made lovely rhythms in the heads and the other lines. The flowers are copied. Evelyn also will think out something beautiful.—G. has done the tree specially nicely. But the house looks as if it will tumble down. Gertrud has made one of the best pictures, entirely her own. Graphically very interesting. And within her present stage. One of the nicest works.—Trude has a very good hand. But she does not progress. She must do her best not to let the things she does become mechanical, but the more she does the richer and fuller they should become. The way in which this boy is climbing the tree is absolutely original and therefore powerful, whereas things copied are schematic.—Her brother Peperl has also made something nice. Personal rhythm, and actually eternal forms. The boy who is climbing the tree shows new ideas.—P. has come out of the scheme in which he began. The home of the hedgehog is very nice too. Peperl has a very beautiful hedgehog and a dog Luxi. They are his comrades and they cannot be left out of any picture. Here he has made a house three storeys high, in each storey there is a dog and hedgehog.—W. has made the tree nicely. The tree already shows the stage where forms are connected. And it shows certain experiences. There is a wealth of form which goes beyond her stage. W., too, will think how this big apple gets on in the fairy-tale.—Elizabeth has done a very nice tree, full of rhythms. She has finished with muddles and begins to find rhythms. *Child :* What are rhythms ? *Cizek :* Rhythms are lines which come when you draw nicely. *Child :* Do I have rhythms too ? *Cizek :* If you begin to draw well, rhythms come at once, and then I shall praise you in front of everybody.

Susi is not yet at the stage where types are formed. The tree is nice. The figures should be shaped more.—Brenda has made her apples especially big. Brenda comes from England, where big apples grow. *Brenda :* Beautiful big ones which I like to eat. *Cizek :* But our Brenda must have more patience, like the little girls who keep on at one thing. Elizabeth, for instance, has this patience, or Cornelia and Trude. *Child :* Me too ? *Cizek :* You don't have it yet. You must learn to draw in one line. Then you will have it too.—Willi did his best to draw the man in a way that is beyond him. It is very interesting, this struggling for a higher stage. If he would draw more simply, not shading, but in one line, he would draw much more clearly and precisely.—Martha has done the tree nicely. Different from Josef, she is absolutely within her stage : figure, tree, and all things are clearly within her stage of creation. That's to be praised. She draws well because she draws with one line. She does not muddle lines, but does everything clearly and distinctly.—S. made the tree very well, according to her age ; it is converging towards the top. It gets painted. From this point apples grow. That also is quite plain and the drawing is clear. The figures too are clear.—Cornelia draws in a very lively way. One sees how her imagination works. She has many ideas, more ideas than creation. But it is so interesting that one cannot easily part with it and that one can look at it and enjoy it for a long time. When Cornelia grows older she will be even more perfect.

Now, every child will think out how the fairy-tale goes on. I shall tell you nothing. You must think out yourselves, and if possible each one should bring a little piece of paper on which the next part of the story is sketched.

7th March, 1936

We had the task to think about the fairy-tale of the apple tree. I very much want to know what you have made out. *Child :* I have made up something very beautiful. I have made a little piece of a house and my sister also made a little piece, so that the children can reach the top.

Child : And a little bit of apple tree and all the children and . . . *Cizek :* And ? *Child :* The tree goes to the window where a little girl with a basket looks out, and below is a balcony with a door. *Cizek :* What has that to do with the apple tree ? What happens there ? *Child* (shows with her hands) : There is the house. *Cizek :* You must say what happens. Do the people shout or do they climb the tree ? *Child :* They go in the house. *Cizek :* What are they going into the house for ? *Child :* In the house they show their parents that the apples are ready. The apples on the tree are not yet ready. *Cizek :* That is quite nice. You can do it. (To another child) What would you like to make ? (Child keeps quiet.) Elizabeth has spoken so loudly that the whole class has heard. *Child :* In our school we have a child who speaks very low. She can't speak aloud. *Child :* The boys are in the apple tree and the farmer comes with a whip. *Child :* An apple tree round which the children are dancing. *Child :* An apple which was not picked up but left lying on the ground was carried by the wind to America. And in the apple were two mice. They have changed into men, like a Hokuspokus, because they were changed from men before. Then Red Indians came and burned them at the stake. *Cizek :* You can do what you have told us. But it must be clear. (To another child) What have you made up ? (*Child :* Because we could not skate we made skating shoes out of wooden bricks.) *Gertrud :* The apples I picked up were brought by Santa Claus. *Cizek :* Strange how much such an apple has experienced ! In one apple mice grew. *Child :* They were not mice but changelings. *Cizek :* We are going to draw the apples as they are picked up by boys and carried to the carts. Then the farmer loads the apples and the cart is drawn to the town ; there the apples are sold. The next time we shall make a drawing of the apples being sold. You could do it in this way : cart, driver, apples, and horses. The farmer's wife and children also go to the town. In the upper part of the drawing one can see the houses of the town. *Child :* Next time I shall draw a market where beautiful apples are sold. *Child :* I shall make a stake. *Cizek :* Use every inch of the paper, because paper is expensive ! We mustn't waste it. Use the whole space ! And make it beautiful ! Express yourselves well ! And draw strongly ! And later we shall paint. But the lines should still be seen after the painting is done. Make your drawing bold !

(Later) Now we are going to discuss the work. Last time we started our fairy-tale. At the beginning we drew a tree laden with apples. Then boys came along, climbed the tree and shook the branches so that the apples fell to the ground. Other children picked up the apples. The next task was to continue the fairy-tale and to make another picture. Why ? Because we want to make our own picture-books. Picture-books made by adults are not good enough for us. The picture-books made by grown-ups, by great artists, you don't understand and you shouldn't understand. You must grow slowly to understand this art, and you will acquire an understanding by your own drawings. Then you will understand it, but not before. Now you understand your own art best, the real child-art. If you go to the great masters in picture-galleries, you will pass the pictures and see nothing. When you return from the galleries you will say : There were many pictures.

(At the discussion.) *Cizek :* Trude formerly was very industrious. At the back of this room you can see pictures which she made when she was three and four years old. She worked very well then. Now her expression becomes weaker. *Child :* What does that mean ? *Cizek :* Where formerly there was a river, now there is only a trickle of water. But she still gives evidence that she could produce something. For instance, her horses are very well drawn. The horses are pulling a cart, and the apples on it are nicely arranged. Why ? Who knows ? I will tell you. If one puts the apples on top of each other, they become bruised and rot and are uneatable. If they are nicely arranged, each apple remains nice and healthy. Now, Trude knows that. Then she has arranged nicely the houses of the town. The houses are big enough for the hedgehog to live in. Trude never forgets the hedgehog. And she does not forget her dog Luxi. He appears in each picture, as also does the hedgehog. The dog is sitting on the horse. Once Trude had a real horse. Luxi prevents people from entering the flat. Trude drew it quite nicely. And she filled the space very well. She knows that paper is expensive. The more she works the more she learns. And what I especially like with Trude is that she keeps to the story she is doing and does not tell a lot of other stories. She hasn't a large imagination, but the little that does occur to her she forms and shapes rightly. This is the task of an artist. To the writer much should occur, to the painter very little, but the little which he wants to represent he should represent well.

To-day I must especially praise Peperl, Trude's brother. Everywhere he has shown Luxi, the hedgehog, and the horse which he once possessed. Luxi always plays with the hedgehog and scratches it. But Luxi knows very well how to avoid being pricked by the hedgehog. When the hedgehog thinks that Luxi is going to scratch him, he lowers his quills. If a man wants to tickle him, he raises his quills and pricks him. The drawing is well done, especially the cart laden with apples. Peperl has done very well. He is improving. His work gets better and better.—F.'s work is well done too. His tree is nice. And he drew a special kind of apple. His idea is of a very modern farmer. He even possesses a lorry. On it are boxes of apples. The lorry is driven to the town. I must praise F.

Trude F. has made no progress. Formerly she worked so well. The reason is she doesn't work so hard. She used to draw at home a great deal. She has less time now, and therefore she does not progress. Still, her farmer is nice, and the different types of apples are also nice.—Martha tries to be naturalistic. She draws things as they are, not as she should do them. But the legs of her horses are all right. Her horses are very fragile. Her buildings are well done. I give praise if I see that children are trying to work nicely. Her peasant woman is well done, because all her clothes and ribbons are clearly shown. Everything should be well formed.—S. makes very little progress. The reason is that she is often absent and does very little at home. It seems to me that she does not like the work any more. Her arrangement is right and her childlike conception is correct, but she lacks the ability to form things well. For instance, her horse's hooves are not complete. She passes them every day in the streets, but she does not notice them. You must always think how things are formed.

T. has twenty thousand ideas. He has thought hard about his stake and done his best. He worked at his drawing of the stake with great pleasure. It is executed very exactly. With the other objects he is satisfied with quick sketches and vague impressions. He suffers from too much imagination. It is so alive that it doesn't leave him time to accomplish a single object. He must learn not only to invent but to complete the drawing.— Marion, of course, is only a little girl. She has no clear idea of things. Everything is only half-formed. She must grow older to imagine things clearer. She is now only dreaming things. And she is satisfied with very futile impressions.

Brenda suffers from superficiality. She makes a few strokes and the drawing is finished. All the details are in her fertile mind but not in her picture. She made the apples large so as to occupy as much space as possible, leaving little room for anything else. That's very clever. But I must say that to-day she drew the horse and the driver neatly and in the right proportion. *Child :* But the driver cannot hold an apple in his hand ! *Cizek :* Perhaps he will ask giants to load the apples for him. Your task is to make a fairy-tale.—Elizabeth has done something very nice. She begins to work her way out of the chaotic. Everything begins to be clearly formed. The house here is nicely proportioned and constructed, and the figure near the house is neatly done. She should go on in this way.— Gertrud drew a horse and cart. Horses and figures are well done. Her apples are already an apple pudding. Her houses are not flats or castles or any particular type of house, but just abstract houses.   G. has the advantage of a clear hand and the ability to draw firmly and correctly.—Cornelia is burdened with too much imagination.   She has so much imagination that her forms are not in accordance with her ideas.   I recommend her to make fewer forms.   She could fill the whole space with three figures.   And they should be worked out thoroughly.—Evelyn is still in the stage of extension and direction.   With her everything is only extended and directed. Her tree is beautifully done.   She should imagine the objects more clearly and think about them more.   What is a leaf ?   Think carefully about it ! How does it really look ?   Have a clear idea of an apple and a tree.

On the whole the drawings were well done.   I recommend that children imagine things more clearly.   They should practise it.   They should, for instance, try to form in their minds the picture of an apple and think about it intently.   And they should make things as they think they are, and not as they actually are.   And the objects they think about, they should draw well.

14th March, 1936

Cizek : We only meet on Saturdays.   That's not enough.   In the intervening time most children forget what they ought to do.   To-day we shall continue the story of the apple tree.   I am sure you have thought about it, as I asked you to do last time.   *Child :* I know.   *Another child :* I too know something.   *Child :* I too.   (All the children put their hands up.) *Cizek :* Each of you should say what you want to do.   *Child :* I should like to draw a part of the house and of the door, so that the children can just touch it, and then I should like to draw a small part of the apple tree.   A little girl walks to the window from which another child is looking out. *Cizek :* We shall not draw small parts, but the whole object.   We shall not draw only the tail of the dog.   We shall not draw only a window of the house or only a small part of the roof, but the whole house, the whole dog, or the whole tree.   We don't want to illustrate, but to form.   *Child :* Apples are sold at the market.   *Cizek :* When the peasant has arrived at the market with his apples, what will he do there ?   *Child :* He will sell them to the shops.   *Child :* The woman who was standing in front of the house has gone.   *Child :* I too want to draw the market.   *Child :* I want to draw the funeral of the two men who were burnt at the stake.   *Cizek :* If I ask you to draw the continuation of the story, you always want to do something different.   You must think about what the people are going to do when they have brought the apples to the town.   What became of the apples ?   *Child :* One man sold them.   *Cizek :* We will now draw the peasant with his cart and the people standing around him. The horse is harnessed to the cart. If the peasant is well-to-do, he has two horses. Now the peasant stands there and cries : '' Apples are sold here, two pounds a penny.'' Then people gather round him with their baskets, and they all want to buy apples. *Child :* But actually the apples are dearer than that. *Cizek :* You are right, but we are drawing a fairy-tale, and in fairy-tales one gets a kingdom for a penny. You will now draw the peasant offering his apples for sale. And the men and women coming with their children and filling their baskets and taking the apples away. The children are hurrying because they are happy at the thought of having apples at home. (Cizek shows them a block.) You can draw the peasant here and around him the parents and their children buying apples. There are men and women, boys and girls, and governesses too. *Child :* What is a governess ? *Cizek :* Brenda has a governess. *Child :* In my drawing the animals come and buy the apples. *Cizek :* I like apples ; who else likes them ? (All the children put up their hands.) I should like to add a word. Those who have drawn the cart and the horse and apples in the lower part will have no space there for people ; they will draw them in the upper part where there is room. We put things where there is room for them. The purpose of paper is not to remain empty.—A drawing must not be very big, but it must be drawn with joy. *Child :* I enjoy drawing very much. *Child :* I am so glad because my drawing is always wonderful. *Cizek :* Who has finished ? (Several children put up their hands.) We all shall have finished in five minutes.

(At the discussion) Now we shall see how the work has been continued. We said, it should be the story of an apple tree and all that happens to it. The tree blooms, bears apples ; the apples are picked by children and grown-ups. The peasant takes them to the town and sells them there. We see how the apples are sold. Gertrud always draws nicely. But to-day she was so unfortunate as to draw the apples as large as blankets. One does not recognise them as apples. One should paint the apples yellow and red so that everybody can see that they are huge apples. The poor horse has a miserable face because it has never had to carry such large apples to town before. Then we see a crowd of people who are gathered around the cart. Everyone would like to buy some apples. A woman even brought a little cart with her but it is not sufficiently large. Gertrud draws firmly ; she does not draw hesitantly so that one can hardly see the lines. I like her style.—Peperl has made beautiful drawings to-day. He has made good progress. To-day he drew a pair of scales, and beautifully. At one side are the weights and on the other side are the apples. He labels the apples " good " or " bad." That is a mental accomplishment. Drawing is only good if it is done thoroughly and if it is well thought out.— Trude has not experienced as much as Peperl has, but she excels him in the strength of representation. She draws her figures with immense vigour, and never rubs out.

The new pupil has drawn a cart which is being driven to town. Instead of apples it is laden with wood. He was not aware of the fairy-tale that we were drawing. He drew what he wanted. His drawing is very alive, but next time he should draw larger, so that the figures can be filled better.— Willi has made quite a good drawing, better than his previous one. His apple tree is laden with apples. His horse works very hard because its strength is not equal to the huge load.—Cornelia is dominated by an over- whelming imagination. Three pictures could be made from her one.— F. has made good progress too. If he could draw his objects at the side of each other instead of behind, it would be much clearer.—Susi is still very primitive.—Brenda, because of what she had been told, did more than usual. Usually she is only interested in one or one and a half things. She is so much accustomed to working on a large scale that she can accom- plish very much with very little. That is art too. But it can't be done without some work.—Our J. will learn gradually to execute more.

T. has a very vivid imagination. He had drawn the whole picture very nicely. A man and a woman are walking. *Child :* No, two men ! *Cizek :* All right, two men are pushing a cart. *Child :* This is not a cart, but a box ! *Cizek :* All right, a box. They are pushing the box and a Zeppelin is flying over them. The Zeppelin wants probably to drop ballast. The ballast is sand. *Child :* No ; the Zeppelin throws out apples. *Cizek :* Sorry, I did not know that. Now, the apple-Zeppelin is quite a new thing. But nobody catches the apples. *Child :* The far-away townspeople catch them. They are in their houses and so one cannot see them. The people had seen the apples falling, but it took time to dress and run down. *Cizek :* Here comes a big cart. The apples are well packed. The driver has a trumpet. He blows : Enter, please !

W. has done the cart very well. The horse is relaxing. Meanwhile the farmer shouts : Buy apples ! and one woman has started buying them. She is carrying them home in her little cart. Being a good housewife, she has carefully packed the apples in her cart. Everything else in this picture is done richly. The representation of the sale is very vivid. It's a good attempt, but next time W. will try to do even better.

Martha started quite well, but she has made too few figures. She is not as vivid as W., but she executes her work better.—Elizabeth has made a cart too. One sees people but no apples. *Child :* The saleswoman has an apple. *Cizek :* She seems to be tired and therefore went to the Park. There she sees Punch and Judy.—Now we come to our friend Schorschi. He has not enough penetration ; he remains at the surface.—S. has worked hard to-day and has accomplished more than usual. Only she should learn to form her figures better.—Trude's older drawings were better. She does not care so much now. It's not that she couldn't draw better, but apparently she is not in the mood. She should draw with more love.—Marion has drawn her apple-cart quite well. We see the buyers coming. It is like a frieze. Next time Marion will draw more details. If one draws as little as Marion, one must do it very well.

(To the parents who are present :) We need the contact with parents. In all schools there are parents' associations. If parents are not interested in the work of their children, it's rather sad. I should welcome contact with the parents, so that the work here and at home has the same quality. It is bad if children are taught differently at home. That may prove dangerous. In our art education the interference of parents is often very detrimental to the development of the children. The reason for the lack of good older pupils is mostly due to the interference of the parents, who often don't know what we demand. If there could be co-operation between the parents and school the development of the children would be unified. Unity in work is always the strongest. Therefore I should welcome a greater interest taken in the children by the parents. Then they would know how to guide their children.

21st March, 1936

Cizek : To-day we shall finish our apple story. Who knows how we could finish the story ? (All children shout : Me ! Me ! Me !) Now, the farmer has gone to the town and has started to sell the apples. What comes next ? *Child :* I shall draw the house where the farmer lives, and people coming to eat the apples. *Child :* In my drawing the farmer drives home. *Child :* The parents who have bought the apples are sitting at home. *Child :* I too should like to draw that. *Child :* I should like to draw the mother making an apple pie, and a child standing at her side with her finger in her mouth. *Cizek :* I expected the apple pie. *Child :* The apples are baked and then eaten. *Child :* The farmer drives home and shows the money which he has earned. *Child :* Santa Claus saves the apples for Christmas and distributes them then. *Child :* Santa Claus is given a few apples, then he buys for $1\frac{1}{2}$d. a thousand pounds which he stores in the warehouse. When Christmas approaches, he distributes the

apples among the children. *Cizek :* You have had plenty of good ideas.
Trude's apples are brought to the man who bakes apples.   Trude wants to
draw Santa Claus giving the apples to the children.   The " Krampus "
helps him.   T. of course has told us a long story.   He will have the paper
full of ideas.   But he should pick out one idea and deal with it separately.
Not too many ideas should occur in one drawing.   Now, everyone will
draw his own idea and in such a way that the drawing completes the story.
And not as if it was just a continuation.   Now start !

(At the discussion) We have finished the story to-day.   It was the
fourth picture in the apple series.   We drew the story of an apple.   Every
child has invented something.   The idea was to make a kind of picture-
book thought out and drawn by yourselves.   I know you don't like bought
picture-books.   For my part I think that each child should make his own.
Why don't we have picture-books made by children ?   It's the parents'
fault.   Booksellers tell the parents : Children like these picture-books ;
they cry for them.   And the parents think that they must buy something
expensive made by an artist.   The artists, unfortunately, don't know what
children want. *Child :* Oh, yes ! My grandfather knows a great deal
about drawing.   He says that children can't draw, but only grown-ups.
Cizek : The best picture-books are those which the child makes for himself.
If Father Christmas brings you picture-books, you should return them to
him and say : " Dear Father Christmas, here is your picture-book.   Give
it to a painter or to a parent."   *Child :* I shan't do that.   I shall keep my
picture-books.   They are much too nice. *Cizek :* You can sit on them if
the chair is too low.   We only want picture-books which we have made
ourselves.   One learns a lot from those self-made picture-books.   One's
best ideas become materialised.   And this is the most valuable gain.   If
you look at the grown-up picture-books your ideas don't become real, but
you are led into blind alleys.   You are led to things beyond your conception.
You admire things which you can't understand.

Now we shall look at what we have done to-day.   One child has made
an apple revolution.   There is almost a riot because so many people want
to have apples.   Everybody is stretching out his hands.   It is a good end
to our fairy-tale.   One realises how children and grown-ups like apples.

Brenda gave of her best to-day.   She has drawn a table at which two
children are eating apples.   If you invent and paint a story yourself, it
must become beautiful.—Pepi's previous work was even better than this
one.   Perhaps there were too many visitors here to-day.   Pepi's work is
always full of experience. *Child :* And Pepi always takes his hedgehog
and Luxi. *Cizek :* And I like it.   They are his friends.   He lives with

them. I am sure that Luxi will get a piece of the apple pie. Where is the hedgehog ? *Child :* It is sitting on top of the chest of drawers. *Cizek :* Josef, our new pupil, has done good work. There is a stair which leads to heaven. *Child :* To the attic. *Cizek :* The people around the table are nicely grouped. *Child :* They take the raisins out of the apple pie. *Cizek :* The raisins are always the best.—Now I think our school year is too far advanced for Josef. He should wait until October when the new school year begins. Then he should come again.—Willi makes progress now because he is forgetting his brother's drawings and the influence of grown-ups. He is relying now upon himself. And that is always the best. You should look into your heads and hearts and not into picture-books. Now, this picture here is made without any picture-book. There is no picture-book where Christmas Eve could be drawn so beautifully. Or perhaps it represents something different ? *Willi :* It's a chestnut-roaster. *Cizek :* T. finishes every story as a drama. Here he has drawn a burglary. Burglars were here who left their tools. *Child :* No ; mother herself has opened the box. *Cizek :* Now I understand. You see why I tell you that you yourselves should make picture-books. You alone can understand them. I myself cannot understand them fully, because I am already so far removed from them. But you understand them fully. T. has done very well. He kept to his subject, which was different from his usual practice.— Martha too has done well. She has drawn a mother who is peeling an apple. And there is a heap of apples in front of her. One would like to have one of them. And who comes here ? A girl ? *Child :* Yes, she is fetching an apple. *Cizek :* She waits until her mother is looking away, and then she will take one.—Gertrud has made one of her carpet pictures. Everything is nicely arranged and side by side. And again, she made a beautiful Santa Claus and " Krampus."—Susi did quite well. She has done a beautiful apple tree and next to it a woman, and the woman has a doll, and she probably wants the doll to eat an apple. That's a very good idea.— F. has drawn well, but not distinctly enough. I told him repeatedly he should press harder and he should work more energetically. It will do him good because it will stop him from scribbling.—In this respect Pepi worked well. Everything is drawn clearly without any scribbling. This shows the strength of his hand. Boldness is the most admirable trait in child art.—Elizabeth has such a vivid imagination that she evades the subject. But she has done a few nice figures full of life. She is improving in her figure drawing.—Trude has a firm hand. What she draws she draws with great skill and firmness. But she should wash her hands more frequently, because otherwise her drawings get smudged.—S. too has worked well.

She used the entire space. But she should try to make the faces clearer, and she should not be satisfied with two lines. She should think about how an eye looks, or the mouth, or the nose.—Cornelia has much movement in her drawing. Her imagination is very disordered. *Child :* What is disordered ? *Cizek :* Sometimes the surface of water is disordered. The arrangement is good.—W. has drawn a nice table laid with a rich meal which she likes. She has furnished the room neatly. I should like all her drawings to be as clearly done.—I liked the work of Marion from the beginning. It is one of the most abstract drawings. The vertical and horizontal distribution of the plane, made alive by the rhythm of her hand, makes this work valuable.—With this our subject is finished. And now we are going to bind our picture-books. Everyone should have his own picture-book. Next time we shall have another subject. *Child :* And what kind of picture-book will that be ? *Cizek :* It won't be a picture-book ; it will be a work of great value.

28th March, 1936

   Cizek : We have finished the picture-book. Now we will paint it. *Child :* Good ! *Cizek :* But think of it : there are four pictures to paint. We shan't have finished until the end of the term. And another thing : Spring is coming. He came to see me. I told him : " Dear Spring, you have come too early. We haven't finished our picture-book." He replied : " It doesn't matter." Now we shall leave the picture-book as it is. Spring looked at the picture-books and was satisfied. Then he said : " Who says A must say B too." Now A stands for apples, and what does B stand for ? B stands for blossoms, for spring blossoms. We are going to draw spring flowers to-day. You know so many flowers. You know more flowers than are in existence. And such flowers we shall make to-day. We shall draw the flowers with charcoal. Each flower has a stem. On each side of the stem are leaves. On top is a bloom or two or three. Charcoal can easily be erased. So you can correct if something is not quite all right. You will draw the flowers beside each other. The paper isn't made to leave blank, but for you to use it. We shall use the space very nicely. You must learn to do that. *Child :* I shall make rocks where edelweiss grows. *Cizek :* We shan't be able to make many edelweiss. *Child :* Because they are so small. *Cizek :* No ; the edelweiss are not small. There is another reason. *Child :* Because they are not spring flowers. *Cizek:* They are spring flowers, but there is a practical reason why we shan't make edelweiss. Because they are white and don't show up on the paper. We shall paint flowers whose colours show up on the paper. It's all right if you keep to your own ideas, so that you can experience for yourself if you are right or wrong.—Now, you will be intelligent enough to paint flowers which show up clearly, and not flowers which one cannot see. There is chamois leather here with which you can erase drawings you don't want. Then we shall use a preparation for fixing, and then we shall paint. *Child :* What is a " preparation for fixing " ? *Cizek :* It is a fluid that fixes the drawing so that it won't move. Now, it should be a spring parade. Those who have a chair which is too low may stand whilst drawing. For painting we have red, yellow, and blue. With these colours you can paint the flowers. Which is the most beautiful colour ? *Children :* Red. *Cizek :* The picture should be finished in half an hour. In half an hour you can do a nice amount of work. And don't make all the flowers red ! Those who have finished must return their brushes. They will be collected, washed, and redistributed.—You can paint the stamens with your beautiful yellow. Do you know what stamens are ? (Nobody replies.) Now, in the middle of the flowers there are little yellow spots ; these are the stamens. You will learn in your botany lesson how they look.—We must learn to work in a good tempo, and we must work well. Who has finished with the blue ? Now hurry ! (Later) Now you get the green colour. Those who have made red or yellow stems may leave them. Only do your best to make the picture beautiful. We shall soon exhibit the pictures and then we shall see who has done the best spring picture.

(At the discussion) Now we have a wonderful spring parade. We worked really quickly to-day. You should always work like that, and if you are given a task, you should think about it quickly, execute it quickly, and work well. That is your task. Not wasting your time ! We have done a really good spring picture full of beautiful colours. Who likes it ? (All the children raise their hands and shout : Me.) *Child :* I like all the spring pictures, but I don't like mine. *Cizek :* Everyone who has finished a picture is dissatisfied. One dreams of a more beautiful work than the actual result. This was the case with all great masters. Now, if " Master " T. is dissatisfied with his picture, it doesn't matter.—Yet with regard to the first picture ; it is really beautiful. Tulips and hyacinths as they grow in spring. And in a good style. It is done by Schorschi. He hasn't experimented much. The arrangement is neat. And the whole picture is based on extension and direction, and nothing else. The colours have only a symbolic meaning. This work satisfies me.

Willi's picture is not so clear. He started by experimenting. He hasn't separated the flowers from each other, as Schorschi has, and therefore the picture becomes confused. The flowers become confused. One doesn't know where one begins and the other ends.   One should avoid that.   One should make each flower separately, as far as it is possible.   The stems and leaves are very good.—The idea of Peperl is grand.   His blossoms show great strength.   It is a latent strength.—Pepi doesn't get excited ; he sits there quietly.   And his strength expresses itself by the grandness, clarity, and purity of his colours.   The work is very good.—Martha started quite well.   But then she only filled the space without any particular meaning. She has only used the space for a decorative purpose.   Willi is so much clearer.   In Martha's picture there is already confusion.   But Martha could have avoided it if she only would have tried to keep things separated from each other.—F. came near to naturalism.   F. thinks that natural science is art.   But this is not true.   Art is that which we invent for ourselves. Natural science is what is in the natural science text-book.   We should not make the flowers as they are in the text-book, but as we think they are. This is art.   *Child :* My aunt has a very nice text-book.   *Cizek :* The things in nature are so beautiful that man cannot improve them.   And man shouldn't try to do it.   Man creates with modest means, with a brush and simple colours.   He couldn't make it as beautiful as God.   Therefore God said : You shall not copy My work, but sanctify it.   And you can only sanctify it not by copying it, but by making those things which I have left for you to make.   God hasn't created art, but nature.—F.'s picture is rather clear, but he leans too much on natural science.

Elizabeth doesn't suffer from imitation of nature.   She doesn't want to imitate nature, but her inner self is troubled.   Her inner self is so full of figures and forms that she is unable to bring them under her control.   She lacks an inner clarity which makes things simple and grand.   But I must appreciate the fact that she made progress.   Her first works were too full of imagination, so that they were very confused.   Here her imagination is more controlled and tends towards a real creative effect.   The flowers here are well shaped.—Trude too is clear and calm in her forms.   Only it is a pity that she has not finished her flowers.   Otherwise she would have added grandness of conception to her clarity.   Her flowers are too small.—Susi doesn't produce works of natural science.   But she lacks strong creative power.   Perhaps she is too young for that.   It will come by itself.— S. was born in the school for applied art, and she grew up there.   Her work shows that she is an applied artist.   She has made applied-art flowers. It is neither kneeling to nature, nor adoring nature, nor is it kneeling to art, but it is merely aiming at an effect without sufficient foundation.   But one must appreciate the fact that S. is happy with her colours.   Previously she didn't like colours, but now she begins to rejoice in colours.   That is always good, because it has a good influence upon the body.   I once talked with a doctor.   He introduced, at my suggestion, painting for sick children under his care.   I told him : If children painted beautifully, it would have a good effect upon their disposition.   The doctor told me afterwards : " My children blossomed under their beautiful work."   Music and colour have a healing influence upon the mind.

Brenda's forms are clear and simple.   They are not too near to naturalism, but self-created.   Brenda worked well.—Fritzi's aim was the same as Brenda's, only her work is not so clear.   Her leaves are confused.   If her work had been more simple, it would have been more beautiful.—Evelyn's work shows a tectonic conception.   Everything has direction.—Cornelia has concentrated on small details.   Previously her imagination was too wild.—Gertrud's position here is unique, because she has an absolute clarity of direction.   Everything with her is direction.   Only rarely does she use a splash of colour.—W.'s conception is very simple.   Simple and grand.   The tulip here has only extension and direction.   These things here are experiences of nature, but not copies.   That can be said of all her work.—Marion is still confused.   She has not yet become clear and able to detach things from the chaotic.   There is always chaos at the beginning.— T. has happily surprised me to-day.   He doesn't rely any more upon picture-books or text-books, but suddenly stands firmly with both feet on creative ground.   He produces flowers from his imagination.   And they are artistically executed, that means, they are not copied.   Everything here shows creativeness.—The medium too plays its creative part.   The materials helped him to be simple and creative.   It is a good example of the co-creative function of the medium.—The work to-day was very good.   And it was cheerful.   Next time we shall do something different.

4th April, 1936

Cizek : To-day is the last lesson before Easter.   There is not another before Easter. (*Child :* But after Easter.)   Yes, after Easter, on 18th April. —Before we begin to-day I should like to show you two embroideries by the S. children.   They are made entirely by the children themselves.   And they are to be admired. (*Child :* But she can't do it as beautifully as that.) You can try it once.   The brother of Sch., for instance, once made a beautiful embroidery.   Boys too can make embroideries.   Formerly only boys and men made embroideries.   Women started much later.   In these embroideries, expression and technique go together.   Usually with embroideries there is more technique than expression.   *Child :* What is technique ? *Cizek :* We can also say : There is absolute unity of creation.—This work here is done by Brenda. She has done a beautiful sweet-smelling flower. It goes well with the embroidery.

Now to-day we shall do what you really want to do. *Children :* Ah ! *Cizek :* You can start by drawing or painting. Or drawing and then painting. You can make what you please. *Children :* Hurrah ! *Cizek :* Writers who report about my school always say that I do nothing here other than look at children's work, and by my looking at it things are created which are admired afterwards by the whole world. We shall try to prove that that is so. Because usually it is not so, as you know. I must always talk to you. To-day I shall not do it, but behave as the writers like me to behave. I shall do nothing but be above you. Now begin with your brush or with your pencil. Those who want it may have a pen and can begin drawing with pen and ink. Who wants pen and ink ? (Nobody replies.) Now do as you like. (Later) Those who want to may begin drawing thinly with their brush. (Later) I can already see that many of you are leaving empty spaces. You shouldn't leave the paper empty. The paper is here to be used. Most of you are drawing something in the middle of the paper, and that is all. That shouldn't be so. Who has finished something ? Those who have a large amount of space left should not show it to me at all. I am no stationer. *Child :* Have I still many empty spaces ? *Cizek :* Look here !

(At the discussion.) We have not sufficient time to discuss everything in detail. If one looks at the pictures as a whole, they give a wild impression. One would think that there were Red Indians all over the place. Now here is our Trude. Look at what she has done ! It is as if she has put her fingers into the paints. Her picture lacks form. She only fills the paper with splashes. No, Trude, you can do much better. You have done beautiful pictures before. Don't be satisfied with splashing colours around ! This part here is quite good. There is a nice feeling for the filling of space. And this here shows the " horror vacui." This fear manifests itself here.— This work here is quite good. It shows a rhythmic forming of the space.— Here we see a confusion of different figures, with no arrangement, just any-how. I know that. If one tells you : Do what you like—wild things like these occur. It looks like Europe. The old nations were uniform in their art—the Egyptians, the Greeks, and the Italians before Raphael. Afterwards disorder began and the over-emphasis of the individual. (To T.) Look here, by making the spinach so tall, the rider is lost in its midst. {*T. :* The riders are behind the wall.) Some details are quite good, for instance the horse. That's beautiful. You should work on a larger scale. If you have a large piece of paper, you must draw in proportion, but not make small drawings on a large paper.   There is no sense in it.   (To a child) That's very good. (To another child) That's a happy work.

Now we have finished school for Easter.   Next time we shall meet on 18th April.   I wish you a very happy Easter.   During the first few days you won't work much, but on the third day a desire for work will come upon you, and on the fourth day you won't be able to resist working.   On the fifth day you will actually work.   You will make some beautiful things and you will show them to me afterwards, as the S. children and Gertrud always do.   Gertrud always does a great amount of home work.   Trude and her brother used to work at home too.   I don't ask for much, but I believe it is good to do a little in order to remember that one is an artist. And another thing : I warn you not to make things like F.   As a rule he works quite well, but then school comes in his mind, and he thinks he should work here as he works at his regular school.   But this isn't a school. We are just young people who want to work without school.   We have no marks here.   Art's aim is not to make something which others have done before.   That's bad.   We want to do what we have experienced ourselves. An experience is always valuable.   If Pepi, for instance, does his Luxi or hedgehog, that's an experience and one recognises at once the close relation between Pepi and his Luxi or hedgehog.   And that is something nice. Good is only what one has experienced oneself and with one's whole soul and body.   But it must not necessarily be something which you have seen. Gertrud looks within herself and finds there wonderful things which she must translate into reality afterwards.   She has the burning desire to realise what she has seen within herself.   And this is really valuable and not what one has copied from a picture-book.   Now I wish you an Easter egg full of intelligence so that you stop copying.   *Child :* May I copy nature ?   *Cizek :* When you close your eyes, many things will occur to you.

18th April, 1936

To-day we shall have visitors from London and America.   They want to see your work.   So you should produce something beautiful in design and colour.   The visitors then will say : " They have colours in Vienna as nowhere else on earth."   Now we shall start with one colour and one brush, and shall make Spring.   We shall make figures : father and mother and children.   We shall make as many figures as we can in the space, all crowded, not every quarter of an hour a little man.   They all want to come and see Spring.   They will all carry flowers, beautiful spring flowers or a bunch of flowers.   Those who want may make very many flowers.   Now, who wants

to start with blue ?   (Only a few children raise their hands.)   Who wants
to paint with brown ?   (Those who want to, get it.)   Who wants to paint
with yellow ?   *Child :* I want to paint with all the three colours.   *Child :*
Me too.   *Cizek :* Now listen, how large will the figures be ?   Who knows ?
Child : From the top to the bottom.   *Cizek :* Right !   The figures will
touch the top and bottom lines.   Children, of course, will be smaller.   First
you must think, how big is the head, how big is the whole figure, how big
are the legs and feet, and then you must work at once.   You will draw only
the outline, and don't make the face blue !   Look here.   (He shows them
a picture which is drawn with only a few strokes.)   You will draw now only
a few strokes, and with the brush.   (Shows them a picture of Gertrud's.)
Only strokes, no filling in !   A picture can be beautiful even if it is not fully
painted.   I am looking forward with pleasure to your pictures to-day.   We
shall have a nice exhibition, and the ladies from England and America will
be surprised.

25th April, 1936

   Cizek : What would you like to do ?   *Child :* I should like to do a
sunset.   *Child :* I should like to do a zebra talking to a horse.   *Cizek :*
Before you go to sleep at night you have many beautiful ideas, and in the
morning when you rise, many things occur to you.   Then you turn over in
bed and think : How shall I draw that ?—Now, this is the way to think,
and you must tell me afterwards.   And you should not be like pupils who
wait until the teacher asks them to do a certain thing.   You must think for
yourselves until something occurs to you.   *Child :* I should like to do a
woman buying flowers.   *Child :* And I a vase of flowers with a feather.
Child : I Schönbrunn and the Gloriette.   *Child :* I should like to draw the
Schönbrunn Zoo with all the animals.   *Cizek :* You haven't sufficient space
for that. We want to draw large.   *Child :* I should like to make Rübezahl.[1]
Cizek : That's again something out of a picture-book.   *Child :* I should
like to draw the Emperor of Abyssinia escaping from his country.   *Child :*
And I the rose, violet, and dandelion festival.   *Cizek :* T. will do his Negus,
and the others will make a spring festival.   Children are dancing in a
meadow, decorated with flowers, flowers in their hair and in their hands.
They are jumping over flowers.   Everything is full of flowers.   This was
Cornelia's idea.   And we shan't make little fleas, but large figures, so that
we can learn something whilst drawing.   The girls skip around and
throw flowers at each other.   Everywhere there are flowers.   Now
quickly !

[1] A fairy-tale figure.

9th May, 1936

Cizek : We are going to draw the Ethiopian lion. How shall we draw the lion ? *A ten-year-old boy :* A lion has a head, a body, and four legs. *Cizek :* A lion has a big head, a huge nose, a big mouth, and eyes like a cat's. Then he has a mane like an artist ; a smooth body with four legs and a long tail. At the end of the tail there is a tuft. Then the lion has huge claws. They are dear in Abyssinia. Little Marion has drawn many animals already, for instance, elephants, but her elephants have no trunks. (Cizek walks around. To a child) The Negus is beautiful. (To another child) Elephants are drawn easily. (To another child) The elephant is all right. (To another child) You should make the Negus so that he touches the bottom line and no space remains empty. (Later) We will begin painting now. You will get nice paints, and you may paint as much as you can. When we have finished with the paints, we shall work with gold and silver.

16th May, 1936

Cizek : We shall finish the Negus to-day. You know that he has left Abyssinia and lives in Paris now. When he has become acclimatised, he will go to London. He has bought a house there already. And there his throne has already been set up. And the throne is freshly gilded. Now we shall finish our work. Many of you have only made a few spots with the brush—yellow and red—but a picture is only beautiful if it is full of colour. Do you agree ? (*Children :* Yes !) T. will have finished his drawing first. He has begun a very nice Negus. It will perhaps be the nicest of all Neguses. He must, however, keep on and execute his drawing very neatly.

Now you must finish your pictures. Paint as much red and yellow as possible ! Those who do the best Negus may use gold. You will paint his crown with gold. (Later to a child) This is worthless. You haven't filled in the outline, but merely dotted with your brush. You must make it more compact. (To another child) Begin at once to paint the head, nose, and mouth. Afterwards we shall have a discussion. (Later) I have been looking forward the whole week to seeing the finished Negus. And luckily you have finished him to-day. Only T. hasn't finished him completely, because he has made a second Negus. It makes me weep when he starts a drawing so nicely and doesn't finish it in the same way. He started the most beautiful drawing of the Negus. I should have liked to have sent it to him on his way to London. Now it is already too late. *Child :* Shall I draw another Negus ? *Cizek :* Yes, you can start again. *Child :* And if it is more beautiful, will you send it to the Negus ? *Cizek :* But you must keep on until the very end with that clarity and beauty.   Your previous drawings always were confused ; true art is clear and beautiful.   The ancient Greeks were always clear and beautiful.

Martha, of course, used strong colours, and only later she used a weak green.   Fortunately, she used the green only in small quantities, and so it has a refreshing effect.   In big quantities it always has a weakening and dulling effect.   Therefore God made the meadows green so that the cows don't get frightened.   If grass were of a strong colour, cows wouldn't eat it. This picture looks like a Madonna picture, but rather weak in design.—Now the two S. children.   They sit very close to each other and one of them has copied.   But I must say that she has painted strongly ; she used a strong red and a strong brown.   The weak green occurs only in small quantities and has a reviving effect.   Then she used a strong blue, not a weak sky-blue, but the strong blue of madonnas.   Her colours are nice. The design is poorer.   Cornelia suffers from a surplus of ideas.   She has so many ideas that there is enough for the whole class.   And she wants to put them all into one picture.   Of course, she hasn't enough room for them. But her things look interesting and original—not dull as some other pictures. With her everything is alive.   I should like to say a word about the proportion of the head and body.   Thank God, the child does not know the proportions as grown-ups know them.   Of course, the proportions of grown-ups are bad, because grown-ups measure everything.   They don't feel, but they have a compass, and measure head, arms, and legs.   This is inartistic and to be rejected.   The child uses the real proportions, which correspond to his feeling.   These are the true proportions.   When a child loses these right proportions and goes over to the scientific proportions of grown-up artists, then art is finished.   Art remains only as long as the true proportions remain.—Gertrud painted a black head, and out of the body grow four legs.   She has the right to do four legs.   Why ?   Because she is an artist and not an anatomist.   An artist produces what he has the divine right to produce.   If she has started with one leg and added a second, she has the right to do a third or fourth, because it gives her artistic pleasure.   That's the essential thing.   Not natural science but art is the decisive thing.   For her the leg is a symbol and has nothing to do with the laws of nature.   And she continues this symbol rhythmically as long as she likes.   What is logical is also right.   And thank God, she still has this logic.   Her colour too is good.   She has the right relation between background and motif.   They are both absolutely artistically felt.   These are artistic and not scientific qualities.—One cannot say, this is art or not art, but one must know if a work has artistic qualities.   This is the decisive factor, not science, correctness, or similarity to nature. Works which are full of art can deny all science and nature. And this is the significance of all the work here. And they have even a greater significance. This genuineness can be transferred to all school subjects, nay, to the entire life. Only then will our life be moral when it is as a child's life.

Elizabeth has a tremendous heritage. Her mother was a pupil here, she is an artist herself, and her children are full of art too. The heritage is rich and is creative because it is encouraged. If it is not encouraged, it slumbers. Strong heritage can break through, but it can be misguided. Our teachers, unfortunately, are guided by teachers. Over there is a teachers' factory. There teachers are manufactured ; out of ordinary men teachers are made. And they are let loose among children, and according to inclination and talent, they encourage or destroy art. They who have no knowledge of the eternal laws of Child Art have no right to educate children. Only those who know what is hidden here and slumbering can have an idea of those qualities.—Bruna worked very quickly. She did not go deep enough. She only wanted to make a second picture. The first picture has all the qualities of Child Art. It is entirely creative. Everything she does is symbolic, even if now and again she has the inclination to change symbols into copies. Copies are inartistic. The symbol is artistic through and through. B.'s work is very interesting. From the point of view of art everything can be justified. What she meant she represented with strong symbolism ; what she did not mean she only used to support the clarity of the whole picture. If here there were not things that were not " meant," the " meant " would be dull.—Pepi also has made an interesting drawing. There everything is symbolical, nothing a copy. He doesn't want to copy nature yet. Everything is symbolical, in drawing as well as in colour. Trude and her brother help each other. Trude is one of the strongest personalities here. Everything she does she makes extremely strong. Everything with her is symbolical. Copying of nature only occurs if the art gets weaker. The weaker art becomes the more the disease of copying nature occurs, and replaces art. Copying nature is a sure sign of creative weakness. Weak men imitate nature, strong men create art.— Marion is a phenomenon. She has brought the " not meant " of the background and the " meant " of the figure to the same level. One is as valuable as the other. This equality of value destroys the strength of symbolism. Therefore the symbolism appears less clear. The whole picture is interesting as a splash of colour, but this is of secondary artistic importance. The main artistic element is weakened.—Marion's colour, too, is beautiful, and would be creditable to a modern impressionist.

because the modern impressionist pays less tribute to the laws of creation than to the laws of appearance.

George is a descendant of the ancient Egyptians. One sees it here quite clearly. Everything is like Egyptian letters and symbols. It is absolute art because there is absolute symbolism. There is not the slightest imitation, and also the background, the " not meant," only helps to underline the " meant."—Pepi always has good ideas. For instance, he depicts the Negus as a red Tyrolean peasant.—Susi's is the result of artistic decadence. Her work reminds me of Klimt's. The whole picture is very beautiful, as all Klimt's pictures are very beautiful. But it is the beauty of decadence. Why ? She does not want the strength of creation, but only the effect of colours. That is of secondary artistic importance. She is swimming in colours and rejoicing in their sweetness.—F. is the opposite. He aims at creation. But he has overdone this figure ; that means there is more work there than creation. He has weakened the symbolism because he has divided it into several sections, each of which is of equal value. There are no main and secondary motifs, but they are all of equal value.—In Jorda's drawing we see an Egyptian mummy. She is not primarily creative. It is not the strength of symbolism, but she is satisfied with adding colours. It is very beautiful but she doesn't aim at real creation. If she would preserve her heritage she would be where we want her to be.

In this second picture there are the same laws of creation. Vertical and horizontal lines are at the strongest angle ; then there is symbolism, and everything is reduced to the most simple and essential form.

Now we have erected a monument to the Negus. You see how a king or emperor incites imagination. How much occurs to one ! Perhaps you will do something similar at home one day ? But instead of a real emperor you will make one out of your imagination. But keep on until the end : Be careful that you represent and create what you have imagined. This is the essential thing. And I must say it and say it again : Do not copy nature ! You must be guarded from this as long as possible.

23rd May, 1936

Cizek : I should like to say a few words about the nice pictures you made at home. (Negus.) The subject of our last lesson (the Negus on his throne) has been nicely executed. I should like to praise especially two girls who were quite thrilled with the Negus. Because their last pictures seemed to them too small, they have now made larger ones. *Child :* I like the rainbow very much. *Cizek :* That's no rainbow ; that's the sun. The picture has nice colours and is well filled. When the Negus goes to London now, we should send him these pictures.—As a reward for your nice pictures of the Negus we shall rejoice to-day by doing what we, individually, want to do. So every child will do the subject he personally chooses. And each will paint with the colours he likes, not with those that are put in front of him. *Child :* I should like to make a very big drawing. *Cizek :* You will have to work hard to finish a large paper.—Now, if you are given a large paper, you must make large figures, of course, not fleas. Why do we work on such a large scale ? *Child :* Because it doesn't take so much time. *F. :* In order to paint it more easily and to be able to see it better. *Cizek :* F. rightly said in order that it becomes clearer and to be able to use more colours in the large space. *Child :* So that not so much paper is wasted. *Cizek :* So that we learn more. The more we learn the larger we draw. Therefore draw large and clearly. And we shall use the paper well, and shall not leave empty spaces of even an inch. Now begin, so that we can be finished by four o'clock. Then English visitors will come. We shall have a talk with them about the Negus pictures. So now draw first, and later we shall paint.

6th June, 1936

Cizek : The few more lessons that we shall have this term we shall use well, I hope. And we shan't stay away. *Child :* I always draw during holidays. *Cizek :* I think you always want holidays. We don't need holidays. We like working.—To-day we want to make something especially beautiful. What is the season now ? *Child :* June. *Cizek :* Yes, June is the name of the month. But what season ? *Child :* 1936. *Cizek :* What season ? *Child :* May. *Cizek :* Let's turn to Elizabeth. *Elizabeth :* I don't know what comes after May. *Child :* June. *Trude :* The spring. *Cizek :* Now then, spring. Do you know the names of the seasons ? *Child :* Summer, autumn, winter, and spring. *Cizek :* First comes winter, then spring, then summer, then autumn, and then winter again. We have winter twice. The ancient Romans were very clever. They started the year with the first of March. So their winter was in one. Our winter is divided. There is a part of winter first, and a part of winter at the end, and between are spring, summer, and autumn. As a matter of fact, there is winter throughout the year, except for a few months. Now what grows in spring ? *Child :* Cherries. *Child :* Flowers. *Child :* Pineapples. *Cizek :* We are going to draw a cherry tree with cherries. Below we can make a garden in which are strawberries. And the rest is left to you. *Child :* May I draw the Negus beneath the cherry tree eating cherries ? *Cizek :* Why the Negus ? *Child :* Because the Negus likes eating cherries. *Cizek ·*

Yes, you can add the Negus.   It's quite good if each one draws his experiences beneath the cherry tree.   For instance, someone has a dog, and the dog's name is Luxi.   Luxi can eat cherries as well.   Another one has a hedgehog.   And if a cherry falls from the tree, it sticks on the hedgehog. Luxi sniffs the cherry and eats it.—Now begin the cherry tree !   Take the paper lengthways.   (Shows how.)   And draw to the top edge.   T., of course, will make a " flea tree."   And beneath it, instead of men, fleas will hop around.   That wouldn't look very nice.   Therefore I should like you to begin at the top edge.   The top of the tree must touch the sky.

(At the discussion) Some of you have done good cherry trees.   Next time we shall draw with the pen, and then we shall paint it.   Now it would not be sufficiently clear.—Marion has done her tree very well.   The branches spread in all directions, not only vertically and horizontally.   Jorum's is not so clear, and she shows much naturalism.

13th June, 1936

Cizek : To-day Elizabeth has shown me an exercise-book in which are beautiful drawings.   She has done flower festivals, a violet, a rose, a marguerite, a narcissus, and a tulip festival.   They were fine and not too big pictures, because smaller pictures can be more easily executed.   To-day we are going to draw such small pictures, straight away with the pen.   We shall, so to speak, write the pictures down at once.   The class will be divided into two groups.   Those at the back are the second group, and those in front are the first group.   The second group will draw, and later perhaps paint their pictures.   The first group will make the following picture : In the background there will be mountains and on their slopes little houses.   The sun will be in the sky, and it will shine warmly on those houses.   The sun will shine as beautifully as to-day.   At the foot of the mountains are little gardens.   They are neatly fenced, so that the flowers don't spread into other gardens.   In these gardens there too may be little houses and fountains.   There we shall draw men working.   And little dogs running about. Goats are bleating. Sheep are grazing. Hens are cackling.   You can draw all that.   And Peperl will draw his hedgehog. *Child :* But Peperl isn't here.   *Cizek :* But I must tell you something very important : you won't fill in with the pen, but make only thin lines.

27th June, 1936

Cizek : To-day is our last lesson.   We shall make to-day a picture of how we are leaving school, full of joy because we have learnt so much, and because it was so beautiful.   (Later) Now draw the school there.   (Shows it.) And here make the children leaving school in a hurry. And there is a reason why I advise you to take the block longways. The children come from the top and run towards the bottom. Now I have already a few very nice drawings.

(At the discussion) We had a cheerful task. Our children are happy because they do not have a report. I met to-day a former pupil. She used to bring me on Saturdays a pile of drawings. You have brought me almost no drawings to-day. Then a doctor visited me to-day. I told him that you were bringing me hardly any drawings. I am ashamed to have to say that in front of so many foreign visitors. But there are exceptions. Gertrud is a good child and she brings me drawings regularly. I am going to show you the nice pictures which she has brought me to-day. She has painted glass as they did in the fifteenth century.—The S. children, too, have brought me drawings. And even Willi once brought me a large number of pictures ! And there is a certain Anni here. She is living in the same house as Willi, and she brought me nothing.—Trude draws well if she is in a good mood. This is, of course, difficult in this great heat.— George has drawn a school. The school was very nice as long as it was full of pupils. Now when the pupils have left, it is nice no longer. The school is very sad at being deserted by its pupils. George has drawn the pupils. They are boisterous. Now, George, you will draw strongly during the holidays. *Child :* I have pressed with such strength that my pencil has broken. *Cizek :* You will learn to draw in such a way that it does not break.—Peperl, too, has made the children very nicely. The children are putting their hands up. That conveys joy.—Cornelia is going into the country, where she will recover from her nervousness due to the heat. In her drawing everything is confused as after the battle of Addis Ababa. Next time she will arrange it nicely.—*Cornelia :* I only drew a school with my pen.—*Cizek :* Gertrud has done a very nice drawing. Her school is quite modern.—In Bruna's drawing one can see how the children really enjoy the long holidays. One can see in their faces that they have long holidays. The movements are good.—T. has made an " international " school. What is that ? *T. :* It is a school where there are different nations. There is a Japanese, a Chinese, a Red Indian, and a Negro. Only one from each nation.—*Cizek :* Each nation is represented by one pupil. *T. :* There are only three, the others having run away because they had bad marks. *Cizek :* Fr. has made an old school. Only girls are leaving the school ; the boys are probably still inside.—Martha has drawn the children as they are. I should like to give Martha a little advice for the holidays, advice which may be helpful to the others as well. Martha should make the figures as she imagined them, and not try to do them as they are in nature.   Do you understand me ?   *Martha :* Yes.   *Cizek :* The vivacity of the children is well represented.—F. has made a very good drawing.   His children are not as boisterous as Martha's or Bruna's, but very serious.   He shows a certain amount of progress because he doesn't try to copy nature, which is beyond his capacity in any case.   Nobody can copy nature.   And nobody should copy nature, because that means an attempt at recreating which will fail.—In S.'s picture the children are leaving with their parents, which is a good idea.—Marion has tried to represent them leaving school in a hurry.   And so her figures became confused. But it doesn't matter.   When Marion is calm again, she will be able to draw her figures.

And now I wish you happy holidays.   During the first few days you shouldn't draw.   You should run about or bathe or lie in the meadow. You shouldn't study at all.   But gradually time will become dull.   *Child :* Not for me !   *Cizek :* No, not for you.   But perhaps for others.   And so you will take a piece of paper, and a pencil, and you will draw something. But by heart, not copy !   Not by lying down in the meadow and copying the grasses.   There is also no sense in copying the sky.   And if you have done many drawings, bring me some of them.   I should be very pleased to see them.

10th October, 1936

Cizek : I am glad that you have all returned.   This year we shall make beautiful things.   The new pupils will sit in the front benches.   And they will draw to-day what they wish to, but perhaps on a small scale.   The old pupils will draw on a large scale, and also do as they wish.   Only one thing I should like to say :   Don't make the figures small !   I should like to have figures as large as the paper.   Why should we draw on a large scale ? Who remembers ?   *Child :* Because otherwise one can't paint the figures. *Cizek :* So that we have a great amount of space to fill in with paints. And we must make everything very clearly—lips, nose, ears, etc.   Those who do something very beautiful will get an easel, so that they can make very big things.   You can draw, for instance, the first school day.   All the children hurrying to school.   Those who have other ideas may carry them out.   It would be nice, for instance, if you would do parents going to town in a cart.   The child is sitting on the coach-box. He goes to school and has a large block under his arm.   On the block he can make beautiful horses, the cart, the coachman, the parents, and the child.   Luxi may run behind.   Now start at once !   I am already curious.

(Later) I am going to tell you a nice story.   But you must continue with your work.   We have a pupil whose name is Trude.   She has brought me marvellous work.   She has drawn so many pictures during the holidays that she had to bring them on a 'bus.   She has brought numerous drawings, and each one more beautiful and more carefully executed than the previous one.   Gertrud comes here because she wants to come with all her heart.   Gertrud could be a model for you.   In former years children came here on Saturdays with a large pile of drawings.   It took me two hours to look at them.   But that is no longer the fashion, unfortunately. They have to do too many things in school now.   So the children get tired. And they no longer want to draw at home.   In school, if nothing occurs to them, the teacher tells them : " You must do this or that."   If one really wishes so, something always occurs.   If one doesn't, nothing occurs.   Some have so many ideas that they haven't sufficient paper.   The ideas must come out of the head.   Those who don't like drawing and for whom drawing becomes dull will themselves become dull.   Therefore take Gertrud as a model !   She does glass painting.   She paints on glass and puts paper behind it.

(Later) Now we will turn the paper and draw longways.   That only applies to the new pupils.   They will draw a gentleman or a lady with a dog longways.   The elegant lady has a dog whose name is " Schipserl."   *Child :* Our dog is called " Schipserl," too.   *Cizek :* One must be able to see that the dog really belongs to the man or woman.   Now go on !   You have plenty of time.   The old pupils can draw this too.   But those who don't want to do this may continue their former drawing.   And don't forget to put on your names !

All the new pupils have been admitted.   Next time they will bring the fee of 18s. for the first half-year.[1]

17th October, 1936

Cizek : Now you are divided into two groups.   First, second, and third bench belong to the first group.   From the fourth to the seventh bench is the second group.   The second group will draw with pen and ink.   You don't need to draw with the pencil first, but you will write down, so to speak, everything with your pen.   I should like to see how you can " write." You can " write " little men, animals, fish, butterflies, birds, trees, whatever you like. *Child :* Shall I draw or write letters ? *Cizek :* You didn't listen. I said : You can " write " men, animals, etc., and not letters.   Here we don't learn how to write letters, but neither do we learn how to draw, as so

_____

[1] The poorer children paid no fee.

C.A.—11

many people think. Here we create, that means that we express that which is within ourselves. You will create and not draw. Drawing is something different.—The second group will do other work. They will continue painting what they started last time. Those who have begun something beautiful will get a larger size to-day and can paint it with fine colours. (To a child) If one wants to paint, one must make big figures, so that the colours have sufficient space. You must think practically.

(Later) If you make a figure, you must do it in this way : The neck extra, the body extra, the legs extra, the arms extra, not the whole thing in one line ! We must draw each part separately. Do you understand ? (*Some children :* Yes.) *Cizek* (to a child) : One mustn't draw two things one on top of the other, because it destroys their clarity. With large figures one must draw clearly and distinctly. So that one learns a lot. (To another child) Here one mustn't do zigzag trees as they do in schools. There are no zigzag trees. Trees consist of a trunk, branches, and twigs. Pine trees have needles. Zigzag trees grow in schools. But they are severely forbidden here. Here we must think : What does a tree look like ? A trunk, then we draw branches, then twigs, then leaves or needles. That is the way a tree is built up. I haven't seen a single zigzag tree in a wood. We do trees which we have experienced ourselves, under which we have walked, where squirrels frisk about. (To the second group) Those who draw on a small scale will not be allowed to paint. The next time only those who have drawn on a large scale will paint. Small things cannot be painted. The brush goes over the line. You must realise that.

24th October, 1936

Cizek : Now you are going to draw a figure. (Shows a block.) So large that the head touches the top edge and the feet the bottom. (To a child) Did you understand me ? *Child :* Yes. *Cizek :* And of course you mustn't make flea-figures. So make a man or a woman with a large head. And the feet must stand here. That is what we are going to draw now. The figure must be large enough to fill half of the paper. (Shows it.) Therefore make large, nice heads ; later we shall paint them beautifully. The paints are already prepared. Of course, we shall not make natural men, but drawn men. A real man walks about, eats, coughs, etc. A drawn man does not eat or cough. Those who make very small heads will not be allowed to paint. (Later) Now comes the most beautiful part of to-day's work : We shall paint flowers and blossoms on the other half of the paper. Leaves will hang down, and the flowers will glow with the most beautiful colours. How large will the blossoms be ? *Child :* As large as a hand. *Cizek :* It can be as large as a fist. But I will explain it more clearly. The blossoms should be sufficiently large to enable us to use many colours. Begin ! Those who have drawn the figure in the middle may draw a flower on either side. And how large should it be ? *Child :* As large as the whole paper. *Cizek :* Or from top to bottom. Bees and humblebees are flying towards the flowers. You can paint the honey as well. (To a child) The stems should start in the earth and not be suspended in the air. (To another child) You must outline the body, otherwise one will be unable to see it clearly. Most of you have drawn the figures too weakly. You must outline them. Because if there are colours on weak lines, one cannot see them. Therefore do outline the figure ! (To another child) That's beautiful ! Now you can put something in the middle of the blossom. *Child :* In the middle I shall put a bee eating. *Cizek :* And another one flying near which wants a nibble. What do bees drink ? *Child :* Honey. *Cizek :* Nectar !—And then you will outline more strongly the face.

Now you are given the paints, and you can paint with red what appears to you to be red. And don't make only a few dots of red. Red is the most beautiful colour on earth.

7th November, 1936

(To the second group) I should like you to do bigger work. We shall take our easels, and paint there, so that we may learn to work on a larger scale. Choose your own subject. You will get sketching paper. If the sketch is good, you will make it larger. But fleas are forbidden. And nothing from picture-books, nothing copied ; you must invent things for yourselves. What is nicely done will be painted. (To the smaller group) Now imagine there is a pond there in which there are fish swimming. What does a fish look like ? *Child :* It is long. *Cizek :* And at one end of this long body is a head. At the other end is a tail. Above and below there are fins. The fins are the feet of the fish. The pond is full of fish. At the edge a boy with a fishing-rod is standing. A fish bites the bait. Those who can count up to ten may make ten fish. Those who can count only up to three may do only three fish. *Child :* I can count up to more than ten. *Child :* I can count up to twelve. *Cizek :* You can make twelve fish, then. I am very anxious to see the fish. Start quickly and surprise me ! (Later, showing a block) This block is the pond. In this pond fish are swimming. If somebody throws in crumbs all the fish will swim towards them, because all fishes would like to have them. That is how you should draw it. (To the older ones) Those who make small figures won't get an easel. (To the

younger ones) What does a fish's eyes look like ? *Child :* Like an O.
Cizek : Who has noticed that fish have scales ? (Nobody.) Who has
noticed that the scales are neatly arranged in rows ? You must learn to
understand that everything in nature follows eternal laws. Scales will
always grow in the same way as long as the world is in existence. (To an
older child) Put more in. It is too empty. (To another child) That's
nothing. You should do big figures. (To another child) Put much more
in ! (To another child) Don't do things which you remember, but things
you invent. (To another child) The figures are much too small. Nobody
should make small figures. (Later) *An American girl :* I can count up to
a thousand, but here are fewer fish, only sixteen. *Cizek :* You must draw
flowers around the pond. Nobody thought of that. Nice flowers always
grow where there is a pond. (Later) Next time the other group will work
at the easel.

14th November, 1936

Before we begin I should like to show you a picture. (He shows a picture
of Doubleday.) This is the battle of Crécy in 1346. That is a long time
ago. The English fought there. The blue ones are the English, and among
them is King Edward III, not VIII. The King is fighting the French.
Here is the famous windmill of Crécy.   I am showing you this picture because
it is done by a pupil of mine. Doubleday is a painter in London and has
an art school there. He has many pupils and they are trained there in the
same way that Doubleday was trained here. He painted this picture when
he was twelve. Now we are going to send him a picture. Therefore we are
drawing the fish to-day. Last time we drew them. To-day we shall cut
them out of coloured paper and paste them. You all know what beautiful
colours we have. You will imagine the most beautiful colours and will
paint some fish with them. A big fish, two small fish, and again a big fish.
If you do three fish to-day, that is enough. *Child :* May we do a fisherman
too ? *Cizek :* To-day only the fish. First you will cut out the body, then
comes the tail, then come the fins, and behind there are other fins. The
four fins are the four legs. If this is done, you may paste the scales. You
can make each scale in a different colour. Begin ! Don't draw anything
at all ! Who wants coloured paper ? Now come here ! (To the older ones)
You will paint the pictures which you started last time. But nobody will
paint who did small figures.

Now you cut out a piece and paste it on. The older ones will draw
with charcoal, not with pencil. (To the smaller ones) You have made
your fish too small. Haven't you ever seen herrings ? Have you seen a

gold-fish ? *All children :* Yes ! *Cizek :* You can make a gold-fish. (To the older ones) One boy drew two knights. He shouldn't have done it because he hasn't experienced it. He has simply copied things from a picture-book. That's forbidden here. You must draw only from your inner experience, and not copy from picture-books.

21st November, 1936

Cizek (to the smaller ones) : Now you continue with your fish. In most drawings there are no fish. There are a few, but they are swimming round singly. We must put in the missing ones. (To the older group) Only those who have drawn their pictures very carefully will paint them. Those who draw carelessly will not be permitted to paint. The clothes should have a pattern, the trousers should be striped, and the blouses embroidered.

30th November, 1936

Cizek (to the older group) : You will hold the block in this way (shows it)—longways, and you will draw two figures, from the top edge to the bottom. Don't begin in the middle and finish in the middle ! You are asked to create. You can make what you like. It may be Santa Claus and " Krampus," it may be father and mother or grandfather and grandmother. That is, you will draw two figures beside each other. Those who have done it best will be allowed to paint. (To the smaller ones) You drew fish. Now you are going to model some. You will get some nice material. With it you can make red, blue, green, or yellow fish. Each child can choose his own colour. You can make yellow fish, for instance. There are yellow fish. And you can give them red fins. Their eyes can be blue, and the scales perhaps green. Just as you like it. There are green fish—the trouts—then the blue carps, and gold-fish are red or yellow. There is no air behind the figures. I can feel that there is no air. It is paper, and I can draw on it what I like. You must think artistically, not naturalistically. We don't learn natural science here.

5th December, 1936

(All the children have got clay.) *Cizek :* To-day you have clay. This is a plastic material. So if you press with your thumb or nose, it yields. Those who don't believe it may try. *Child :* I have already tried it. *Cizek :* Clay has a quality for destroying bacteria. Therefore it is a healthy material. One of the reasons why we use it is that there is so much scarlet fever about now. We shall make little clay figures for joy.

Those little figures have heads, necks, bodies, arms, and legs. On the arms are hands. And what is on the hands ? *Child :* Fingers. *Child :* Five fingers. *Cizek :* Yes, several fingers. More than one finger. You can make a man or a woman. *Child :* May I make an animal ? *Cizek :* Now begin and make your little figure. It makes no difference what kind. It should not be a cobbler or a greengrocer or a clerk, it should just be a little man. One should not be able to see that it is a Mr. So-and-so. It should be just a nicely formed little man. *Child :* May I make a rider on a horse ? *Cizek :* You should make a little figure. Later we shall make animals.

12*th December*, 1936

Cizek : Now the older ones will get a task. I had a wonderful experience. It was on Santa Claus Day.[1] Two Santa Clauses and two " Krampuses " came to our house. One pair went up to the upper storeys, and the other pair to the ground- and first-floor. I was working when suddenly I heard frightful shouting. I opened the door, and I saw in the corridor " Krampus " beating some children. Now I should like you to draw " Krampus " thrashing children. The children resist him and pull his tail. " Krampus " turns round and tries to hit them with his broom, but a few boys have entered his basket and are pulling faces at him. The girls are shouting. That is what you should paint now, and straight away with colours, and without much drawing. " Krampus " may be as big as the whole paper. *Child :* Must we do Santa Claus as well ? *Cizek :* No, only " Krampus." He was as black as the devil, and he had a long tongue, green eyes. He had a golden basket, and a birch broom, which was bound together with a red ribbon. We shall have an exhibition of the finished pictures.

(To the smaller ones) You will have the block lengthwise. You will put it on the table and will begin to paint straight away what you like. You can make figures, but big ones, or trees, perhaps Christmas trees. Do whatever you like, but do it on a large scale. And start painting at once ! Wet the brush first ! (To the older ones) Your Krampus should beat the children and should move his hands and feet.

19*th December*, 1936

(They are modelling in clay.) *Cizek :* Don't bang on the table ! We shall model with clay, and not the figure as a whole, but in parts. First we shall make the body, then the neck, then the legs, and finally the arms,

[1] 6th December.

hands, and the rest.   Only when you are much older and have learnt much more will we make forms in one piece.   Pointed things like a pointing finger or a very long nose are apt to break when the clay dries.   Therefore one should not make them.   One should do nothing which projects too much.   One cannot make out of clay everything one wishes, but only that which the clay permits.   The clay dictates its treatment.   That's what you should learn.   (To other children) You can choose what colours you like for embroidery.   You can make black faces, or red faces, if somebody is excited.   *Child :* Red Indians are also called Redskins.   *Cizek :* There are people with blue faces when they are cold, or green faces if they are envious, and yellow faces.   *Child :* If someone has jaundice.   *Cizek :* Like Chinese.   There are faces of all colours.   (To a child) We are not going to stroke the clay, but press it with our thumb.   Then it will become nice. One feels the work of the hands.   But if you only stroke the clay, it will not become sufficiently clear.   And the different parts must be well connected.

Next time we shall meet on January 9th.   And now I wish you a Merry Christmas !

9th January, 1937

Cizek : I know that Father Christmas brought you nice things.   *Child :* Yes !   *Child :* I got a doll's kitchen with dishes.   *Cizek :* I know.   Now we are going to do a very interesting task.   We shall take the block long-ways.   (Shows it.)   And we shall draw an oblong.   I'll tell you a secret. The oblong represents a court.   Do you know what a court is ?   (*Child :* Yes.)   Who doesn't know what a court is ?   (Nobody.)   A court is the free space between different buildings.   We shall draw a house above. It may be a villa, a little castle, or a farmer's house with a big roof and chimneys.   Now we shall do the upper part of the house.   (Later) Listen ! You shouldn't make the roof project.   The roof shouldn't be larger than the main body of the house.   That's much nicer.—It doesn't matter if the ground-plan of the house is not exactly square.   Peasants often build like that.   A peasant builds just as it occurs to him.   And he is right. Those who are not gifted, take the ruler.   (Later) Now we'll go on.   Most of you have done the house quite nicely and have decorated it richly.   One can see that wealthy people are living in them, perhaps the Duke of Windsor. One of you has drawn an elephant in the house of the Duke of Windsor. If a Duke has an elephant, he will put it in the stables and not in his drawing-room.   Now we shall draw the stables at the right side of the house ; that's where the door is.   Horses and cows are there.   Are the animals already looking out of the stables ?   (Later) Now the house, villa, or castle is finished and so are the stables. At each window an animal is looking out, for instance, an ox, a cow, a donkey, a hen.   Now comes the barn.   What is a barn ? *Child :* That's a house of wood where wood and hay are stored. *Cizek :* Yes, it can be of wood.   In countries where there is a lot of clay it may be made of bricks.—Here is a house without any window.   It has only a big door.   Through this door the carts go in laden with straw, hay, or corn. In this house all these are stored for the winter.   Later the corn is ground, and out of the flour cakes are made.

16th January, 1937

Cizek : We have finished the court.   We have turned the block round. Whatever one draws, one can turn the block round how one likes.   The old masters used to turn their drawings round.   What shall we put in the court ?   Who knows ?   *Child :* Animals and men.   *Child :* A peasant woman.   *Child :* A cat and a dog.   *Cizek :* In the middle of the court there is usually a dung-heap.   Do you know what that is ?   *Child :* Where all the manure goes.   *Cizek :* On the dung-heap hens run about.   They are scratching for worms.   The hens strut on the dung-heap.   The chicks walk with them.   The cock crows for joy because the hens have found something to eat.   Beside the dung-heap there is usually a fountain where clear water comes out.   There are no water-pipes in the country.   Pigs are running about.   Somewhere there is a dog's kennel.   And beside the kennel there is Puffi.   *Child :* Or Burli.   *Cizek :* Everyone will do their own dog. The dog will keep watch to see that nobody steals the hens.   Of course, there are also men walking around.   Some go to the fountain, some carry dung from the stables to the dung-heap.   You can draw a lot of things in this court.   Begin at once !   (Later) The dung-heap is a mountain.   (Later Cizek shows the big drawing of a manure-heap that was done years ago.) This is a manure-heap with little hens running about.   On top is the cock. The farmer's wife is feeding him.   He opens his beak so wide that the food reaches his stomach.   The cock likes the food.   It keeps him quiet.   Here you see the small hens flying about.   They would like something to eat as well.   Here is the hens' roost.   There Mrs. Hen is sitting and hatching eggs.   That's all very nicely depicted.   This child had ideas.   She did not come to me and say : " I don't know what to do."   She did not ask. Her head was full of ideas.   Something always occurred to her.   And the same should happen to you.   (Walking round.)   This child has done a very nice manure-heap, fountain, and dog.   The dog is keeping watch to see that nothing happens.   Now there are empty corners.   Would you

not like to make trees and bushes in these corners ? Do fill the corners.
Those who have no ideas should make a peasant and his wife. (While
walking around, he says to most children) Put trees in the corners ! (Later)
Now be quick. We want to begin colouring. Who has finished the outline ?
(To the ten- to fourteen-year-old ones.) I am not very satisfied with
your drawings. You bring me too many things from outside for which
we have no use. That's all that terrible caretaker's naturalism. Those
who produce art are walking in sunshine, and not in the dark of vulgar
people. We don't want you to bring this vulgarity from your schools.
That's all right there. There they give marks and correct. There you
can make things like that. But here is a temple, and you should do that
which is the highest within yourselves. That is realised here in lines, forms,
and colours. So don't make things as they really are, but as *you* can make
them. That's art. Those who want reality should go to the technical
school. They can learn photography there. And there they will get
reality.

We do not make reality here, but truth. We represent the truth as
we believe it to be, and as we must represent it according to the eternal laws
of creation, and not according to the laws of caretakers and servants.
By the way, those maids often understood more about art than artists.
I mean bad artists, who mix nature with art, who believe that nature is
art. We want to avoid that. There are thousands of schools for that kind
of art. We don't need to be the thousand-and-first. Otherwise we should
be superfluous. But we are not superfluous. We do " Gestaltung." What
is Gestaltung ? Does anyone know ? Nobody. I believe that you don't
know it. Most of the drawings that I have seen are not " Gestaltungen "
(shaped, formed), but copies of nature. Copies of nature are never " Gestaltung." " Gestaltung " is what I imagine with my eyes closed. That's
Gestaltung. Those who go out and copy nature are not artists but copiers
of nature. Artists are those who shape nature, form nature, make this form
express and impress their will on this form. Those are the artists. In
such a way Rembrandt painted his landscapes. All the famous Dutch
painters have shaped nature in this way. They have placed nature under
their artistic will. Dürer hasn't copied his marvellous landscapes. He
created and formed. That's what you must learn. You must learn
" Gestalten." But don't make inferior copies of nature. Every " Gestaltung "—even the most simple one—is more valuable than the most faithful
copy, because " Gestaltung " comes from within, enriches, whereas copying
impoverishes. Copying makes rich nature poor. Every individual " Gestaltung " makes the world richer to its extent. And therefore we shall

have a class work every two or three weeks.   Then you will "gestalten."
And because it is now carnival time, full of balls and masquerades, we
shall make something connected with it.   We shall make two figures.
(Shows the block.)   You take the block and draw a man and a woman.
These two are quite satisfied with their mere existence.   You will draw
the figure in such a way that you make the head separately, and also the
neck, the body, the legs, the feet, the arms, etc.   You will build up the whole
figure out of different pieces, and not the whole figure in one piece.   I
don't want to see a figure in one line.—When you have finished the drawing
of the two figures, you will clothe them, but not with existing costumes, but
with those of your own invention ; no copies of rococo costumes or picture-
book drawings, that means things which you did not invent yourselves.
You will begin with a man's or a woman's figure.   You may draw at once
with charcoal.   The charcoal drawing will be sprayed with varnish—when
it is finished to the last detail—and then you will paint with tempera.   The
drawing should be finished in thirty minutes.   Often those who can't draw,
start with a group of forms.   That's forbidden.   Details must be put
together.   Then, don't make the heads too small, because there would be
no room for colours.   You must not forget that.   When you have finished,
we shall have a discussion, and we shall see who has done the best work.
(To a child) I did not tell you that you should make soldiers, but masks.

23rd January, 1937
    The subject is " trees."

30th January, 1937
    Cizek : Before we start drawing to-day I should like to say a few words.
Twenty-five years ago my first assistant, Miss Kolbe, felt ill.   She went to
the hospital and realised that she would never recover.   On her death-bed
she told me : " It was so beautiful in the Juvenile Art Class.   I should
like to have a successor who will be as enthusiastic as myself.   The only
one possible is Miss Staudek."   So Professor Staudek came to us twenty-five
years ago.   And to-day we celebrate the twenty-fifth anniversary of her
entrance.   And we shall welcome her as heartily as we did twenty-five
years ago.   We have enjoyed her activity for twenty-five years.   Her
work was outstanding in view of the difficulties here.   She is not a teacher
in the ordinary sense, but a co-worker in a difficult task.   Here we have
to explore an unknown territory and a territory which embraces all mankind.
So far, this territory has only been felt.   Most teachers know only what
they want to know or what they are expected to know.   Professor Staudek

helped to find clarity, so that everybody who deals with Youth knows what to do and how children should be guided. I thank Professor Staudek for her courage in this struggle for eternal truth. What the children do here is God-wished, it is innate, and they must do it. The world becomes richer because of it. Whoever makes something good makes the world richer. Those who do bad work do harm to the world. She always encouraged the production of good things, and especially in her own sphere of textiles. I am very fond of textiles. But only the talented should be permitted to do textile art. Those who do textile art here are chosen for it. It is in textile art, more than any other, that that which is God-wished and innate within all children is revealed. In no other medium does it become so clear. Why? Because textile art prevents superficial working and encourages the rhythm of work. This rhythm is innate within all children. This rhythm weakens in adolescents, and disappears entirely with adults, because they discourage it and their profession absorbs it. But children have this rhythm within themselves. You all carry this wonderful rhythm with you. And this rhythm is nowhere revealed better than in textile art. Because textile art keeps off the copying of nature it plays an important rôle in Child Art. We thank Miss Staudek for having tried out those things, always following the eternal laws of creation in material. The work and material become a unity, and in addition to that there is the unity of the child, which is a psychological element. It is unity which makes a work of art. Look at the great works of art—there is always a unity within them. And the same thing applies to Child Art, as far as it is uninfluenced by grown-ups. It is a sin if adults disturb this unity. It is a forgery of documents. Miss Staudek knew how to let children work in their own spirit and not under an alien influence. We thank her for her sense of duty, her devotion, and her joy in work. She understood from the very beginning that there is no question of mere play here. We hope that she will be able to carry on with her work happily, and that she may see the day when my work (my " Last Will "[1]) is finished, which is supposed to be something unique and which perhaps never will be finished. But it should come to some kind of an end. And I ask Miss Staudek to work with me towards this end. I thank her again most heartily.

Miss Staudek: I thank Professor Cizek for the kind words. I have always the feeling that I have done nothing here. *Cizek:* All the modest men who have accomplished something have had this feeling. They always think they should do more. But we can all be very satisfied with the work

[1] For many years Cizek was working on his " Work " which should contain all he knew about Child Art. The Yale University Press had supplied the funds for paper and printing.

Miss Staudek has accomplished.   *Miss Staudek :* My most ardent desire is to be able to help with the work.

Cizek : Now we are going to celebrate this festival, which isn't one, with drawing.   You have a frame and within it you will draw a festival.   You should draw a procession of children.   You have purposely been given a smaller frame so that you can finish the drawing to-day.   You will draw children marching towards Miss Staudek.   They all carry bunches of flowers.   Some carry wreaths with the inscription : "Twenty-five years." Those who wish to may write the date : 1st February.   Or you can make something special.   Just what you like.   Two or three boys are carrying a huge wreath.   The girls may make a big girl being carried by three girls. One can make a great variety of things.   You can depict for yourselves this festival in your imagination.   So begin !   Those who wish to may draw Miss Staudek.   Now begin !   (The children shout and throw flowers at her.)   (Later) You don't need to make many children.   If there is sufficient space, you can draw more children.   A picture like this is only beautiful if there are a great many children.

(Later) Now each one has made a picture.   But there are still many blanks in the small frames.   Even if I gave you only a quarter of an inch square you would leave half of it blank.   (Later) Those who have outlined their drawing must improve it with a pen.   Don't spoil work with your pen, but improve it !   That's the reason for pens.   Next time we shall work with new colours.   Those who have enough room at the edge may draw birds or flowers there.   Or the birds may be bringing congratulations.

13th February, 1937

Cizek : To-day is the last day of term.   Imagine you have got your report and are bringing it home.   Depict on your paper what occurs ! One child has a report with only very good marks.   What will mother do ? *Child :* She will rejoice.   *Child :* Rewards !   *Child :* The mother will look surprised. *Cizek :* The mother will say : " I couldn't imagine you being as good as that."   And father will give you a kiss.   *Child :* My father is not in Vienna. *Cizek :* Now depict the children coming home from school with their reports.   You can show how those children are running home out of sheer joy at being able to give their reports to their parents.   Of course you also can depict some bad children.   They hide their reports, so that they cannot be seen.   Or you can show children shouting in the street, holding up their reports so that everybody can see their good marks.   And other children with their fathers looking earnestly at their reports.   The children are afraid of what will happen to them.   Others are thinking of the rewards they will get for their good behaviour. You can depict all that. So we shall get a different picture from each child. (Takes a block.) Begin drawing, but make the figures sufficiently large. We need big boys and girls. Once in a drawing a boy ran from here to there. (Shows it.) So everyone will imagine the subject in a different way, but will always draw it with big figures.

I was very satisfied with to-day's home work. You have learnt a lot. I should like you to continue in this way. You need not do twenty different drawings—one or two are quite sufficient ; but you must draw at once with the pen. Most of you have made good progress. Carry on ! And now, Good-bye.

20th February, 1937

Cizek : To-day we begin the second term. It will last until the 30th June. It is the summer term, and it makes no difference if it snows or hails. For us summer begins to-day. We are always in advance of our time. We shall have a subject which we all like. We shall draw a car (takes the block broadways) in this way. With this car we shall drive into the summer. Each of you knows what a car is. When you went to school this morning two hundred and fifty cars passed you. And now you must draw one of those cars. *Child :* I shall make an Easter car. *Child :* I shall make a summer car decorated with flowers. *Cizek :* We shan't think about minor details, but about the main thing. *Child :* The carburettor. *Child :* The wheels. *Child :* The engine. *Cizek :* The main things are the wheels on which the chassis is built. *Child :* But really the most important are the wheels and the engine. And it can be driven without windows and doors. *Cizek :* I think the chassis with the wheels and the seats and the bonnet with the engine. Of course, the most important thing is the chassis with the people. Now they produce small chasiss. And they have the shape of a snail. One must get in and roll up like a snail. And if one wants to leave, one must roll out like a snail.

Now, we are going to draw the car with charcoal. (Shows a block.) Here is the bonnet, here the chassis with the people, and under the chassis four wheels with mudguards. They prevent mud from flying from the wheels on to people. Through the windows one can see into the car. One can see clearly who is driving. You will do that. Each one will put into the car whoever he wants to be there. Let the Duke of Windsor sit there, and his bride. You must draw the car nicely, because afterwards we shall paint it.

(Later) Many have already finished their 'bus or car, and many have much space left.   (Takes a drawing.)   We shall draw in this empty space a cyclist.   Those who haven't an empty space cannot draw a cyclist.   They must wait until they get the colours with which to paint the car.

(Later) We shall paint now.   We shall paint the car.   *Child :* With all the colours ?   *Cizek :* That's impossible.   People would think there was a parrot coming.   *Child :* I must paint my car blue and brown.   *Cizek :* We have neither brown nor grey nor black.   Therefore we must use other colours for the car.   *Child :* Red.   *Girl :* I should like green.   *Cizek :* In order to match your clothes.   We shall now go around with several colours and each child will choose the colour that he likes best of all.   But we shan't choose the colours of the cars driven along the streets.   If I had the money I should buy a gilded car.   *Child :* But one cannot make a gilded car.   *Cizek :* The King of England drives in a golden car.   *Child :* He drives in a black-blue one.   *Cizek :* The King and Queen are sitting in a golden carriage, and this golden carriage is drawn by sixteen horses. *Child :* Yes !   *Cizek :* And the latest car at the Coronation was entirely gilded.   *Child :* That's impossible.   That would cost innumerable millions.   *Cizek :* Unfortunately, we have no gold paint.   Otherwise I would give you some.   Now then.

(Later) To-day I think I am in America, where almost everybody has a car.   There legs are superfluous.   And this room is full of cars just like America.   But we don't have dull cars as those which are driven in the streets, but really beautiful cars, the most beautiful ones.   We leave the black cars to the chimney-sweeps, and the grey cars to the road-sweepers. We possess the really beautiful cars.

Unfortunately I cannot discuss every individual work because there isn't time.   But I should like to say that many cars are very nice.   They are not copied in a dull way from real cars, but have been invented by the pupils themselves.   They have built up the cars out of the different parts as they imagined them.   These are the right type of cars.   Cars which are copied are the wrong type.   We are driving only in our own cars, invented and planned by ourselves.   They are not machines, but works of art.   The whole is a work which we have thought out and shaped ourselves. Art must not be like nature, but how the individual does it.   I draw the car and the cyclist to the best of my ability.   What we have tried to do here you should also do at home.   Don't take books or drawings in your hand, but produce your drawings out of your own head.   It's the same with poets.   A poet won't take a book and copy poems, but he will first think and will translate his thoughts into prose or verse.   That is then a created work, a work of art.

Many of you have not made the steering wheel. (*Several children :* I did it.) If you have made it, that's all right. But those who haven't made it can't drive their car. They must wait until the car has a steering wheel. On the whole, your work is quite nice. And the drawings look quite cheerful. Drawings should not look sad, by the way. Now pack up your things, and go home. At home you will do the same with a pen. With a pen one can make cars much nicer ! Next time bring me your cars drawn with a pen !

27th February, 1937

Cizek : Last time the cars were very well done. Some children really invented their cars and did not copy them from cars driven in the streets. Some did cars as they imagined them, plus a little bit of realism. These drawings are less strong. And then there were drawings which were mere copies of cars that are driven along the streets. They, of course, have least value. They are just copies, whereas the former ones are imaginative creations, that means something which I imagine and then work out from my inner self. I don't need to know what a car looks like, but I construct the car as I want it. Those who work in this way are artists ; those who copy real cars are copiers. They may be very skilful men, but they are not artists. To your credit I must say that there were very few copied cars. Eighty per cent. of all drawings were good.

To-day we drove with our cars into the second term, and we are driving into the country ; we don't return from there, but we climb into an aeroplane and return by it. Who knows what an aeroplane looks like ? (Most children raise their hands.) Who hasn't seen a plane ? (Nobody.) It is a pity you all have seen planes ! If you hadn't seen them, you would have drawn them better. You would have been forced to invent them. Now you have seen the planes high up in the air. Of course, you couldn't see all the details. *Child :* I once passed a plane in a train. *Another child :* I have been to Aspern.[1] *Cizek :* We shall try to describe an aeroplane now. Who can ? *Child :* Above it is broad and below it is narrow. Then there are propellers and a wheel. And two seats. *Cizek :* Now we know. So T. means that there is first the body of the plane. What does the body look like ? *Child :* Like a fish. *Cizek :* Right ! and one can crawl into that fish. The fish has a long bright body, and on the left and right sides are windows. In front there is also a little window out of which the pilot can look. What is attached to the body ? *Child :* Two wings. *Another child :* And a tail behind. *Cizek :* Yes. And what else is attached

[1] Aspern is the aerodrome near Vienna.

to the plane ? *Child :* A rudder. *Child :* A propeller. *Cizek :* The propeller is the most important part because by it the plane is driven forward. Now we shall draw such a plane, but not as small as a flea but as large as it can be drawn in the space here. (Shows the block.) That's what you are going to draw now. And as large as possible. But nothing should be left out. *Child :* Shall the plane be on the ground or flying ? *Cizek :* It is best to do it flying, but don't leave out the wings and the tail ! Those who wish and can may make a window or the number. Each plane has a number. When we are given colours, we shall paint the number.

(Later) Those who have finished will get pen and indian ink. Listen ! You shouldn't make clouds. Once I saw a picture of a plane and at the side of it there were large white blankets. We shall put in the empty spaces something different from clouds or blankets. Or we shall leave these empty spaces. That will be beautiful. (Later) Who has finished ? (Most raise their hands.)

(Later) One child has put flying blankets in the empty corners. We shall do something different. We shall put flying birds there. And a small plane far behind. But one can see it. Those who have finished should bring their drawings here.

6th March, 1937

Cizek : We shall exhibit in Paris. There are many young people who long for it and can't do it. It is a great distinction that you are able to exhibit in Paris. Our Juvenile Art Class has already exhibited once in Paris and was rewarded with a gold medal. Now we have to make a few stories for this exhibition. One story will be that you will draw a street, and the second what happens in this street, what the people are doing. Now give me an example. *Child :* For instance, somebody has an accident. *Cizek :* Yes, somebody falls on his nose or breaks his knee. That's an accident. That can happen to anybody, and it can be drawn. I shouldn't recommend a street, because that's beyond your stage. A street would be all right after the eleventh year of age. Who is already eleven ? (Two raise their hands.) Those who are eleven may do a street. What do you understand by street ? *Girl :* At one side houses and in front a cyclist and cars. *Cizek :* It may be a street like Fichtegasse,[1] or like the big " Ring," [2] or a country road with trees. You can make that, but it is difficult because perspective [3] enters into it, with which you who are between seven and eleven should have nothing to do at all. Only after eleven

---

[1] Where the Cizek school was.   [2] One of the main streets of Vienna.

[3] The first time he used that word.

can one try to represent things in the right perspective. Now begin, but do your street urchins from the edge to the bottom. And beside them a girl is standing and saying : " Stop your fighting ! I shall tell mother." Or a coal-cart is passing by, the horses are pulling it. Children are going behind it and picking up the coals which are falling off. They have bags with them, in which they will take coal to their mother. The mother will be very pleased, because she won't have to buy any coal. She has no money. So the children help their mother. Then you can do a cyclist. He can be made very interesting. He may carry a pannier. Who has another idea ? *Child :* How a car is being driven along or a horse-cart and children are running behind and are trying to climb on to it. *Cizek :* Have you any other idea ? *Child :* A girl is falling over in the street and the boys are laughing at her. *Cizek :* You can do that, but you must use the paper very carefully, so that you can draw the figures large. I should be delighted to be surprised by you. I am sure everyone will have a good idea, without any suggestions from myself. We did this subject twenty years ago. Then a boy did a water-cart, another did a peasant-cart. The cart is jolting over a stone, a wheel is breaking, and the barrels are falling off. Another boy did a coach with two horses. The horses are shying and running away. Men and women are thrown from the coach. A policeman is running after the coach. People are helping. Now all that was thought out by the pupils. And you must have ideas like that, so that the Parisians can see what Viennese children have invented. And rewards will only be given to those who have used all their paper. And then, there must always be something happening ; for instance, a chauffeur is colliding with a cart, he loses his balance and is flung out of his car. Or you may depict the different types of people in the street. Or a dog is running after some hens. (After the children have finished their drawings) Last time, you remember, we did an aeroplane. Do you remember ? (*Children :* Yes.) Each aeroplane has a special sign. *Child :* On each wing. During the night it has red lights on its wings. *Cizek :* Our plane flies only by day. Its sign is a coat of arms, or a star. The commercial planes between cities have numbers, for instance 5560. You may draw a 5 or 7. Or you may put your initials. We shall not paint the plane. Only the letters or signs will be painted in green, red, blue, gold, or silver. The wings and the plane will not be painted to-day, but only next time.

13th March, 1937

Cizek : To-day we are going to draw flowers because spring is coming. The car and aeroplane which we did turned out quite nicely. One could see how much you have learned. You have learned to think. What does a car or plane look like ? If I don't know, I invent something for myself. This is most important : that we learn to invent forms ourselves. And the best works were those where the smaller ones made their own plane. They had invented and drawn it quite well. But some have not learned to think. Some have not invented a drawing, but just copied. A boy, for instance, copied a form without thinking for himself. And he repeated that form. In this way inferior works are produced. But if somebody strives to build a car—whether good or bad makes no difference—he has done some real work, and that is the main thing. I was pleased to see that even children who used to think in a very complicated way have proved that they are not dependent on copying forms. T. has invented forms out of his head. That's progress. And many other children, too, have shown this progress. Only a few proved that they can't invent their own forms, but must copy other forms. The great value of our way of working is that we learn to think. Forming means thinking. You will take that with you all through your life, and, having been accustomed to think in relation to nice subjects, you will go on trying to be thinkingly constructive in all spheres. Thinking young men !

But to-day we will do flowers. We shall try to remember forms. And where the memory is not enough we shall think for ourselves. We shall say : a flower has a seed-box and around it petals are grouped in different rhythms. The seed-box can be divided by rhythms. The leaves may have different forms. You will invent them. You get a suggestion from nature and go on thinking or yourselves. There are flowers outside. Go and look at them, and when you come back you will draw flowers.

But you must draw them as you can and just as you can ! Then we shall paint the drawings with nice colours. But you must not make photographs. And those who don't need to copy from nature will invent their own flowers. They must not necessarily be real flowers. We have no natural flowers here ; we have here art. Nature has her flowers, and art has hers. You can do the flowers you like. (Later) Now you will get the colours. (*Some children shout :* Hurrah !) Red, blue, yellow. And you will paint the flowers as you imagine them. But don't colour beyond the lines ! (Later) Colour is discipline, not licence. The ancient Egyptians knew only four colours !

20th March, 1937

Before we did the flowers we did cars and planes. We had different ideas about them. It was like that : abstract forms as Gertrud makes them.   Hers is the primitive and the most valuable stage.   There man is all-important.   He doesn't copy, but makes only what God tells him. Man at this stage does not represent objects, but symbols of objects.   There are strokes, for instance, and they symbolise an aeroplane, a car, or a flower. Little Gertrud doesn't make flowers, but she makes the direction of the stem and the extension of the blossom.   That is the strongest and simplest way in which one can express a flower.   Gerti does not yet imitate nature, but she is still an artist and a creator.   She gives the flower only that which is most artistic and essential.   And that is direction and extension. Gerti in this sense is the strongest of all.   She is a rare case of a child left to her own resources and a good testimony to her parents.   Parents who leave their children entirely to their own devices know what treasure they possess. Therefore they leave them untouched.   All parents should know that. But unfortunately many of them don't ; most parents want to have their children as they wish them to be and not as God wants them.   And therefore they spoil them.

Now we shall look at the works.   Here is a very good drawing.   At the edge there are rhythms.   This is the very beginning of order.   Drawing does not mean, as the famous word goes, leaving out, but order.   To order one's ideas, that is drawing.   And we can see that here.   There is a simple symmetry and the rhythm of double and fourfold symmetry. This work later gets more confused and becomes copying.   The work ceases to be art but becomes natural science.   Not only is the form copied, but the colour also.   In the upper part there is pure rhythm.—Erica, too, begins with rhythms.   Then her drawing becomes almost writing, and then she copies nature.   But still, her copies of nature are bearable, because her naturalism is not dull and stupid but to a certain extent symbolic.— It is a pity that Peperl isn't here.   He has done a good drawing.   First he begins quite rhythmically, and this is a quality which no one can take away.   Everything here is rhythm.   In the lower part of the drawing we can see clearly the rhythmic construction of the whole.   The work is not imitative.   It contains contrasts.   And thus style is created.   There is lack of style if all colours are imitative.   So copies come into existence.

Runa started quite nicely.   Her rhythms are fine.   Girls have more innate rhythm than boys.   Boys' rhythm is often disturbed by their greater vitality.   Runa started well, but she broke the colour rhythm by her use of blue.—J. started quite nicely, but her green shows that she has copied.   The whole is like a carpet.—K. is a special case.   He is precocious and therefore copies.   This produces confusion.   He is over-clever, and so becomes confused.   Where intelligence is too strong in the realm of art, it causes damage.   It is a pity that K. copied, otherwise a fine rhythm would have been created.   Again, we do not deal with natural science, but with art.

Uta, too, brought green into her painting.   They all must have green, because the present generation is so weak.   Weak generations love green, blue, and mauve.   The green wouldn't have been so bad if she had used less.   But because she has used green in the same strength as the other colours, the colours have become equal.   And equality means death.— T. did some quite good work.   Some of his flowers are nice.   But why does he introduce suddenly into his vertical rhythm a trend in an opposite direction ?   Thus confusion occurs.   The order which is the significant quality of art is disturbed by it.   This work is very interesting from a psychological point of view.   It reveals the draughtsman.   Other people would have used the space better.

B. has a strong personality, which reveals itself in the drawing and in the peculiar rhythm.   She constructs things which do not occur in nature, but which she invents for herself.   Everything is abstract and far from nature.—Herbert, of course, went through a school which was very naturalistic.   So he copies forms from nature.   It is a mixture of banality and personal rhythm.   Let us hope that in the end the personal rhythm will triumph in this struggle of forms.—Helli's work has a few nice qualities. Everything is nicely filled, not overladen, and there is a good rhythm.   And she has used the colours very nicely.   An imitative colour is always banal. One could say : Vulgar people tend towards the copying of nature, better ones tend towards art.   I am not against nature—quite the opposite.   If I go into the woods, then I want only real flowers, and the taste and smell of real strawberries.   But in art I want only art, not nature.   In art I want forming, shaping, spiritual construction, self-invention.

Gertrud's work is rhythmically nice.   What she constructs is self-invented, not natural science, not copied from a picture-book.—The copying of nature is not art.   Art is when forms of our own spiritual conception occur.   *Child :* They said that great artists have copied nature.   *Cizek :* Tell those who say that : " You understand nothing of art ! "—The next drawing is a fine example of rhythm without the copying of nature.   There is a fine rhythm in these movements.—The flowers of Sybil (two years five months old).   She is still in the scribbling stage.   (Some children laugh.) She simply creates spots.   Everything with her is extension.   When there is direction, drawing begins.   Here we see the beginning.   The colours are a kind of contrast ; they have no unity, but they are kept from each other in a form of contrast.   Sybil's other picture shows the same good qualities. Here are the contrasts of green and red; they are the strongest contrasts we have.—On the whole, this flower exercise was a good exercise. You have proved your capacity and possibility of development by fine examples. Let us hope that you will continue straight upward, and not in a broken line, confused and disordered.—I wish that your parents will help us and that they won't lead you towards naturalism.

Subject: Prams seen from above. (After half an hour) *Cizek:* Most of you drew the pram without any love or devotion. You should get accustomed to working neatly. Those who work carelessly won't progress. Those who make an effort will have success under all circumstances. Actually you should be ashamed of yourselves. You have been here for such a long time. For instance, I told you: "You should sign the drawings." And still many of you hand in the drawings unsigned. You should learn to listen. And you should learn to think about what I say. We shall take the block now. (Shows it.) You will make a spring landscape, an Easter outing. You know that we always progress with the time. But some people say that we are old-fashioned. We are not only old-fashioned, but we go back to the oldest roots of art, to the eternal truth.—Now we shall do what we always did at Easter time: an excursion. Who knows what an excursion is? (All raise their hands.) We shall make an Easter excursion. We shall climb a mountain. Now draw the mountain here. (Shows where with his finger.) And all over the paper. In the upper part there will be sufficient space to do a building. We shall make a dairy with cows which give good milk. This good milk is the reason for which we shall climb the mountain. I believe you are no friends of alcohol? (*Some children:* Oh yes!) Now you will draw the mountain and the building in the upper part. It will be a house, and beside it there will be stables and through the open doors one can see the cows. They are standing with their backs towards the door, so that one can see them. They are waiting to be milked. A woman is milking the cows and afterwards she will carry the milk away. In another building the milk is sold.—Now we are climbing this mountain. Draw the mountain first. Its top must be flat, because a house has to be there. A house can't stand on a pointed mountain. On the building there will be the inscription: "Dairy."

3rd April, 1937

Cizek: Last time you made a mountain. On top of it there is a restaurant such as is on the top of Kahlenberg[1] or another mountain. At this

[1] Mountain near Vienna.

restaurant you can get refreshments, water, milk, lemonade, or chocolate. Two roads lead to the restaurant. You should do these roads. One of the houses is a stable with the cows inside which give milk for the children. In the other house all the drinks are retailed. And near the third house is a fountain.—Now you will do the roads which lead straight to the doors of the houses, but don't make turnings. They should all be straight. And make all the windows and doors very carefully. A short time ago I saw drawings from all over Austria. Most of them were beautifully executed. Now listen : You have three roads. How many roads have you ? *Child :* Two. *Another child :* One. *Cizek :* Those who make two roads should do them in this way : on the left road a car will be driving up the mountain, a big modern car of 100 h.p. It shoots upwards, but not on the middle road which leads to the stable.—I must praise J. Everything in her drawing is in order. Drawing means putting into order, putting thoughts in order, and not making confusion. Her road is full of cows. Only the men don't know where they belong.

10th April, 1937

    Cizek : Yesterday there was a thunderstorm. Who saw it ? (Most children raise their hands.) Did the lightning strike anything ? *Child :* Yes. *Cizek :* Did it strike your house ? (*Child :* No.) Then it must have struck something in the country. It was a terrible thunderstorm. Then it poured with rain. The newspapers report that many houses were flooded. Two women had to save themselves, but only with great pain. Water entered the basements. It was terrible. Now we are going to draw this thunderstorm. *Child :* Did somebody die ? *Cizek :* A thunderstorm occurs in this way : first there are spots on the sun. If such spots occur, then there is usually an earthquake, hail, or a thunderstorm. When the sunspots disappear, then is fine weather again. (*Child :* April weather.) Now we shall draw people in the thunderstorm. You won't draw a line, but the whole paper is the street. (Shows a block broadside.) And in the street you will show many people walking along with umbrellas. Those who have no umbrellas wear mackintoshes with hoods. The hoods are pointed and water is running down. Now we shall draw the people with the umbrellas. *Child :* And hoods ! *Cizek :* Schips, the dog, will go with them and will get very wet. He starts shaking himself and later the flat will be quite wet. Now we shall not draw that, but only imagine it. Now we do only the street in rain. The people have their umbrellas open, and you will try to draw the raindrops. (*Child :* I know it.) Many know it, others will try it, and everybody will do it nicely. Then we shall draw the lightning striking something. *Child :* May we also draw the women escaping with great difficulty ? *Cizek :* You will do the figures, real men, and not fleas. Schips is pulling a man along. You will have many ideas. You will draw them all. And those who do the sun must make it with sunspots, so that one sees that everything is the fault of the sun. The sun will not have its usual friendly face. Now begin ! We shan't draw cars, but only men and dogs.

(Later) You must do your umbrellas nicely curved, with many spokes, and with a big handle with which you hold the umbrella. People are hurrying along the street, because they want to get home soon. (Later) Many of you do the figures with arms hanging down. They can't hold an umbrella in this way. They must raise their arms. Only a few did it in this way. Some have the spokes projecting. They look quite pointed. If it rains heavily, streams of water will be pouring off them. You should do it in this way. You must, so to speak, write down and draw your observations. Only experiences like that can make a thunderstorm interesting.

17th April, 1937

(On April 10th a Maharaja with his wife and daughter had visited the Juvenile Art Class.) *Cizek :* Last time you saw the Indian prince with his wife and daughter. He was dressed like an ordinary man. The Maharaja is going to the Coronation in London. There he will wear his full regalia : gold, and a turban with wonderful jewels. In India the Prince does not drive in a car or a tram, but he has an elephant. The street urchins would like to run after him, but the police do not permit it. Now let us make an elephant ! On top the Maharaja is sitting. What is an elephant ? He has legs like columns. The head is very big with huge ears and a long trunk. Then he has two tusks and two little eyes. What kind of tail has he ? *Child :* A wee tail. *Child :* A dear little tail. *Cizek :* Yes, it's like string. And the elephant is longer than it is high. (Later) Now, you should listen to what I say. I told you that you should make an elephant. Some have finished their elephant and have drawn the Maharaja like a stupid doll on top of it. Some have made a crippled elephant. No Maharaja would sit on it. *Child :* I haven't done one stroke of the elephant. *Cizek :* That's right. But one child has done two Maharajas and her elephant has crippled legs. It can't walk. And the trunk comes out from its nose like a big drop. That's no trunk. The trunk is thick and strong at the upper part and gets thinner towards the end. Listen ! First draw the elephant well. And look at the drawing to see if it is well done. Don't mind the Maharaja !

The Prince climbs only on a well-made elephant. We have much to do with our elephant. The elephant has legs like columns. The legs are as strong as trees, and not as a walking-stick. Who did it rightly ? Look ! (Many children raise their hands.) I see a few hands which I shouldn't see. Then look at the tusks ! Those who have made the legs too thin will erase them and will make new and thicker legs. Those who have already made the Maharaja should erase him. Those who have made the trunk too thin should erase it and make a thicker one in its place. (Later)Now the elephant is more or less finished. We are going to put the Prince on it. Of course, he won't sit on a bare elephant. Indian elephants have precious trappings. Some Princes have little temples on their elephants. Then they have a kind of canopy. But that is only at festivals. In ordinary times and if it is not rainy he has only precious carpets and no canopy. Now, you will not make the Prince, but these precious carpets and nice ornaments, which we shall paint later in gold and silver. There are special painters in India who paint the decorations of the Princes' elephants. *Child :* I can only paint those ornaments. *Cizek :* All right, you will paint them. Some of you have decorated the elephant's legs with ornaments, and on each leg a different ornament. That means confusion. No elephant would know which leg was which. (Later) Now hurry with your Prince, so that next time you can paint. You will get gold and silver.

24th April, 1937

   Cizek : The Maharaja is already in London. He wrote a letter. He sends you his greetings. He is glad that he has been here. On his return he will perhaps come here again. Then he will look at your pictures and will perhaps take some of them with him to India. You must make those pictures very nicely. Perhaps we shall exhibit them here and invite people to see them.

   You will get thin colours now. Those are colours where the drawing remains transparent. We shall paint with them, and on top of them we shall use thick colours. You will use only a little of the thick colours, so that the picture doesn't become smeared. Those who want yellow and red may take those colours. But you can have blue or green as well. One colour after the other. And those who have painted especially well will get silver and gold. Now, who knows how to paint the elephant ? *Child :* Brown. *Another child :* Gold. *Child :* Grey. *Child :* Grey-brown. *Another child :* With different colours. *Child :* Red. *Cizek :* You must not think in terms of natural science. You must not forget that the elephant is painted with colours, and not just grey and brown. In the

Zoo elephants are grey and brown, but an Indian Prince doesn't ride a grey or brown elephant.

We haven't had such a nice subject for a long while. Since the Abyssinian Emperor. So you must take care. (Later) Some draw carefully, others smear. Others paint one colour on top of the other. Those who have done the picture very nicely may make it on a larger scale. (Shows the size.) Who would like to make it so large ? (All children raise their hands. Later) You must hurry. Otherwise it lasts too long. You work a little bit too slowly. (Later) You must become more absorbed in your work. Next time we shall finish and then we shall have a discussion. *Child :* Will there be a tombola here ? (Cizek had promised something like it.) *Cizek :* We shall see about that after the discussion.

8th May, 1937

(The children continue to paint the elephant. When finished, Cizek depicts in the most vivid colours the Zeppelin catastrophe.[1]) There was a short circuit, and the whole Zeppelin exploded. Thirty men were burned. Think, as many as we are here. Twenty-five years ago a huge ocean liner— the " Titanic "—hit an iceberg in the Atlantic. Three thousand people were drowned. Only a few were saved. Our children then made pictures of this catastrophe ; they painted it very well, how the " Titanic " went down and the people tried to save themselves. We always paint such catastrophes. Thirty years ago we depicted the eruption of Etna. This is a high mountain in Sicily which is a volcano. Thirty years ago it sent forth so much fire and lava that the great city of Messina was destroyed and thousands of people perished. In 1908 our pictures of Etna were exhibited in London. And now we are going to paint the explosion of the Zeppelin. (Shows a block.) In the upper part you will make the airship. And below the thousands of people who are waiting for it. It is a huge crowd. At last the Zeppelin arrives. It tries to land, but suddenly a lightning flash. And that's what we are going to do now. The Zeppelin is as long as the distance between the " Burg " and Parliament.[2] What does an airship look like ? *Child :* Like a sausage. *Child :* Like an egg. *Cizek :* Yes, like a sausage, only with a sausage both ends are pointed ; but otherwise the Zeppelin is like a gigantic sausage. Under the balloon hangs a gondola where the people are ; and there are a few smaller gondolas for the propellers. They are, so to speak, the wheels which move the Zeppelin. Now begin ! First the Zeppelin and then the twenty thousand people

[1] The Zeppelin " Hindenburg," when trying to land near New York, burst into flames.
[2] The Imperial Castle and the Parliament—two huge buildings on the " Ring."

below.   And then draw how they throw ropes from the Zeppelin, how the people below try to catch them, how the people jump from the Zeppelin at a height of 150 feet in order to save themselves.   Then you will draw the Zeppelin burning.   Who has not seen a Zeppelin ?   (Only a few raise their hands.)   Now, the Zeppelin looks like a gigantic sausage.   Below hangs a kind of cabin with people inside.   It's like a 'bus.   Oh, you will do it quite easily.

22nd May, 1937

(Continuation of the Zeppelin.   Red and orange are distributed for the flames.)   *Cizek :* Those who made the nicest pictures may do the Zeppelin afterwards as large as that.   (Shows it.)   Who wants to make the Zeppelin as large as that ?   (All raise their hands.)

29th May, 1937.

Cizek : To-day, because the sun is shining so nicely, we shall paint with colours.   We shall paint a nice picture.—On Mondays the children from Meidling come.   Last time one of those children finished her picture and I told her : " Now, quick.   Make another picture, which you can finish in one and a half hours.   That's the whole time you have."   And the child drew quickly with charcoal.   Then I gave her colours and the girl finished the picture.   (Cizek shows the girl's picture.)

Now then, to-day we shall make a picture with charcoal and afterwards paint it with beautiful colours, so that we shall not draw much to-day. We shall take the block in this way.   (Shows the block longways.)   And there you will paint figures and not fleas.   Why should you make large figures ?   Who knows ?   *Child :* So that we draw as much as we can in the space.   *Cizek :* Yes, so that the paper is well used and we shall not get half-empty papers.   In addition to that, you learn more.   The figures should be executed with the brush and not with the charcoal.   It makes no difference what kind of figures you draw : man, woman or child, or all three.   But arrange them nicely !   You can also draw people with ruck-sacks who are going to the market.   Those who have sufficient imagination can draw the Queen of England.   She has very beautiful clothes and a nice crown.   And the Princesses too.   And T., who knows Red Indians, (*T. :* Fine !) may draw Red Indians.   *T. :* May I do Old Shatterhand and his wife ?   *Cizek :* Yes, but nicely !   (Later) You must draw something interesting, and not a few dull figures !   You must make something which is really interesting, and where you can use nice colours.   Not a baker's boy who has no colours or only dirty ones.   We don't have dirty colours here. You must do something which has beautiful colours. And you must make everything big : hands, feet, head, so that a great amount of colour can be used. I can only paint large spaces with a brush. You should know that already. (Later) Now, some are already beginning to make little dots. You must paint large spaces. Brushes are to be used for painting spaces. Those who want to draw should take a pencil. A colour only has an effect if it is used to fill large spaces. Coloured dots have no effects. One cannot even see them from a distance. You should not use charcoal as a brush. You should distinguish between the two. One draws with charcoal and paints with a brush. If a space is painted, one can make a decoration with a second colour, but first the space must be painted.

(At the discussion) We had beautiful colours. But if one looks at these works here they look like smeared colours. Only chocolate and grey. Why ? You had such beautiful pure colours. The reason why you get the colours separately is so that you shouldn't mix them. *Child :* But, Herr Professor, with some pictures it is quite nice. For instance, the one by S. Or the picture with the boy and girl. They are full of colour. *Cizek :* But there are only a few nice ones. *Child :* The picture of the Tyroleans. *Cizek :* Young X. has worked very well. He knows how to keep the colours pure. But most children stir the colours like gravy. Then their colours have a result like this. (Points to a picture of two Red Indians.) Nobody told the boy to paint the space with the Red Indians as an extension. He only made the extension. That would be quite nice if he knew it, but the bad thing is that children want to do things for which they have not matured. In their impatience they want to do something of which they are not yet capable. They should be satisfied with what they are capable of, and should be humble like a grape which matures slowly. And some of you only dabble with the colours. One sees how much you have to learn.—The picture of Ilse would have been quite nice but for the blue globes she painted below. If she had not got blue colour, she would have been spared. It is not for pedagogical reasons that we distribute the colours separately, but because we aim at a unity of colour.—There is a poor child from Meidling. She is very economical with her colours because she is used to being economical and modest at home. She chose the warm colours out of innate taste, and with one single colour she achieved a sub-division full of taste. But with the others neither drawing nor forming of colour has been achieved. It is true that sometimes wonders of art come into existence because of absolute freedom. But here we aim also at " culture," which means the highest freedom within the smallest space. Freedom in a concentrated form.   Freedom in the infinite may become wildness. If a child has an innate feeling for harmonies, it arranges colours naturally, following laws which are effective unconsciously.   And the same can be manifested in the realm of rhythm.

This exercise has shown that you, first of all, must be economical with colours, that you must begin with two, three, or four colours, but not more. The ancient Egyptians' colours are so wonderful because they had so few. And their colours were not chemical products, but natural products.   They ground their colours.   One has found colours of an unbelievable beauty which have lasted to this day.   Nowadays one has hundreds of shades of brown.   One has a huge selection of red.   Nowadays one has too many colours.   Parents should be careful not to give their children too many colours.   A nice harmony of colours comes out of only a few colours.   Limitlessness leads towards trash and chaos.   I advise you to be economical at home and tell your parents : " Give us only a few colours."

Negroes have a few colours only because there is no colour factory in the jungle.   Some insects supply them with colour, but so little that they can paint only with a few colours and in small quantities.   They will paint a clay figure with a few red or brown or yellow strokes, and that's enough. There is a harmony of colours.   But here you want to use thousands of colours and you mix them into an ugly gravy.   We want to avoid that. We shall be satisfied with two or three glowing colours which are congenial to your youth.   No unity of colours, but, according to your stage, abstract symbolic colours !   Now you have heard something new about colours. Remember it !   If you use colours, use only a few !

5th June, 1937

Cizek : Because it is so nice to-day we shall do an outing, and not by railway, because that's dull.   What is interesting ?   *Child :* The mountains. *Child :* On top of a mountain.   *Child :* In a meadow.   *Cizek :* To walk on the summit of the Grossglockner [1] or the Montblanc.   That's grand. *Child :* I have been there.   *Cizek :* At your age I did not know that there was a thing called Montblanc.   Now we are going to draw a road. (Shows the block.)   We shall climb here, then continue walking along, and then climb again.   It is more like a zigzag road.   (Shows a reversed S.)   We shall make a bend.   But first the road.   If the road is correctly drawn, then we shall walk on it.

(Later) Now you have finished the road.   We shall draw the people

[1] Highest mountain in Austria.

now. They are climbing. They are all enjoying the fresh air. Now what are you going to put on the road ? *Child :* Cars and people. *Child :* Children with rucksacks and dogs. *Cizek :* Dogs are the main thing. Children can't separate themselves from dogs. So we shall draw dogs as well. Dogs run the distance ten times over. They run ahead and return to their master, greet him and run away again. The dog is happy about his being with his master. My sister, when she was your age, had a dove. It followed her like a dog. When people came the dove flew up.—Now you will draw man, woman, and child, and a dog. And at the side of them cars, and those who can do it, cyclists and motor-cyclists as well. Do make the whole thing very cheerful and the road full of life. But be careful ! I noticed already with one child that she made ants instead of men. That would be an ant road. (Children laugh.) One could do it, but then one must know how to draw ants. Or you could make a road full of dogs only. Now, we shall be satisfied with a road on which there are man, woman, child, cyclists, and cars. That's enough for us. (Later) Now we shall see who has done it the best. Those who have done a nice meadow which is not open to the public may put up a notice : " Trespassers will be prosecuted." (The children draw with indian ink.)

12th June, 1937

Cizek : Now we shall take the block broadside again. (Shows it.) We shall draw this. Until now we have always been satisfied with the outside world. To-day we are going to draw the inside of a room. You haven't done it yet. You know, children are going to school in the morning. Mother says : " Hurry ! It's high time. It is a quarter to eight."[1] The children crawl out of their beds. How does one crawl out of one's bed ? First one starts with one's feet. Left or right first. Now we shall draw when we have already got out of bed. We are washing. You will draw the room with the bed unmade. A girl or a boy is standing at the basin and washing. It is not difficult. There is nothing easier than to wash. (A child laughs.) Of course you will draw large figures. Why ? *Child :* So that one doesn't think that they are ants. And so that one can see them better. *Cizek :* That's right. And because one can execute large figures more easily than small ones. One cannot do much with small figures. Draw in a way that one can see the head clearly, also the nose, the mouth, the eyes, the fingers, etc.—This is the foot basin (shows it) and this the bed, and beside the bed is the washstand and a chair. It may be only a stool on which the basin is stan ing. And then there is the boy or girl who is

---

[1] Continental schools begin at 8 o'clock as a rule.

washing.   (Later) Now we shall outline, but we shall be careful not to spoil the drawing.

(Later all the children get new paper.) You all have got new paper. On this paper you will draw the head of an ox, front face.   Who knows how to do that ?   What shape has the head of an ox?   *Child :* Oval.   *Cizek :* All right, oval.   We shall draw an oval head.   Then we shall draw two eyes, two nostrils.   Then there is a cow standing with her tongue out of her mouth, and rejoicing. (*A child shouts :* Moo !) The nostrils of the cow are near to its mouth.   On its head are two horns.   And below left and right an ear. They are so big that the cow can kill fleas with an ear.   So strong is a cow's ear.   And that's what you will draw.   Then the two eyes.   They are not small, but large.   And the nostrils are large.   Try to draw that.   I should like to see how you imagine these things.

19th June, 1937

Cizek : Last time you crawled out of your bed and you were washing. To-day we shall draw how you dress.   That means clothes and shoes. Again you should make a room with a bed and other things.   And a boy or girl.   They are dressing.   Those who have no brother must invent one, and those who have no sister must wish one.   Next to the bedroom there may be another room.   Start drawing.   Everyone should put on his shoes. So you get a nice movement of the body.   While dressing, one can also stand.   Hurry, so that we can have a discussion ! (Later) Again you are doing such small figures !   Why do we have paper ?   Not in order to leave it empty.   You must draw large figures, so that you learn something. (Later) Until now we have always done landscapes.   But now we have done for the second time a room.   We divided it.   Last time we did children rising and washing.   You all did it very well.   It was a new task, but you solved it quite originally.   To-day we did the dressing.   One girl had a very interesting idea.   A boy put on his shoes in this way : a boy loses his balance and while he tries to put on one shoe hops about the room.— Lia did a girl who is buttoning her blouse.   Very good.   A real child's conception.

Jori, too, had an original idea.   She must have thought hard.   Yes, every child has thought.—Trude's work is rather conventional ; she has not progressed in recent years.   She is new only in that she tries to find new situations in her conventionalism.   The way in which the boy is putting on his shoes is nicely done.—Fritz has filled the space very well.   He hasn't left empty spaces.—Hilde has done the dressing well, and just according to her age.—K. has worked somehow indistinctly.   He is quite original.   He depicts the putting on of the shoes.—One sees that T. has no sister. His sister in the drawing is like a brother. He has made some progress because he is becoming clearer. He doesn't go off on to so many side-tracks now, but keeps to the main idea. I hope he will continue in this way.—Erica's work is modest.—Gertrud has good direction. There is little movement. She is not old enough to represent movement or change of movement. She is satisfied with hints of movement. That corresponds to her mental stage.—Liesl hasn't finished yet.—Tuna is full of immense imagination. One can see that clearly with the boy who has his hands in his pockets. It's tectonically good. This is perhaps the most precious stage in a child's work. There are not yet connections of forms for children of this stage, but they build the figure up tectonically out of separate parts.

I am happy that most of you have made progress, not due to copying but through your own experiences. To the parents I say : Don't unfold the bud, but let it open of its own accord, slowly. Violently opened buds perish. Everything should mature slowly. Nothing should be forced.

*　　*　　*

More and more people accept Cizek's principles, but some of the "theories and practices imputed to Cizek are without foundation," as an Inspector wrote to me after the first edition of this book was published. " But I also find," continues the Inspector, " a number of practices which are apparently at a discrepancy with his declared principles. As I understand you, Cizek's aim was to enable children to express their imaginative experience freely and without adult imposed interference—hence his insistence on the child's not being discouraged from non-naturalistic productions, and on a child's being urged to imagine what a thing he wants to paint is like, rather than being told how to represent it. (This would not, of course, rule out the all-pervasive influence of the teacher's personality, nor the need for stimulus and encouragement—even quite definite suggestions as to what the children should try to draw.) I was therefore somewhat unprepared for the following points in Cizek's procedure :—

" 1. His insistence on detail ; e.g. p. 115—the buckles, hair, eyes ; p. 118—the Christmas tree ; p. 134—the apple tree.

" 2. His showing children drawings made by a former group of children.

" 3. His frequent adverse criticism of children's drawings, sometimes apparently on the ground that they are not sufficiently ' like ' the natural object ; e.g. p. 139—the horse's hooves ; p. 117—Santa Claus's legs are ' wrong way round ' ; p. 152—' Don't make the face blue.'

" 4. His insistence on hard work and discipline. Of course the children must learn that this is necessary, but I am surprised at such pas-

sages as the following, which struck me as being 'teacherish':—
p. 127, 'T. should stick to one thing and do that well'; p. 130,
urging the children to work at home ; p. 138, 'Trude was formerly
industrious. . . . Now her expression becomes weaker'; p. 143,
'S. has worked hard to-day and has accomplished more than
usual. Only she should learn to form her figures better'; p. 159,
'I told him that you were bringing me hardly any drawings. I am
ashamed to have to say that in front of so many foreign visitors.'

" 5. His comparing one child's work with that of another, often to the
detriment of one.

" 6. I am wondering whether the remarks about the children's drawings
belonging to this or that 'stage' were addressed to the children
or to visitors and students ?

I know, of course, that one cannot, from your verbatim accounts,
judge of intangible things like the relationship between Cizek and
the children, and the general atmosphere. Many things can be
conveyed by a tone of voice and a look which the bare words, set
down in print, seriously misrepresent. It is for this reason that I
hope that you will be able to clear the matter up."

Here is my reply : . . . In the past only the adult counted, now some
are so afraid of influencing the child that they do not want to encourage
production at all. Cizek's "Leave the child alone" is misunderstood by
some. They are a small minority, but I found lately in several places
opposition to the idea of suggesting, without compulsion of course, occasionally a subject. Cizek did suggest subjects, and always without compulsion, and most children were grateful. Now with regard to your direct
questions :

1. Cizek's occasional insistence on detail (e.g. p. 115) is to be explained,
partly, by his encouragement to fill the space.

2. The room was always full of children's works. They were surrounded by them. When Cizek showed them, though very rarely,
drawings made by former pupils, his purpose was to fill them
with confidence that they too could produce something good, but
never in order to make the children copy.

3. Cizek was always against naturalism. On the same page (139)
where you find criticism apparently on the ground that the drawings
are not sufficiently "like" that natural object, he says about
Martha (line 6) : "Martha tries to be naturalistic. She draws
things as they are, not as she should do them." To say of S.'s
horse's hooves that they "are not complete" does not mean that

she should make them naturalistic. Cizek finishes his remark about the hooves by saying " You must always *think* how things are *formed*."

The criticism " Santa Claus has legs the wrong way round " (p. 117) is made by a child, not by Cizek. Children do criticise. " You will draw only the outline, and don't make the face blue ! " (p. 152) may have meant : draw only, don't paint. Occasionally Cizek experimented with colours. This may have been his intention in this case. Anyway, the " lessons " are put down in a very concentrated form. So a sentence by itself may give a wrong impression.

4. There was in Cizek's school a most cheerful atmosphere, and only the discipline of work.—Cizek individualised. The child T. (p. 127) had too many subjects in his mind at the same time. It was good *for him* to be encouraged to concentrate.—Work at home (pp. 130 and 159) was never compulsory, but Cizek thought that 1½–2 hours once or twice a week was not enough. Many children brought him their homework. Pp. 138 and 143. Again the two extremes. Formerly, the child was seldom praised, only criticised. Now some think there should be only praise and not the slightest hint that there is room for improvement even in children's works. Granted the danger of too much criticism is greater than the opposite, but positive criticism, extremely tact-fully handled, is good, certainly with some children.

5. Children, occasionally, compare their works. Cizek himself did it occasionally when the same subject was treated by the class or by most in the class. He knew where comparison did no harm.

6. A good number of remarks in those " lessons " were addressed to the visitors. Often Cizek spoke intentionally above the heads of the children.

You rightly sum up by saying that intangible things cannot be judged from verbatim accounts (necessarily shortened, and without the background of the personality of the child and the special atmosphere of a special " lesson "), and there is a danger that bare words can seriously misre-present, as you suggest. I only hope I have conveyed some idea how Cizek dealt with his children. But no gramophone record or film could reveal the whole wisdom of the master.

PLATE 1

CHARCOAL AND BRUSH DRAWINGS.—GIRLS, AGED 3-5.

CHARCOAL.—GIRL, AGED 4.

PAINTING.—GIRL, AGED 4.

PLATE II

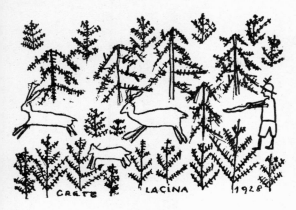

GIRL, AGED 7.

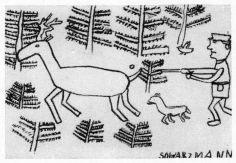

BOY, AGED 7.

BRUSH DRAWING.—GIRL, AGED 8.

PAINTING.—BOY, AGED 8½.

GIRL, AGED 8.

GIRL, AGED 8.

PLATE III

GIRL, AGED 8.

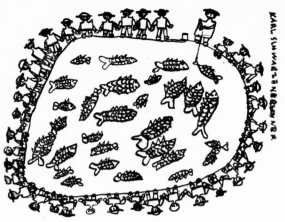

BOY, AGED 8.

BOY, AGED 8.

BOY, AGED 8.

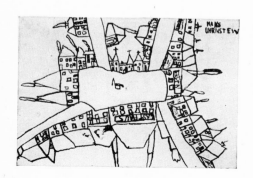

BOY, AGED 10.

GIRL, AGED 8.

PLATE IV

GIRL, AGED 8.

BRUSH DRAWING.—BOY, AGED 7.

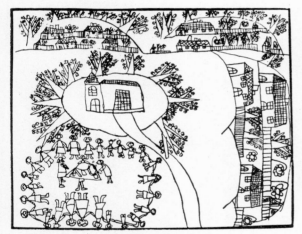

GIRL, AGED 9.

BOY, AGED 7.

GIRL, AGED 10 (SOME ADULT
INFLUENCE).

ETCHING IN ZINC (RARE MEDIUM FOR
CHILDREN).—GIRL, AGED 8.

PLATE V

GIRL, AGED 7.

GIRL, AGED 8½.

WATER-COLOUR.—GIRL, AGED 14.

PEN DRAWING.—GIRL, AGED 14.

PLATE VI

WATER-COLOUR.—GIRL, AGED 14.

LINO CUTTINGS.—GIRL, AGED 14.

SILHOUETTES, MADE DURING THE LAST WAR.—BOY, AGED 12.

PLATE VII

PAINTINGS : SCENES FROM VIENNA.—BOYS, AGED 13-14.

PLATE VIII

CLASS WORK IN CLAY.—BOYS
AND GIRLS, AGED 6–7.

PLASTER OF PARIS.—GIRLS,
AGED 10.

CLAY.—GIRL, AGED 10 ; BOY, AGED 9.

PLATE IX

"BEGGAR MUSICIANS" : BAKED CLAY.
—CHILD, AGED 11.

"FAMILY" : PLASTER OF PARIS.
—GIRL, AGED 10.

PLASTER OF PARIS.—GIRLS, AGED 8.

PLATE X

"SANTA CLAUS AND KRAMPUS" (SEE FOOTNOTE, PAGE 112): CLAY.—GIRL, AGED 10.

FIGURE IN CLAY (PROFILE AND FRONT VIEW).—GIRL, AGED 12.

PLATE XI

FILET WORK.— GIRL, AGED 9.

WOOD WORK.—BOYS AND GIRLS,
AGED 10–12.

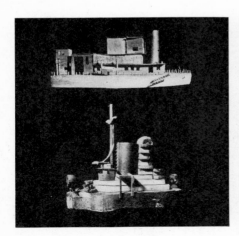

SHIPS, MADE FROM SCRAP
MATERIAL (WOOD, CARDBOARD,
AND PAPER).—BOYS, AGED
9–10.

HOUSE, MADE FROM WOOD, CARDBOARD,
AND PAPER.—BOYS, AGED 12.

PLATE XII

CLAY.—GIRL, AGED 12.

PAINTED WOOD.—BOYS AND GIRLS, AGED 12-14.

INDEX